SECRETS

OF THE

ROYAL DETECTIVE

Don Hale

WRITERSWORLD

Secrets of the Royal Detective
Don Hale

ISBN 1-904181-47-3

Cover design by
www.tinracer.com

Layout and typesetting by
www.dwrobinson.com

WRITERSWORLD
9 Manor Close
Enstone
Oxfordshire
OX7 4LU
England

www.writersworld.co.uk

ABOUT THE AUTHOR

Don Hale, OBE

Don Hale has gained an enviable reputation as one of the country's most controversial and high profile investigative journalists and human rights campaigners. He became a specialist in dealing with reports and inquiries involving true stories, true crime and potential miscarriages of justice, and has been uniquely involved in the quashing of many wrongful convictions.

The most newsworthy case was probably that of Stephen Downing, who spent twenty-seven years in jail for a murder he did not commit. The story became front-page news in nearly 30 countries worldwide at the time.

In 2002, Don was awarded an OBE for 'campaign journalism' and received the award from HRH Prince Charles at the behest of Prime Minster Tony Blair.

Don also wrote about the Downing campaign in his best selling book, 'Town Without Pity', which was short-listed for the Crime Writers' Association's Gold Dagger Award for non-fiction. An adaption of the story later became a successful BBC TV drama called 'In Denial of Murder', and was broadcast during February and March 2004. It starred Stephen Tompkinson as newspaper editor Don Hale, and attracted a nine million audience.

He has also written numerous other books, on a variety of subjects ranging from rock star Joe Cocker's autobiography and ex-footballer Peter Swan's problematic career, to Sounds of the Sixties biographies and the dramatic history of the record-breaking steam engine, Mallard.

The national record books suggest that Don has won more awards for his writing than any other journalist in British history. Some of his most notable honours include 'Journalist of the Year', and the 'International Freedom prize'.

He began his career as a professional footballer, representing Bury, Blackburn Rovers, York City and Shrewsbury Town before retiring from the game due to injury and taking up sports commentating before eventually getting involved with specialist features and hard news.

Don also worked with the BBC, Manchester Evening News, and many national newspapers, before spending more than twenty years editing a number of award winning regional newspapers.

He has appeared on countless mainstream television and radio programmes and is a regular speaker at Universities and Union meetings. He is married with two sons and two grandchildren, and lives in North Wales.

ACKNOWLEDGEMENTS

I should like to express my special thanks to my wife Kath, and all my close family, for enduring many missing hours spent researching, or busy writing up my notes, and for their continued support and encouragement.

Also, to my elder brother Geoffrey, and his family, for his help with preserving some of this valuable archive material. And belated thanks to my late parents Doreen and Charles Hale, my grandparents Thomas and Minnie Stinton and, in particular, to my great grandparents James and Letitia Wood, for ensuring that the many interesting and valuable items survived for many decades.

In addition, I would like to thank: -

Duncan Broady, the curator of Greater Manchester Police Museum, at Newton Street, and to all his hard working and supportive colleagues.
The Chief Constable and members of Greater Manchester Police.
Manchester City Council Library & Information Services.
Manchester City Council Archives Department.
Manchester Archivist, Ms Paula Moorhouse.
The editor, the Guardian & Manchester Evening News.
The editor, the Times, London.
The editor, the Guardian.
The editor, Blackley Guardian.
The editor, Oldham Evening Chronicle.
The London & North Western Railway Society.
Mr Noel Cashford, MBE.
Debbie Freeman – author of the Victorian play, 'Fire in the Park'.
The Wise Monkey Theatre Company & production team.
The Gresley Observer & members of the Gresley Society.
Steve Foote and James Morgan at Tin Racer.
Den Robinson, Robinson Associates.
Graham Cook at Writersworld Ltd.
The Police History Society.
The New Moston History Society.
The Manchester United Supporters Club.
The Red Café.

My special thanks goes to the Manchester City Council Library & Information Services, and the Manchester City Archives department for permitting the use of many important and nostalgic archive photographs. And similar praise must also go to the Greater Manchester Police Museum for again allowing exclusive use of some of their most treasured archive pictures.

Finally, my sincere apologies to anyone that has helped in the development of this book but has been omitted in error from the list of tributes and acknowledgements. Every contribution, no matter how large or small, is fully appreciated.

Don Hale
September 2004

CONTENTS

THE ROYAL DETECTIVE'S SECRET FILES

INTRODUCTION

For the best part of half a century, a rather dominant, yet dark, dour and dismal portrait of my great grandfather, James Wood, dressed in his rippled-effect and military style uniform, hung on the landing of my grandparents' home at Cleveleys, near Blackpool.

It always reminded me of Lord Kitchener's haunting face from the famous Great War recruitment posters, with a large handlebar moustache, and those jet-black penetrating eyes that seemed to follow you around the room, and made you keep turning back to see if he was still watching. As a child, it seemed quite scary and probably left a rather fearsome impression on my vulnerable young mind.

I always presumed it was a reminder of his wartime service; but nearly twenty years later discovered the picture actually commemorated his appointment as the youngest Superintendent at that time for Manchester City Police – and was commissioned many years before the outbreak of hostilities.

Regrettably, this large picture has since disappeared, although some smaller copies remain, together with other softer and more flattering photographs of the man.

They were all found within some dusty, half-hidden boxes and secret files of family archive material passed down the generations following the loss of my parents. When I examined the contents it seemed like stepping back into the mists of time, and unfortunately raised many questions that no surviving family member could ever answer. I kept wondering why so many key issues had never been discussed before, and felt disappointed that much of his work had remained a secret for so long.

The information, however, certainly provided in me the inspiration to review many myths and rumours, and investigate a number of claims, to finally establish the truth about his remarkable life and career. Additional research, and the discovery of other archive records, allowed me to finally piece together a rather fascinating jigsaw, not just about my great grandfather, but also about major changes to social life around Manchester prior to 1914.

Quite incredibly, some other family papers related to James's own great grandfather, James Wood senior, contained a daily diary about his position as one of the city's early Watchmen for the period of 1825-1833. He recorded the details of crimes and incidents on the streets of Longsight, Gorton, Ardwick and Ancoats – prior to the introduction of cars, telephones and electric lighting – and more than a decade before the local police force was even formed!

Many of these documents were of little or no monetary value, but their historical importance was priceless and, surprisingly, most had been extremely well preserved.

James spent fourteen years with Queen Victoria's Army of the Empire and a further twenty-four years with Manchester City police. During his career in the force he worked in all departments, and at one time was even a Detective Sergeant to Jerome Caminada, who was one of the city's most famous Victorian detectives.

James too became a highly proficient detective, earning many plaudits for arrests and convictions, and was a proud instigator and enforcer of changes in legislation on street trading laws, the licensing of theatrical children and registration of servants.

He also helped organise, supervise, or became involved with, a host of major city events, including the Daily Mail Air Race and arrival of the very first 'flying machine'. He was also involved with Manchester United's name change – and their later move to Old Trafford – and with several memorable royal visits.

In addition, he retained a close association with many of the personalities of the day, including Lord Northcliffe, Prime Minister Arthur Balfour, and Sir Nigel Gresley!

Undoubtedly though, his main claim to fame was probably as Manchester's first royal bodyguard to the Prince and Princess of Wales around the turn of the century.

He was also responsible for the protection of many other prominent visiting VIPs, and for nearly a decade was the city's explosives officer in charge.

This was also, of course, during a time of great international drama and political unrest, with threats against the monarchy and government from 'foreign agents and agitators', and with Victoria's mighty army engaged in constant overseas conflicts.

This book takes the raw seeds of discovery and converts them into a rich harvest of nostalgia and memorabilia. It also provides a unique insight and a remarkable behind the scenes look at some of Manchester's major historical moments during a revolutionary period of development.

Unfortunately, James died at an early age, and yet the impact of his work was such at that time, with so many wanting to pay a final tribute, that his slow funeral cortège practically brought the city to a standstill. This book is primarily written to commemorate the 90th anniversary of his death. I believe it is now time to review the contents of his secret files and appreciate the sacrifice that he, and many others, made to help establish Manchester's proud heritage.

CHAPTER 1

Serving Queen and Country

I always remember being in awe of my great grandfather for decades without really quite understanding why, or what it was all about. Any mention of his name at the dinner table soon attracted coughs, grunts and weird stares, followed by a vigorous shaking of heads. It was the children must be seen but not heard syndrome.

All this seemed very odd to a young kid of seven or eight anxious to play out at the seaside and hardly interested in family secrets. It seemed even odder in later years, when I realised that Letitia, James's widow and my great grandmother, lived in that house at the time and remained a feisty 97 year-old to the bitter end! Even more surprising, was the fact that more than fifty years after James's death, she still protected his possessions with a fierce and passionate determination, converting her private room into a near shrine to his memory.

I recall the room as always being very dark, heavily scented, and draped in long flowing black fabrics. It was also packed with memorabilia from their life together, and from his extraordinary career. Letitia always seemed exactly as she was, like someone slightly out of place, from another time, another world!

She was always a very trim and petite lady, desperate to cling to her treasured memories. At home, she seemed to be in constant mourning and wore long dark clothes and a shawl or bonnet, and was wafer-thin with soft, delicate, wrinkled skin.

The memory plays tricks as you get older but Letitia seemed to move around as if she was on casters, and I can never recall her showing any great emotion, or displaying any sight of her legs, ankles or hint of flesh!

I was always inquisitive and perhaps fortunate to gain the very occasional brief chat with her amidst the many competing and ticking clocks, dusty ornaments and clinking glassware. And yet, despite her rather abrupt manner, I couldn't help but like her!

1

Letitia kept herself to herself and was always a very proud and very private person, who had been widowed for such an intolerable time. She only appeared in public on very rare occasions, as if by prior appointment, and enjoyed most of her meals alone.

She had a very dry sense of humour though, and enjoyed twice-weekly sessions of ballroom dancing at a small friendship club somewhere down past the tram tracks; continuing her hobby until the last few years of her life - claiming she only stopped due to a lack of suitable company, rather than any lack of mobility.

The Grand Old Lady
Letitia Wood

Her husband James had been a boy soldier in Queen Victoria's junior Army. He was just nine years of age when he first signed up to represent the Sovereign, initially joining the Cadets, and then her Army Reserve.

It was a glorious era for the dedicated soldier, and a time when most geographical maps of the world and school atlases were plastered in a deep red colour to signify the arrogance and absolute dominance of the great British Empire.

James was born in May 1868, within the run-down and poverty stricken Parish of Hulme in Manchester. He was the son of Job (pronounced Jobe) and Agnes Wood. His father was described in early census forms as a cellar man, and later as a bottle dealer.

The records also suggest James was christened the following year in the city's cathedral, and that he had three sisters and a younger brother.

It seems, that it had always been James's ambition to join the Army and he remained with his cadet colleagues until he eventually reached the age of eighteen, and then signed-up on a semi-permanent basis.

His school report declared him to be a 'bright young scholar,' and he left at the age of fourteen to try his hand at a number of varied occupations. At one time, he was shown to be a joiner's apprentice, and he may even have helped his father at some stage in the licensing trade.

Realistically though, he was only passing time and had only one true ambition, to join the Army as soon as possible, but still had a staggering four years to wait!

In the meantime, it seems that when another more interesting temporary opportunity came about, he took it with both hands, joining the London & North Western Railway Company as a clerk at Victoria Station in Manchester.

He remained in that post for about two years before finally signing on for the 1st Battalion of the Royal Lancaster Regiment as a promising young infantryman.

His Army records confirm he first attested for the services at Ashton-Under-Lyne on June 16th 1885, when he was just eighteen years and one month old. James was five feet, six inches tall, and had grey coloured eyes and light hair. He signed for a period of seven years in the Army, and a further five years in the Reserves.

James was an avid reader and loved the colour, splendour and spectacle of parades and the promise of excitement and adventure told on the parade ground by Army veterans and officers.

RECORD OF ACHIEVEMENTS

Immediately prior to joining the Army full-time, his new regiment completed a tour of duty in the West Indies, and had representatives at convict settlements in New South Wales, Australia; and in India.

Earlier, the regiment also served in the Crimea and helped in the suppression of an Indian mutiny. They also provided generous support with an expedition to Abyssinia (now Ethiopia) in 1868, and also took part in the famous Zulu wars of 1879. James noted that important regimental battle honours had been won at Alma, Inkermann, Sevastopol, and in India.

His company were known as wanderers, and just four years before James joined they were finally awarded a new and more permanent base at Bewerham Barracks, near Lancaster. Shortly afterwards, they sent members of the 2nd Battalion to South Africa, where they took part in the relief of Ladysmith.

His regiment were known as the 'King's Own' and were one of the oldest units in the British Army. Records state they were initially raised in 1680 by the Earl of Plymouth, for service in Tangiers; and uniquely, the regiment wore the 'Lion of England' on their cap badge.

Additional campaign honours highlighted meritorious service in the Napoleonic wars, the Crimea and in Abyssinia; and interestingly, the 4th Regiment of Foot - to which he was attached - were also employed in personal service to the Sovereign.

It is clear to see from his documents, that the opportunity to join such an illustrious company of men at that time must have felt like a dream come true for the enthusiastic young Mancunian.

Many records still exist within the regimental museum at Lancaster and displays, exhibits, and illustrations of various campaigns during their 250-year history can still be seen both there, and at the Chapel, which also retains four Coptic crosses found within a heap of scrap for recycling into guns at an arsenal in Magdala.

They date back to the 4th and 5th century, and carry engraved illustrations of Bible stories. One cross is now displayed and occasionally used for processions within Westminster Abbey.

Army personnel records from that period however, remain extremely fuzzy, and disappointingly do not provide much detailed information about individual soldiers.

Sergeant James Wood,
Royal Lancaster Regiment

Fortunately, James's own records paint a more accurate picture and highlight many important facts.

It seems James saw action in parts of South Africa, sometime between 1885-1890. And there is also a 'Soldier's New Testament' for 1900/01, which infers he returned to South Africa, probably with the

Army Reserves at some time during the Boer War. The conflict certainly raged prior to his final discharge.

Despite the fact these items are more than one hundred years old, many details are perfectly recorded on long lasting parchment or wax paper.

They also confirm that Sergeant, No 1087, James Wood of the Royal Lancaster Regiment of Infantry was discharged from the Army – slightly ahead of schedule – in consequence of promotion to the rank of Sergeant in Manchester City Police.

The records claim he served five years and thirty-four days in the regular Army, and nine years, two hundred days in the Reserves (and cadets). His total service was said to be fourteen years and two hundred and thirty-four days. The Officer in Charge, 4th Regiment of Foot, signed him off.

James readily added his own signature to the papers, agreeing to return if needed, and confirmed his intention to continue to serve with the Reserves.

Included within the paperwork is a small crème coloured record sheet providing details of his discharge on February 4th, 1900 - after more than five years of dedicated service to his queen and country, together with a copy of reports and recommendations.

ARMY DISCHARGE PAPERS

Soldier's name and description: James Wood
Attested for the: Royal Lancaster Regiment on the 16th June 1885, for: 7 years in the Army and 5 years in the Reserve in the County of: Lancaster at the age of: 18 years and 1 month.
Born in the Parish of: Hulme, in or near the Town of: Manchester.
Trade or calling: Clerk. Last permanent residence: blank.
Height: five feet, six and a half inches. Eyes: Grey. Hair: Light.
Marks: Mole below left shoulder blade.
Religion: Roman Catholic.
Signed: J. Wood.

Remarks: When a soldier has any complaint to make, he should appeal to the Captain of his Company; his tone and manner should be temperate and respectful. He should be accompanied by a non-commissioned officer, if possible, of his own Company.
No soldier, on any account, is to presume to make a complaint to his

Officer for another soldier, who he believes, is aggrieved, and not more than two soldiers should approach the Officer to make a complaint at one and the same time.

Copy documents of Army Form B. 128
Should this parchment be lost or mislaid, no duplicate of it can be obtained.
Name: James Wood.
Of: 1st Battalion, Royal Lancaster Regiment of Infantry.
Born in the Parish of: Hulme, near the Town of: Manchester.
In the County of: Lancashire. Attested: Ashton-Under-Lyne, on the: 16th June 1885.
For the: Royal Lancaster Regiment, at the age of 18 ½ years.

He is discharged in consequence of: Promotion to the rank of Sergeant of Police.
Service towards completion of limited engagement: Army: five years thirty-four days. Reserve: nine years, two hundred days. Total service fourteen-years, two hundred and thirty-four days.
Medals & decorations: Nil, 2nd class certificate of education.
Place: Lancaster. Date: 4th February 1900.
Signature of Commanding Officer: Commanding 4th Regiment of Foot.
Discharge confirmed: 4th February 1900.
Remarks: Any person finding this certificate is requested to forward it in an unstamped envelope to: The Under Secretary of State for War, War Office, London.

CIVIL EMPLOYMENT:

A register for civil employment is kept at the Head Quarters of Regimental and Recruiting Districts, in which are entered the names of men of good character discharged or transferred to the Army Reserve, who reside in the Regimental District.
Applications for registry should be made to the Officer Commanding the Regimental District within one year of Discharge or transfer to the Reserve.

Description on Final Discharge:
No: 1087, Sergeant J. Wood of the Royal Lancaster Regiment of Infantry. Age: 32 and nine twelfth years. Height: 5 feet 9 ½ inches. Complexion: Fair. Eyes: Grey. Hair: Light. Trade: Clerk.

Marks or scars, whether on face, or other parts of the body: Moles below left shoulder blade, and two warts left groin. Intended place of residence: 69 Rutland Street, Hulme, Manchester.

Discharged the service at: Lancaster this 4th day of February 1900.

Army Discharge Certificate, February 1900

ENLISTMENT INTO SECTION D, 1st CLASS ARMY RESERVE

Men who have been discharged on termination of their first period of limited engagement from any form of the service may be enlisted for

Sec D, 1st Class for four years, within 6 months from the date of their discharge.

Cavalrymen will be enlisted on the understanding that, on mobilization, they will be liable for employment as officers' grooms, or as drivers, either in the Cavalry or in any other arm of the Service.

Only those Infantry men will be enlisted who have trained as Mounted Infantry or are accustomed to riding or driving. Their enlistment will also be on the understanding that, on mobilization, they will be liable for employment as officers' grooms, or as drivers, either in the Infantry, or in any other arm of the Service.

In the case of Infantry or Artillery Reserve, men discharged with character other than 'Bad' or 'Very Bad' will be eligible for enlistment. In other arms of the Service, only those will be eligible who received at least a 'Good' character on discharge.

RE-ENLISTMENT IN THE MILITIA

Men discharged from the Army with not less than three years service can re-enlist in the Militia of the County in which they reside on advantageous conditions, which will be communicated to them by the Adjutant on application.

Pamphlets showing the conditions and advantages of the Militia are supplied gratis at every Post Office.

There was also a small blue coloured note advising him of a possible need in the future for the Army Reserve, and a stern warning of what would happen if he failed to attend, if requested!

ARMY FORM D-463. ARMY RESERVE

Notice to join the Army for Permanent Service.
Name: Wood – James. Rank: Sergeant. Regimental No: 1087, Royal Lancaster Regiment.

Here enter the Regiment, Artillery, Division, or Corps to which the Reservist belongs. You are hereby required to join: The depot, Royal Lancaster Regt.

Should you not present yourself on the: 11th February 1900, you will be liable to be proceeded against. You will bring with you your 'Small book,' your Life Certificate, Identity Certificate, and Parchment Reserve Certificate.

Take this notice to your nearest Money Order Office and the Postmaster will on your signing the attached receipt, pay you the sum of three shillings as an advance of Reserve Pay, to be adjusted when you join.

If conveyance is necessary, take this Notice to the nearest Railway (or Steamer) Station from which you can depart for your destination. On presentation, the Travelling Warrant will be detached by the booking clerk, who will issue to you a through ticket to enable you to join.

Signed: Major, Station Paymaster, Officer Paying Reservists by order of the Commanding Officer. Dated: February 3rd, 1900. Stamp of Paying Reservists.

Reservist Papers, February 1900

SOLDIER'S NEW TESTAMENT
South Africa 1900-01.

A small pocket sized blue book with red and silver writing.

The New Testament of Our Saviour Jesus Christ with engravings from drawings made in Bible lands by H A Harper and J Clark. Printed in London by The Scripture Gift Mission, 15 Strand, WC.

'In my opinion, there could be nothing more suitable for the spiritual comfort of a soldier on active service than this Testament.

'The size permits him always to carry it in his khaki jacket pocket. And each soldier will have something of far greater value to him than the proverbial marshal's baton.'

Signed: Father M. Wolseley.

* It is clear from some of the documents now available, that there are certain minor discrepancies with ages, and dates etc., in current records, but I can assure readers that all the information inserted here has been taken from the original papers.

MANCHESTER CITY POLICE FORCE 1890

Archive records and details of former police personnel, including James, are retained at The Greater Manchester Police Museum on Newton Street.

They verify much of the information contained with his personal papers and I noted that this building was a former police station, opened in 1879, where James probably spent some time during his early career – and ironically was also a place Detective Caminada once recommended for closure!

Thankfully, many of the original features of the premises have been retained. And visitors are still able to examine the charge office with its bizarrely shaped polished counter and see the wooden records cabinets and authentic furniture.

They can also see the heavily worn indentation in the counter where the desk Sergeant would lean to hear the circumstances of arrest and examine several old cells and facilities used throughout the Victorian era. There are also numerous displays and it is certainly worth a visit.

James Wood first joined Manchester City Police as a young constable on October 30th 1890. It was more than five years after he had first joined-up with the Army, and just under ten years before he eventually received his final discharge papers, following promotion to Sergeant.

He was an experienced soldier, and seemingly a very brave infantryman who had seen action overseas, and was said to be an excellent shot with a rifle.

He worked with a variety of weapons throughout his time in the Army and was used to handling both firearms and explosives. Prior to discharge, he was promoted to Sergeant of Infantry and is described in records as a 'popular and reliable soldier'.

The city force were recruiting quite heavily during 1889/90 and particularly welcomed men with military experience, people used to handling weapons, and others able to deal with an assortment of potentially hostile situations. James matched these relevant criteria.

Manchester police records confirm that he had grown an inch and a half from first joining the Army at eighteen - and was now five feet, eight inches tall! Some later documents indicate that he continued to grow, this time reaching a final mark of five feet, nine and a half inches.

His complexion was described as fair, with light brown hair, and acknowledged that he was a former clerk with the L & NWR Co, and an experienced sergeant with the 1st Battalion of the Royal Lancaster Regiment.

A copy of details taken from his personnel records held at the police archives at Manchester City Police Museum on Newton Street: -
Name: James Wood. Rank & Number: Police Constable.
Joined: 30/10/1890. Height: 5 ft 8 inches. Complexion: Fair. Eyes: Brown.
Hair: Light brown. Born: Manchester, Lancashire. Religion: Catholic.
Trade. Clerk. Employer: London & North Western Railway Company.
Status: Single. PPS. 1st Battalion, Royal Lancaster Regiment. (Five years).

APRIL 1899.
Personnel records at Police Museum.
APRIL 1899. Reward for meritorious service.
APRIL 1899. Reported for meritorious conduct – diligence.
AUGUST 1899. Lives at China shop.

* In August 1899, the records show that Detective James Wood lived over a china shop at 69 Rutland Street, Hulme. It said he occupied a

portion of the premises. This was the same registered address shown on his paperwork on joining the Army in 1885.

FEBRUARY 1900. Recommended for promotion to Sergeant.
FEBRUARY 1900. Promotion list.
FEBRUARY 1900. Promoted to Srgeant.
DECEMBER 1901. Recommended for reward.
DECEMBER 1901. Report of meritorious conduct.
OCTOBER 1902. Reward.
OCTOBER 1902. Report of meritorious conduct.
JANUARY 1903. Recommended for inspector under Explosives Act 1875.
FEBRUARY 1903. Made inspector under Explosives Act 1875.
DECEMBER 1903. Promoted to an Inspector.
JANUARY 1906. Applied for superintendency.
JUNE 1907. Report requested for police courts.

His initial police record card claims he was single at the time of entry into the police service, but James was actually married by then!

I have managed to obtain a copy of his marriage certificate, which confirms he had already wed his local sweetheart from Hulme, Miss Letitia Little. Perhaps he had been single at the time of the original application?

They were married on March 8th, 1890, at the Parish Church of St Michael's in Hulme. The Rector was J.A. Pocklington MA. Young James was only twenty-one years of age, and Letitia nineteen.

As this was immediately prior to joining the Manchester police force, his occupation was stated on the certificate to be a Sergeant in the King's Own.

Confirmation was also given relating to his father's occupation as a cellar man, together with the details of Letitia's father, William Little, who was a French polisher. Their future address was shown as 27 Dearden Street, Manchester.

Despite obvious hardships, this was certainly a time of great promise and opportunity for the young couple and allowed James to finally settle down after many years of military service.

It meant a new beginning and he soon decided to dedicate himself to a bright new career as a young policeman. Although he had no idea of what lay ahead, he continued to enjoy a relatively short, but extraordinary career, that most other officers could only dream about...

James and Letitia's Certificate of Marriage
St Michael's Church, Hulme, 8th March 1890

NO ORDINARY POLICEMAN

James Wood was certainly no ordinary policeman. Any student of law or media researching his police career would soon note his remarkable achievements, steady promotions, commendations, awards, rewards and many letters of meritorious service.

He became an established explosives and firearms expert, utilising his varied military experience, and was frequently used by the Government to review and supervise explosive operations, and to implement and oversee potential matters of national security.

It is quite clear that he also helped in the protection of royalty and other visiting VIP's. And yet quite bizarrely much of his career had passed unnoticed for more than a century until these personal boxes of treasured memorabilia came to light.

The museum records confirm he joined the Manchester City Police force in October 1890. He was a very young man, and yet had already gained more than five years front-line military experience, with additional experience in the Army Reserves and cadets.

James could handle a weapon, be it a gun, bayonet, or knife; and knew much about explosives and a specific need for their very delicate care. He was also very confident that he could handle himself in any situation.

He had only been married to Letitia for seven months at that time, and left the barracks and military field tents behind to take advantage of a new and shared opportunity with his wife, living and working close to the area where he was born, and where he had first

Little Bo Peep
James Wood's daughter, Minnie

met his childhood sweetheart as an awkward teenager.

His time in the services obviously gave him the edge over other trainees and he helped many settle down to their chosen career and those difficult first few months away from home and normality during a very strict induction programme.

His military experience was vitally important too whilst patrolling the uncertain streets of Manchester city centre and the suburbs in this dangerous period of change.

Many inhabitants refused to go out at night, especially alone, for fear of attack and robbery. How little seems to have changed over the past century! Many gentleman of that era also hired private security guards to watch out for their person and property and often carried a weapon of some description about their own person.

Even some police officers were armed! Most Constables just carried a wooden truncheon for protection but Detectives had access to, and often carried, firearms.

The Manchester Detectives were a much feared and respected team. This specialised unit had developed rapidly over the fifty or so years since their initial introduction but remained in constant danger from potential attacks due to their obvious capabilities and reputation.

In the city areas, they were known as 'D's' and it was said there was an air of expectation and anticipation when Detectives suddenly appeared on the scene to begin asking difficult questions. In many slum areas they were often accompanied by a back-up group of Constables, and generally worked in pairs.

It is not quite clear as to how many wore plain clothes at the time of James's early career, as some Detectives worked undercover, or wore a disguise.

Additional officers, cleared for the use of firearms, attended incidents with pistols or rifles, and some constables with army training were often called in support.

James was just such a person. He was young, bright and keen. He was also a very ambitious officer who later helped many of his colleagues to understand the use of weaponry, and the need for self-defence. His experience must have proved invaluable.

He started as a Constable and according to the files, gained his first successful entry nearly nine years later, during April 1899, with a file note of meritorious service.

James worked with a number of particular officers and was often paired off with others, whose names also appeared in dispatches and within shared newspaper reports.

Perhaps it was his basic training as a teenage clerk with the railways, and with the Royal Lancasters, but James meticulously maintained his own private cuttings book with photographs, and fascinating details of many major incidents that he was involved with throughout his police career from 1890-1914.

In addition, he also kept many copies of letters, memos and any other relevant paperwork relating to his actions, which have since proved extremely useful in trying to piece together precise career achievements.

The author's grandmother, Minnie, as a child. An interesting study of late Victorian fashion and perceptions.

CHAPTER 2

Case Notes and Cuttings from 1898 Onwards

James gained several rapid promotions following his initial period of training and probation, quickly moving from an ordinary beat bobby to a fully fledged Constable; from Constable to Detective Constable; Sergeant to Detective Sergeant; Inspector to Detective inspector; Detective Inspector to Chief Inspector; and finally from Chief Inspector to Superintendent.

He worked in all departments of the service – and especially enjoyed his time in the Detectives' office – helping to solve numerous crimes, and both catching and convicting a host of notorious North West villains.

This time around the turn of the century ensured James's military and policing skills were utilised to maximum effect, helping to organise feasibility studies for special events and numerous VIP visits to the city. He was also asked to submit other key reports to the Chief Constable on a number of other important matters, including royal visits.

Many promotions were preceded by use of a temporary rank as an acting senior officer; with some postings, this often took up to, and at times over, twelve months, before official confirmation took place.

The following information has been taken directly from James's prized personal files and paperwork, and from other official documents currently held at the Greater Manchester Police Museum at Newton Street. Additional information was collated from newspaper archives and by records held at the Manchester City Library.

It should be noted however, that the personnel records do not always contain a full account of all the promotions or case history, but do confirm a substantial number of rewards and recommendations received during service.

Within this book, I have included a number of examples from many of the varied and fascinating cases he worked on throughout his twenty-four year police career. The first cutting dates back to August 1898 and relates to one of the quickest ever recorded arrests and convictions recorded at that time within the history of the Manchester City force.

The other cases highlighted, together with copies of supporting paperwork and archive material, provide a unique insight into the workings of the police and about life in general in the city during an incredible period of change, and quite remarkably all have remained locked away within family papers for generations.

Manchester horse trams at the turn of the 19th century

August 25th, 1898

JEWELLERY ROBBERY IN MANCHESTER

A smart arrest

A daring jewellery robbery has been committed in Manchester, and the city police have affected a smart arrest.

This morning about one o'clock the window of Messrs W and F Terry, jewellers of Victoria Street, was smashed from top to bottom and five silver watches were taken.

Information reached the police and efforts were at once made to arrest the culprit. The case was placed in the hands of Detective Sergeants

Wood and Jakeman, who, some little time after the robbery, came across a young man named Thomas Halstead, of no fixed address, resting on the forms on the Infirmary Esplanade.

He was bleeding profusely from a wound to the wrist and was accused of having broken into Messrs Terry's shop. He was taken to the Town Hall, and when acquainted with the charge that would be preferred against him, admitted that he was the offender. The watches have been recovered.

THE CULPRIT IN THE DOCK

At the City Police Court this morning, before Mr Headlam, City Stipendiary, Thomas H Alstead, a slim young fellow of about 19-years of age, was charged in custody with having broken into the premises of William & Frank Terry jewellers, of 8 Victoria Street, in this city, and stolen eight silver watches valued at £25 from the window.

The story of his arrest provided a very good illustration of the ingenuity and expedition of the city police methods of detection.

Sergeant Wood, who first gave evidence, stated that he and Sergeant Jakeman, who were on special duty in the neighbourhood, were informed by Constable Harrington soon after one o'clock this morning of the occurrence.

On going there, they found the window (which is valued at about £25) was smashed, and a heavy file was lying inside. Two pieces of broken glass were stained with blood. A tray containing the eight watches was missing. At a subsequent period they obtained from one of the carters employed by the Evening Chronicle, a description of a man whom he had seen running away from the direction of the shop.

The two officers adjourned to the Infirmary Esplanade, where they made a survey of the somnolent occupants of the seats. They examined the hands of each person, and at last came across the prisoner, who had a newly made cut on his wrist.

That was at 5.15 am and even then, the cut, which they presumed had been caused by the broken window, was bleeding. Sergeant Jakeman put his hand in the prisoner's trouser pocket and pulled out three of the watches. They charged him with breaking into the shop and stealing the watches, and he replied: 'The game's up, I did it!'

In the meantime, Constable Harrington found two of the watches between the window and an outer covering, and two others on the footpath in the vicinity. Corroborative evidence was given by several other witnesses.

The prisoner was committed to take his trial at the next Sessions.

An undated case from around the same period
THEFT FROM A SHOP DOOR

This morning at the City Police Court before Mr J Buckley and other magistrates, John Kerr of Rumford Street, Salford, and Harry Escott of Bloom Street, Salford, were charged with stealing two pairs of boots from the shop of Mr Walter Beardow, Stretford Road, Hulme.

Detective Wood was passing along Stretford Road the other evening when he noticed a pair of boots showing under Kerr's coat. The two men were together and seeing that they were observed, they ran away.

The officer gave chase and subsequently arrested them, and it was then discovered that the boots, of which Kerr had two pairs in his possession, had been stolen from Mr Beardow's shop door a few minutes previously. Escott was sent to gaol for a month, and Kerr for 14 days.

Evening News. February 13th, 1899
HIGHWAY ROBBERY OFF DEANSGATE

At the City Police Court this afternoon before Mr F J Headlam, Andrew Gunn, labourer, was charged with highway robbery with violence and also with receiving a stolen gold watch, knowing it to have been stolen.

About half past eleven on the night of the 7th of the present month, Duncan McKinley, who lives in Hamilton Street, Old Trafford, was attacked in Severn Street, Deansgate, and robbed of his gold watch and chain, and 45s in cash as he lay on the floor.

Two men have since been committed to the Assizes on the charge of being concerned in the affair, and Gunn, and a number of others, were arrested in a lodgings-house in Gartside Street by Detective Sergeants Wood and Woolvern.

They were taken to the Town Hall, and prisoner was then identified by a beer house keeper as the man who had left a watch with him some time previously. In answer to the charge of highway robbery with violence, prisoner said that he was not there. With regards to the charge of receiving stolen property, he replied that he found the watch.

The prisoner was remanded until tomorrow with a review to his committal to the Assizes.

Follow-up article

THE HIGHWAY ROBBERIES OFF DEANSGATE

Andrew Gunn, the young labourer, who was yesterday remanded by Mr Headlam on a charge of being concerned in the recent highway robberies in the neighbourhood of Deansgate, was today committed to take his trial with the two men already committed, at the Liverpool Assizes, a woman named Martha Fawcett, of Severn Street, having identified the prisoner as one of three men who robbed Duncan McKinley, of Hamilton Street, Old Trafford. Detectives Wood and Woolvern arrested the prisoner in a lodgings-house at two o'clock on Sunday morning.

Further notes from his cuttings file confirm:

Tried at Liverpool Assizes on 23rd February, 1899, found guilty and sentenced to 3 months imprisonment and 20 strokes with the 'Cat'. Ten lashes at each six-week's end.

MARCH 1899. E Division

Rewards to Detective Officers for extraordinary diligence and activity in the discharge of their duties during the months ending 31st March 1899.

PC Wood, award of 7s. 6d.
Other officers rewarded, included: - Chief Inspector Hargreaves £5, Inspectors Corden, Dutton, Edwards and Watson, rewards of £10 each. Signed: S. Hargreaves, Chief Inspector.

February 1900. Memorandum

RECOMMENDATION TO SERGEANT

The sub-committee considered the appointment of Sergeants to fill existing vacancies in the Force. Resolved: That the following Constables be recommended to the Watch Committee for appointments as Sergeants, viz., PC D203. Taylor; PC Davies; PC Wood and PC Goodwin.

* **BRAVERY REPORTS**: The same report also contained some interesting notes of bravery by other constables and detectives, with a particular mention of a PC Webster. He helped in the rescue of three

people trapped in a flooded cellar and shop. The report said when he was alerted, the cellar, surrounded by a window and wall, with a floor falling into the cellar, contained about 5 feet of water.

It stated: 'The constable without divesting himself of any clothing at once sprang into the water and at great personal risk rescued a boy as he was about to sink. He carried him to a place of safety and entered the building a second time and rescued a woman and child who were clinging to a floating counter.

'With assistance, he got them out and they were taken to a place of safety. Through Grafton's exertions and exposure he was taken seriously ill with cramp and was on the sick list for several days.'

The police report confirmed. 'PC Webster rescued a youth from drowning who had fallen into the cellar attached to the shop at 371 Hyde Road, and would have doubtless been drowned but for the constable's exertions.

'I have received a number of letters from the neighbourhood speaking very highly of the courageous way in which the constable acted, and it

The Thriving City
Junction of Market Street and Exchange Street, 1902

22

is the general opinion that there would have been a serious loss of life but for the constable's exertions in getting people out of the shop and other buildings.'

It was resolved that the recommendations of the Chief Constable be adopted, viz., that Detective Sergeant Woolvern be granted a reward of £5 and the Watch Committee's Medal for Bravery; that Detective Sergeant Ashton be granted a reward of £5; that PC 629 George Grafton be granted the Watch Committee's Medal for Bravery; that PC 98 David Webster be granted the Watch Committee's Medal for Bravery. Also that the medals be presented to the officers named at the first available general parade of the force.

E Division, December 1901
SPECIAL REPORT OF MERITORIOUS SERVICE

Sir,

I beg to submit for your consideration the under mentioned report, the particulars of which I have fully inquired into, and believe to be substantially correct, and I recommend the parties named in the margin as deserving of reward.

Apprehension: By Sergeant Wood

Whilst in charge of detective office on 29th May last, Wm Cannon came enquiring for a woman supposed locked-up. He was persuaded to wait until records were searched. The sergeant, knowing that a woman was in custody on suspicion of larceny then telephoned and obtained assistance of Inspector Woolvern and PC Lea, and from enquiries made, it was found that Cannon had committed a burglary at the house of Mr H. Hill, Rusholme. Jewellery to the value of £10 being stolen – this was afterwards recovered.

He was sent to the Sessions and sentenced to 9 months imprisonment. He had served several terms of imprisonment for shop-breaking etc., including a sentence of 4 years penal servitude in London.

Signed: Philip Corden, Chief Inspector.

Evening News. July 24th, 1902.
ALLEGED THEFT OF JEWELLERY
Owners Wanted

Detective Sergeant Wood and Detective Dorricott, passing along Victoria Street, City, on the 18th inst, observed a man named Charles

Thompson, who lives in Drake Street, Strangeways, closely examining a watch he had in his possession.

Questioned as to how he came by it, Thompson said that it belonged to his wife. The officers did not consider the man's answer satisfactory and took him into custody.

Subsequently, when at the Town Hall, a gold ring, chain and pendants, besides the watch were found upon him, and he at once confessed to having stolen them from a house in Dover Street, West Gorton, which was occupied by Elizabeth Wilson, who had missed the goods during her temporary absence.

At the City Police Court this morning, Thompson was sent to the Sessions on a charge of stealing the articles named.

A second charge is about to be preferred against the prisoner of being in possession of stolen goods. When his house was searched on Saturday, the police discovered a quantity of jewellery, which the prisoner says he has found.

The following description of the property has been published: -
Gentleman's English Lever, No 28,049, lady's Geneva watch 'The Marvel,' No 280,354, silver and pearl fruit knife, a pair of gold-rimmed spectacles, enamelled half-crown brooch, English penny brooch, floral design on one side with the name of 'Ada' in the centre, silver curb brooch with heart in the centre, lion shilling, ivory handle razor - marked 'one of the best', a gentleman's blue cloth overcoat with a velvet collar has also been found.

E Division, October 19th, 1902
SPECIAL REPORT OF MERITORIOUS CONDUCT
Sir,
I beg to submit for your consideration the under mentioned report, the particulars of which I have fully inquired into, and believe to be substantially correct, and I recommend the parties named in the margin as deserving of reward.
Apprehended on the 18th July 1902, one Charles Thompson, charged under h & a 'jewellery' value £10, proceeds of larceny from dwellings. Committed to Sessions (two cases) sentenced to 9 months.
Remarks: Good strong case. R. Dorricott and Sergeant James Wood given 7s. 6d each reward.
Signed: - Philip Corden, Chief Superintendent.

Evening News. December 4th, 1902

EXTRAORDINARY ALLEGATIONS OF FRAUD

A typewriter agent's stay in Manchester

Some extraordinary allegations of fraud were made at the City Police Court this afternoon. A respectably dressed man named Charles Goad, apparently about 40 years of age, who spoke with a strong American accent, was charged in three instances with obtaining money by false pretences, and in the fourth with embezzlement.

He was apprehended a few days ago by Detective Sergeant Wood in a Blackburn hotel, and before then, he had lived at Liverpool, Blackburn and Manchester.

The charges were of embezzling £11. 11s, the moneys of Palmer Howe, Princess Street; obtaining £100 by false pretences from Emma Louise James, Moss Side, under the pretence of supplying Lever Brothers, Port Sunlight, with typewriters; obtaining under similar instances £40 from Walter Seddon, Moss Side, under the pretence of supplying Ogdon's Ltd, with typewriters; and obtaining £80 from Sarkis Taselodjiu under a similar pretence.

With regard to the case in which Mrs James prosecuted, it was stated that the prisoner went to her as a lodger in January of this year, and on October 31st he disappeared. During his stay near the end of June he told her, according to her evidence, that he had an order from Levers' for a number of second-hand typewriters.

They agreed to share in an undertaking to find the money for twelve machines. Her share was £48 for six machines, and she was to receive in return, £10 for each machine. On the 13th August, he paid her £12, which he said was interest on the £48.

Later, she received a letter from him in the course of which he said he was about to purchase more machines and suggesting that it would be better for her to entrust her money to him and he would yield her a bigger interest than the four or five per cent she was at present getting.

'If you feel you can trust me,' he added. 'I shall be glad to do all I can for you. Assuring you of my desire only to promote my own and your own welfare, yours faithfully, Charles E. Goad.' On the strength of this note, the witness advanced another £52 making in all £100.

Mr Murray: 'So out of the £100 you gave him, you got £12 back?'

'Yes.'

A representative of Messrs Lever, Sunlight Works, Birkenhead, said he did not know the prisoner, and stated emphatically, that the firm did not buy second-hand machines.

In the charge of defrauding Seddon, the prosecutor said the prisoner represented to him that he had a number of second-hand typewriters which he had obtained for £5, and that he had an order from Messrs Ogdon by which he would make £8 each. On this statement he obtained £40 from Seddon, who was to share in the profits of the transaction.

The prisoner pleaded guilty to these two charges, and the others were not proceeded with.

Inspector Clegg said the prisoner had undergone a sentence of twelve months' imprisonment for false pretences, and he had also been in the State Prison, Connecticut, for some offence of which the police did not know the nature.

Detective Sergeant Wood remarked that he had received information that the prisoner had received close on £500 in seven or eight cases of a similar character.

The prisoner was sentenced to six months imprisonment in each case and three months in the other – making nine months in all.

Evening Chronicle 1903

A BIRMINGHAM TRAVELLER'S LOSS
Mysterious robbery in Manchester

Sidney Aronsberg, jeweller's traveller of Portland Road, Birmingham, brought an action in the Manchester County Court before his Honour Judge Parry this morning, against Mrs Cater, proprietor of the City Hotel, Long Millgate, Manchester, for £4 10s.

Mr Leonard Harris appeared for the plaintiff and Mr J A Buckley represented the defendant.

The plaintiff stated that on the 23rd October last, he travelled from Birmingham in the afternoon and took his baggage to the City Hotel, which was a temperance hotel. His baggage consisted of a skip and two bags, and of the latter contained a purse and the sum of £4 10s, which he put in after he had had his dinner and before he went out.

In the evening, he went to the Queen's Theatre, and when he returned to the hotel, he went into the baggage room and found that the purse was in the bag, but the money had been taken out. The bag at the same time remained locked, as he had locked it, and apparently in the same position in which it had been left.

The plaintiff in reply to Mr Buckley, said he had stayed in the hotel previously and had seen the notices 'The manageress will not be responsible for valuable articles unless given to her personally'.

He went to the pit of the Queen's Theatre after he left the hotel. He could not have had his pocket picked of the amount because it was not in his possession. There was jewellery of the value of £3 and £4 in the bag with the purse and the money, but that was not touched. Asked why he immediately examined the bag when he returned from the theatre, he said he wanted to take his money upstairs.

His Honour remarked that this was a little peculiar proceeding, seeing that he had left the money in the bag during the evening.

In further cross-examination, the plaintiff said that other bags contained jewellery of the value of more than £100. They were not tampered with. He acquainted Miss Cater with his loss as soon as he learned it. The defendant the next morning lent him a sovereign for which he gave her an IOU.

Miss Cater, daughter of the proprietor, stated that she was on duty on the evening referred to, and it would have been scarcely possible for anyone to enter the baggage room and to remain there for a few minutes without her noticing it. The plaintiff remarked to her that the purse must have been left in the bag so as not to incriminate the person who took the money.

Detective Sergeant Wood stated, that he was consulted about the affair, but he failed to trace the money. Answering Mr Harris, the witness said he declined to express an opinion whether there had been a robbery or not. He simply made the usual inquiries.

His Honour spoke of the plaintiff's story as extraordinary. The most likely thing was that he put the purse without the money, into the bag. How he lost the money it was impossible to say, perhaps he had his pocket picked. Judgement would be for the defendant with costs.

CHARGE OF THEFT AND FORGERY

A youth named William Isherwood Eatock, clerk, who lives at Mount Ive, New Lane, Winton, and a young man named George Marriott, warehouseman, who lives in Malcolm Square, Coupland Street, Chorlton on Medlock, were charged at the City Police Courts this morning, before the Stipendiary Magistrate, Mr F.J. Headlam, with stealing two cheques, one of the value of £20 and the other £10, and with forging the endorsement of them.

The prisoners were employed by Messrs William Cambell & Sons, rope manufacturers, Cannon Street, and yesterday, they were visited by Detective Sergeants Wood and Ashton and were charged with the offences named, also with uttering the cheques.

A search of the premises was made and the sum of £20. 10s was found under some roping. When the prisoners were being taken to the Town Hall they admitted the offence.

It seemed that the prisoners obtained a couple of blank cheques, which had already been signed by one of the members of the firm. The name of "E.H. Cambell" was put in as the other signatory and it was endorsed in the same name, which, in the three instances where it occurred, was in the same handwriting.

The bank cashed the cheques, but almost immediately afterwards discovered that the signatures were frauds. Marriott was asked to write the name "E.H. Cambell" and it was then found that his writing was identical with that on the cheque.

The prisoners were sent to the Assizes for trial.

* Continuation of case at Manchester Assizes. Crown Court - before Mr Justice Wills.

A MANCHESTER FORGERY CASE

A youth named Wm Isherwood Eatock, and George Wm Marriott, pleaded guilty to a charge of having stolen three blank cheques and with having forged two of them for £10 and £20 and cashed them.

Mr Tipping, who conducted the case for the prosecution, said that the prisoners were employed by the firm of Messrs Wm Campbell and Sons of Cannon Street, Manchester, Eatock being a clerk and Marriott a warehouseman.

One member of the firm was an invalid, and in the office were a number of cheques, which bore his signature, as he filled up a number so that they could be used for payment of accounts even when he was not at the office.

The prisoners got hold of three of these cheques, and Marriott filled in the name of another member of the firm on two of them, and cashed them. The fraud was discovered through the bank clerk having his suspicions aroused by the signature, which had been placed on one cheque by Marriott.

When the prisoners were arrested, the sum of £20 was found in a cellar of Campbell's warehouse, and later on a sum of £1.10s was revealed. Both prisoners pleaded guilty and Mr Ambrose Jones, addressing the Court on behalf of Eatock, said he had borne a very good character, and was the son of a very respectable man.

Marriott had been the tempter in the case which, counsel thought, was one where the provisions of the First Offender's Act might be applied. Evidence of the character was given for Eatock, who was then bound over to come up for judgement if called upon, his Lordship warning him that he must be careful in his conduct.

Marriott was sent to gaol for three months in the second division. His Lordship commented upon the creditable preparation of reports presented by police in the case.

Social contrast
The well-to-do and the poor on the streets of Victorian Manchester

CHAPTER 3

Explosives Expert and Social Reformer

James Wood was always a great champion of administration and of ensuring that everything was kept neatly in its place. This was the probable result of more than twenty years of military style duties but he always insisted on looking clean and tidy, with his uniform pressed each day and buttons and boots shining in regulation order.

He was also keen to ensure that his men followed suit and that they also had a good grasp of weights and measures and trading standards law.

When he was first appointed as Manchester's Explosives Officer in the early 1900's, he again accepted the challenge with relish. He put his Army experience to good use again and was used to dealing with high explosives and gunpowder storage.

According to the city's Watch Committee reports and Government Inspectorate, the stores were in a terrible state when he first took charge and he worked hard and systematically to put matters right. And working with a small hand picked team, he was soon able to maintain order and continued to supervise these standards for about another twelve years or so.

During this period, he also undertook a number of other senior duties but this was a highly regarded and prestigious role, which brought him into contact with Government officials and Ministers of the Crown.

Every so often, in his dual role as a law enforcer under the Explosives Act, he also took action against unlawful traders and firework manufacturers. He helped to clamp down on unauthorised sales and hit traders who either had no licence to sell fireworks, or were well over their agreed and permitted quota.

His Chief Constable insisted on prosecutions, although I gather in certain cases he left this task to the discretion of the senior officer. I have enclosed some examples from within the newspaper cuttings to show what the traders could expect if they got on the wrong side of the law, together with copies of letters and relevant correspondence from regulating committees and Government.

Once again, it provides an interesting insight into the thoughts of senior officials at this period in time.

COPY OF LETTERS FROM TOWN CLERK
APPOINTMENT AS INSPECTOR
Meeting of the Watch Committee of the Council held on 8th January 1903.
Appointment of Inspector under the Explosives Act 1875.

Resolved: - that Sergeant James Wood be appointed as Inspector of the Local Authority of the City of Manchester under and for the purposes of the Explosives Act 1875 (a true extract).
Signed, Wm Henry Talbot. Town Clerk.

** COPY OF LETTER FROM CITY COUNCIL*
The Explosives Act 1875, Section 69

The Lord Mayor, Alderman & Citizens of the City of Manchester being the local authority for the City of Manchester within the meaning and for the purposes of the Explosives Act, 1875, hereby appoint JAMES WOOD as an officer of the Local Authority for the said city, under and for the purposes of the said Act and the Acts amending that Act.
Dated the 18th day of February 1903.

By order of the Council of the said City.
Signed: Wm Henry Talbot. Town Clerk.

Evening Chronicle. March 22nd, 1903
IMPROVEMENT IN REGISTRY OFFICES

There was a note of optimism about the report to which the Manchester and Northern Counties Branch of the National vigilance Association listened this afternoon.

It recorded 'a year of increased effort and enlarged success', described the outlook as 'distinctly hopeful', and saw 'indications of a most encouraging character'.

A most marked improvement in regard to registry offices for

domestic servants was noted. The municipal byelaw wrought a great change both in the number and respectability of these places.

CITY NEWS. October 18th, 1903
FIREWORK SELLERS FINED

Firework Sellers Fined – At the City Police Court on Wednesday, Michael Riley, trading as Riley & Sons, Lever Street, Piccadilly, was fined half a guinea and costs for permitting fireworks to be conveyed in an open cart without sufficient covering, and Henry Mann, the driver, was fined one shilling and costs.

For improperly packing three parcels of fireworks, Riley was also mulcted in the sum of three shillings and costs. The Midland Railway Company was fined ten shillings and costs for insufficiently covering fireworks in a conveyance, and the driver, George Prescott, five shillings and costs.

For other offences under the Explosives Act, 1875, chiefly for exposing fireworks in shop windows, the following persons were fined: Elizabeth Howard, Lower Moss Lane, Hulme; Elizabeth Coleman, Hamilton Street, Rochdale Road; each one shilling and costs.

Katherine Walsh, Burton Street, Rochdale Road, half a crown and costs; Emily Edwards, Coupland Street, eight shillings and costs; Isaac Bradshaw, Mill Street, Bradford, five shillings and costs.

Inspector Wood prosecuted, the offences being proved by police constables Jones, Fisher, Scott and Brindley.

CITY NEWS. October 17th, 1903
SHOPKEEPERS & THE SALE OF FIREWORKS

Further prosecutions against shopkeepers for offences under the Explosives Act, 1875, were heard at the City Police Court on Thursday.

Nellie Kenworthy, Stockport Road, Longsight, was fined twenty-one shillings and costs for storing fireworks in unregistered premises. Ephraim Dickenson, Shakespeare Street, Chorlton on Medlock, and Charles Wielding, City Road, Hulme, were each mulcted in like sums for storing more than fifty pounds' weight of fireworks.

The prosecutions were at the instance of Inspector Wood, the offences being proved by officers Jones, Fisher, Scott and Brindley, who had previously warned the defendants.

Evening Chronicle. October 19th, 1903

ALARMING THE LADIES

For discharging fireworks on the highway, John Hawe (14), Weaste, and Thomas Scalsh (15), Patricroft, were fined 5s each at Eccles today and warned that they were liable to a penalty of £5.

On Sunday night, as people were leaving church, the two boys were using 'throw downs,' among the crowd and alarming the ladies. They claimed that there was no fire and the crackers were harmless.

Albert Street Police Station
In the early 1900s

Evening News. October 29th, 1903

FIREWORKS DEALERS FINED

At the City Police Courts this morning, the following shopkeepers were fined for offences under the Explosives Act, 1875: William Tierman, German Street, Oldham Road, for keeping four and half pounds of fireworks on unregistered premises, 5s and costs.

Betsy Greatorex, Upper Medlock Street, keeping seven pounds of fireworks on unregistered premises, 20s and costs. Ann Bailey, Moston Lane, exposing thirty-three and a half pounds of fireworks in a shop, 5s and costs. John Williamson, Moston Lane, keeping one hundred and eighty pounds of fireworks, or one hundred and thirty pounds in excess of the quantity allowed, 20s and costs.

Christopher Croasdale, Hyde Road, Ardwick, for keeping one hundred and forty-seven pounds in excess, 20s and costs. George Myers, Thomas Street, keeping one hundred and twenty-one pounds in excess, 20s and costs, and for not keeping in accordance with the Act, 20s and costs.

Henry Perks, Edge Street, keeping twenty-seven pounds in excess, 20s and costs, and not keeping in accordance with the Act, 20s and costs. Henry Clinton, Every Street, Ancoats, keeping three and a quarter pounds of gunpowder on unregistered premises, 5s and costs. Henry Lanson, Ashton Old Road, keeping two hundred and two pounds in excess, 20s and costs.

The prosecutions were taken at the instance of Inspector Wood, and the offences were proved by police constables J. Scott, Fisher, Jones and Brindley.

Evening News. November 12th, 1903
THE STORAGE OF EXPLOSIVES
Prosecutions in Manchester

The following persons were summoned at the City Police Courts today, under the Explosives Act, 1875, and were dealt with as follows:

Hannah Whitehead, 82 Medlock Street, Hulme, keeping sixteen pounds of gunpowder in unregistered premises, 1s and costs. Robert Henry Hunter, 35 Rochdale Road, keeping sixty-seven pounds of fireworks in his shop, being nineteen pounds in excess, 10s 6d with costs, and for exposing eight and a half pounds on shelves, 2s 6d with costs. Sarah Woodhall, 26 Queen Street, Ardwick, keeping eight and a half pounds of fireworks, not being registered, 5s and costs.

Samuel Holmes, 109 Ashton Old Road, keeping four and a half pounds of fireworks, not registered, 5s and costs. Thomas Gee, 259 Stockport Road, keeping eighty-five pounds of fireworks, or thirty-five pounds in excess, 10s and 6d and costs, and for exposing thirty-one pounds in a glass case, 1s and costs.

Edward Tipping, 7 Ladybarn Lane, keeping sixty pounds in unregistered premises, 21s and costs. Ernest Holland, 2 Burgon's Buildings, Fallowfield, keeping eighty-six pounds of fireworks, unregistered, 5s and costs. George Brown, 3 Burgon's Buildings,

Fallowfield, storing eighty-six pounds of fireworks, or thirty-six pounds in excess, 5s and costs, and for being the owner of eighty-seven pounds of fireworks and allowing the same to be stored in unregistered premises, 5s and costs.

Inspector Wood prosecuted and the offences were proved by officers Richard Dorricott, Scott, Fisher, Jones and Brindley.

Evening News. November 25th, 1903
OFFENCES AGAINST THE EXPLOSIVES ACT

At the Manchester City Police Court this morning, James Pain and Sons, firework manufacturers, were fined £5 and costs for having fireworks packed in cardboard boxes instead of cases of wood or other solid material.

They were also fined a similar sum for not labelling packages with the word 'Explosive'. The main parcel company were fined 21s and costs for having exposed iron on a lorry whist conveying explosives. Mr Bell of the Town Hall Clerk's department prosecuted, and Inspector Wood and other officers proved the cases.

Evening News. December 17th, 1903
AN ERRONEOUS IMPRESSION

James William Parrish, Dry Salter, of Caernarfon Street, Cheetham Hill Road, was fined 10s 6d and costs at Manchester City Police Court this morning for storing thirteen pounds weight of throw-down crackers without being registered.

This will serve to show that the impression that these crackers are not explosives is erroneous. Sergeant Wood and police constable Dorricott proved the case.

BLOWN TO PIECES

The East Lancashire Coroner was informed today of the shocking death of Robert Ratcliffe, of Snodworth, Billington, near Blackburn.

He was engaged yesterday in blasting operations at Holly Head Quarry, Wiltshire, when a fuse, which he was lighting, exploded unexpectedly.

Ratcliffe was literally blown to pieces. He was only 25 years of age and unmarried.

THE CLOTHING OF DESTITUTE CHILDREN

One of my great grandfather's most noteworthy achievements was in working with a team of fellow Manchester police officers to provide destitute children with sufficient food, warm clothing and shelter throughout many desperate winters.

He also encouraged constables to report any incidences of potential neglect with children left wandering the streets in need and in need of assistance. These cases were dealt with sympathetically; every effort was made to locate and provide help and support to the parents and families, and wherever possible to secure regular employment for the head of the household.

Some examples of this work are highlighted within this book.

The Police-Aided Association for Clothing the Destitute Children of Manchester was formed in 1901. The following article appeared in the Manchester Chronicle during 1903, giving an account of some of their early work.

James Wood was also appointed a member of a special council committee and had peculiar responsibilities to oversee and execute regulations relating to Street Trading, the Licensing of Theatrical Children and the Explosives Act of 1875.

Manchester Chronicle, October 17th, 1903
MANCHESTER'S DESTITUTE CHILDREN
Clothed by the Aid of the Police

The policeman whose duty it is to patrol the streets of Manchester probably sees more of the squalor and poverty inevitably associated with large cities of population than anyone else, not even excepting the self-sacrificing ladies and gentlemen who visit the poor in the interests of one or other of the many organisations designed to help the poor and unfortunate.

And so the Police-Aided Association for Clothing the Destitute of Manchester – now in its second year – is doing splendid work among the wretched little children who run about the streets in tattered garments, or are confined to the house because they have not sufficient clothing even for decency's sake.

The system under which the Association carries on its essential work is briefly this: -

The police undertake to ascertain the homes of any insufficiently clothed children they may see in the streets, to find out the causes, which have led to their apparently destitute condition; and then to fill up and return to the Association, forms giving all the particulars thus ascertained.

These forms are then handed over to visitors appointed by the Association, who have voluntarily undertaken the work of making further inquiries. In the first year of the Association's beneficent operations, 335 children were clothed. This year, the number has reached 567 boys and girls.

This morning what may be described as the winter session was entered upon at the Albert Street police station, where clothing was distributed to 51 children. In this work, the police play no part. It is expediously but very kindly performed by members of the committee, of whom Mr James Scotson and Mrs Manton, assisted by Mr W.R.C. Clarke, the secretary, were present this morning.

The children, accompanied by their mothers or fathers in nearly every case, are received in the parade room, and then, one by one, in their 'shreds and patches,' are taken to an upper room, where in the case of a boy, he is given first a new shirt, and than a suit of warm navy blue serge clothes.

As may be imaged, the transformation is in nearly every case, a startling one, and it is to be made complete when the well-worn shoes have been cast off and warm stockings and clogs substituted.

Never was the old saying: 'Fine feathers make fine birds' better illustrated. Boys who had entered the building looking half-starved and pitiably miserable off-springs of a poverty-stricken home – and natural inheritors of all that such conditions involve – looked positively well on the way to become sturdy little fellows with the makings of men and respectable citizens in them.

For that reason, the mothers looked thankful and, not infrequently, the busy workers of such a great good shed tears of joy as the little ones pattered off in their warm clogs and clothing.

* Further examples of the success in monitoring street trading and the difficult life of children on Manchester's streets are further explained and highlighted in the Manchester Courier of Tuesday May 9th, 1905, and by 'A Distressing Case' published in the Manchester Evening News of Saturday December 9th, 1905.

December 10th, 1903

MANCHESTER WATCH COMMITTEE REPORT

Re: Promotion of Street Trading Department Officers

The Chief Constable begs to bring before the Committee the following facts and recommendations relative to the Officers of the Street Trading Dept.

The Street Trading Department was established nearly two years ago under the Manchester Corporation Act, 1901. Sergeant Wood was selected to take charge of the new department, and he was given the assistance of constables Charles Dorricott and Richard Dorricott.

The officers entered thoroughly into the spirit of the Act and have by their exertions contributed in no small degree to the success that has attended the establishment and operation of the department.

They have given entire satisfaction to the Chief Constable and the Committee, in their first annual report, issued last May, made the following comments respecting the officers named, viz.,

'The members of the Sub-Committee desire to express their appreciation of the admirable work done by the officers appointed to the specific duties of the department by the Watch Committee and the Chief Constable.

'These officers have exercised a friendly supervision over the juvenile traders of the city, and have encouraged them to improve their personal appearance. In several instances, they have been the means of obtaining permanent situations for boys previously engaged in street trading.

'They have also brought cases to light where parents have ill-treated their children, and where their earnings are squandered in vice and debauchery... and have taken steps which led to the punishment of the offending parents and the protection of their off-spring.'

The Chief Constable fully endorses this report. Sergeant Wood is also duly appointed (by the Watch Committee) inspector under the Explosives Act for the City of Manchester. In the discharge of his duty, he is assisted by the constables Dorricott.

The same energy has been shown in the administration of the Explosives Act as has been shown in dealing with Street Trading Regulations, and the Explosives Act is now better administered in Manchester than at any other period.

On Saturday last, Major Cooper-Keys, HM Inspector of Explosives, made a surprise visit to the city, and after examining the books, registers, etc., expressed his entire satisfaction with the same and intimated that he would have pleasure in presenting a favourable report.

The Chief Constable proposes to relegate the work in connection with the Registration of Domestic Servants (which comes into active operation on the 1st January next) to the Street Trading Department. It is advisable that an officer having such responsible duties should have a substantive rank.

Sergeant Wood has served in the Manchester City Police Force for over 13 years, has held the rank of sergeant for nearly four years, is an officer of exemplary character, and during the whole of his service has never been late for duty, nor had any mark of any description recorded against his character.

PC Charles Dorricott has served 13 years and has only two minor offences recorded against him, the last being nearly 10 years ago. The Chief Constable therefore recommends that Sergeant James Wood be promoted to the rank of inspector; that PC Charles Dorricott and PC Richard Dorricott, be each promoted to the rank of sergeant.

Resolved: That the report now read, be approved, and the recommendations therein adopted, viz., that Sergeant James Wood be promoted to the rank of inspector, and that PC Charles Dorricott and PC Richard Dorricott, be promoted to the rank of sergeant.

1905 onwards.

The Manchester Courier. Tuesday May 9th, 1905
JUVENILE STREET TRADING
Manchester byelaw at work

Whatever may be the evils of street trading – and that they are considerable cannot be denied – they are being reduced to something like a minimum in Manchester. This much may not unreasonably be claimed as a result of the limitations now in force.

Three years' working of the byelaw adopted by the Manchester Corporation has produced striking results. The child of really tender years has been eliminated from the ranks of the street sellers, while the conditions imposed on those who remain have led to the practical disappearance of the old-time gamin.

The Manchester juvenile street-trader in the main is of a sturdy type, healthy and comparatively well clad, and except on occasions when the weather is unusually bad, rejoicing apparently in the free and unconfirmed nature of his calling.

The City Police Courts
Minshull Street, 1902

Scope of the Regulations

To recall briefly the purport of the bye-law of the Manchester Corporation, which came into operation on the 25th March, 1902, it may be stated that it provides, among other things: 'That no licence shall be granted to any child under twelve years of age. All children over that age, being boys or girls under sixteen, shall be entitled to be licensed, provided the Corporation are satisfied – (a), that they intend to trade in the streets of the city; (b), that they are not unfit to trade through being sickly, blind, deaf, dumb, deformed, or mentally deficient; (c), that they have the consent of their being licensed of the persons purporting to have the custody, charge or care of them. If such persons are fit persons, and have fit homes. Provided that in the case of girls under the age of fourteen, it shall be a condition of the licence that they shall not trade within an area of one mile from the Town Hall.'

Certain conditions have to be observed by the holder of a licence. These require that: - 'No licensed child shall be in any street for the purpose of trading after eight o'clock at night between October 1st and the 31st March, or after nine o'clock at night between April 1st and September 30th.

'No licensed child shall trade in the streets unless decently clothed. No licensed child shall, whilst trading, be assisted by any unlicensed child. No licensed child shall trade at any time unless wearing his or her badge in the appointed way. No licensed child, unless exempt from school attendance, shall trade on the streets during such hours.'

Humane & helpful

So much for the restrictive side of the Corporation's endeavours. But the city authorities do not stop at a merely negative policy. Acts of Parliament and local byelaws depend for their success very largely on the spirit in which they are put into operation. One of the most gratifying features of the Manchester juvenile street-trading byelaw is the humane and helpful personal interest it has called forth in those who are concerned in the administration of the regulations.

The licensed sellers in the city – and one has reluctantly to point out that in this movement, Salford as yet, takes neither part nor lot – are the objects of an almost parental attention from the members of the Street Trading Committee of the Corporation, of which Councillor P Whyman is the chairman; the Street Trading Department of the City Police Force, over which Inspector Wood presides; and the Police-Aided Association for the Clothing of Destitute Children, of which Mr W R C Clarke is the secretary.

The last named organisation came into being contemporaneously with the department, and is doing incalculable good in seeing that those holding licences are something like reasonably clad.

No deserving case reported to them by the police fails to receive assistance, and it will be readily understood that such cases are of constant occurrence.

The harvest of the street

The Association, in conjunction with the Street Trading Department, also exerts itself as far as possible to find regular employment for such of the juvenile traders as desire it. One of the great dangers of street trading is that those engaged in it may come to lose the taste for more staid and settled occupations.

It is a primary object of the Street Trading Department to try and counteract this tendency and to discourage a continuance in street trading beyond the age at which more settled work would be commenced. As showing the attention bestowed on this matter, it may be stated that regular employment has been found of the lads since October last.

But the emoluments of street trading are in some cases considerable, and to those who consider the present rather than the future, they offer some temptation to continue in the calling. We are credibly informed that some lads, while attending school full time, can earn as much as seven or eight shillings a week from the sale of papers.

Regular vendors of newspapers on the streets, during the racing season, are said in not a few instances to clear from thirty to thirty-five shillings per week. Apparently, there is money to be made out of enterprising street hawking.

One veteran for many years, a familiar figure on Market Street, is credited with being the possessor of a bank balance running into some hundreds of pounds. But the prosperity of the few must not be taken as bearing any relation to the condition of the many.

Regular street hawkers for the most part fail to make their vocation yield anything more than a very precarious livelihood, sometimes, we fear, scarcely that. The general all-time average earnings of the juvenile section of street traders are estimated at from three to four shillings weekly.

Beneficial effects.

The effect of the byelaw in thinning the ranks of the street hawkers has been enormous. In the days of unrestricted street-selling, it is estimated that something like five thousand children were so engaged in Manchester, their ages ranging from so low as five years, and they were to be found on the streets at late hours of the night.

The average number of street traders licensed is now about eleven hundred. Nor can it be said that the reduction has entailed hardship on poor parents. Before licences came into operation, it was found that lads took to the selling of newspapers of their own accord, and without the knowledge of their parents, spending their earnings on sweets and cigarettes.

A vast number was also turned out on to the streets by callous parents, anxious only that their offspring should provide them with money for drink. Needless to say, anything of this character is practically impossible now.

Gambling among the hordes of street trading children, at one time said to be alarmingly prevalent, is now almost non-existent, while improved school attendance returns attest the beneficial effects the new regulations have had in checking a prolific source of leakage in the education arrangements of the city.

Evening News. Saturday December 9th, 1905

A DISTRESSING CHORLTON CASE

Prompt relief work

Particulars of a lamentable case of destitution in Chorlton-on-Medlock, have been supplied to us by Manchester Police. The story is a distressing one, but it serves, at any rate, to show how promptly and effectively existing organisations are able to give relief when the necessity arises.

Sergeants Dorricott and Cox, whilst passing down London Road, met a poorly clad lad, who they thought was begging. They took him to his home in Tell Street, Chorlton-on-Medlock, where they found that the lad was the son of a commercial traveller named John Carroll, who has been out of employment for six months.

Mrs Carroll and six children were in a destitute condition. The ages of the children ranged from 18 months to 17-years, and the eldest lad had been unable to do any work for eleven weeks owing to an injury to his wrist.

The youngest child was suffering from measles. The only furniture in the house was a table, a chair and an old sofa; everything else had been pawned to buy food. When the officers visited the house there was not a scrap of food in the property.

The case was reported at the Town Hall to Inspector Wood, who communicated by telephone with the Rev William Johnson at the Central Hall. Within half an hour, one of the two sisters was at the house.

She obtained two shillings-worth of groceries for the family, left them tickets for more food for the weekend, and through the Lord Mayor's Charity, coke and coal were supplied.

Clothing for the children was sent by the Police-Aided Clothing Association, and this morning, the father and his eldest son, went to the Central Hall, where temporary employment was found for them.

CHAPTER 4

Famous Friends, Pyrodramas & Reformatory Ships

In his capacity as a senior police officer and royal bodyguard, James came into contact with many personalities, ranging from sportsmen to government ministers, to major business entrepreneurs.

In particular, James was more than well acquainted with his Manchester Member of Parliament, Arthur Balfour, who remained a family friend for many years.

He also knew Ned Hulton, the founder of the city's Sporting and Evening Chronicle; Alfred Harmsworth, who later became Lord Northcliffe, owner of the Manchester Evening News and founder of the Daily Mail; and Nigel Gresley, who was later knighted for his outstanding achievements as a railway engineer and creator of numerous powerful and record breaking steam locomotives.

His association with Hulton was probably more distant, and I believe stemmed in the main from at least one family member, William Stinton, who worked as a sub-editor and journalist on the news desk for a city newspaper, or from his brother Thomas, a printer and linotype operator on the same paper.

Indeed, it is possible that it was via this print connection that James's only daughter, Minnie, first met her own sweetheart, Thomas junior.

Ned Hulton had also worked for other city papers and controversially left to start his own rival publications in Manchester during 1897.

Arthur Balfour's name was first mentioned within the Wood household during his election year of 1885, when political leaflets started to be pushed under the door of their flat at 69 Rutland Street, Hulme, by the prospective Conservative MP for Manchester East, and/or his assistants.

The small premises, just above the old china shop, was situated within his constituency and ironically the election came at a time when

James couldn't vote as he was under age, yet bizarrely was old enough to sign up for queen and country!

Consequently, it was to be another five years before he returned to the same property.

Looking back through the archives, it seems remarkable to consider that when James and Arthur Balfour officially met some fifteen years later, my great grandfather was responsible for the safety of visiting VIP's, and Balfour was Prime Minister!

The two however, had met before and discussed certain Manchester affairs. Balfour also appreciated his work on various council committees, with particular regard to the care of destitute children and reforms to protect youngsters from exploitation by trading and theatrical laws.

Balfour's first visit to East Manchester must have been a huge culture shock for the experienced politician, who enjoyed a privileged and pampered lifestyle.

Well spoken and well educated, Balfour was born in 1848 on the family's estate in East Lothian, Scotland. He was educated at Eton and Trinity College, Cambridge, where he studied philosophy.

He was first elected to the House of Commons in 1874 at the tender age of twenty-six and was soon appointed private secretary to his uncle, the Marquis of Salisbury, who was then the Foreign Secretary within Disraeli's government of the day.

Shortly afterwards, Balfour again hit the fast-track button, enjoying promotion to Secretary for Scotland, when the Marquis himself became Prime Minister.

In later years, he was appointed Chief Secretary for Ireland, First Lord of the Treasury, and eventually Leader of the House in 1892. And in 1902, Balfour was elected Prime Minister, replacing his uncle in Downing Street.

He continued in this role for a further three years before being forced to resign in 1905, following a major political row over tariff reform. This argument eventually forced a general election, which the Conservatives spectacularly lost, and led to a remarkable Liberal landslide.

Balfour had been credited with ending the controversial Boer War, and retained a keen interest in philosophical studies. He was a renowned philosopher, a prolific writer, and publisher of a number of acclaimed papers, especially on his favourite pet subject.

The first, in 1879, appeared shortly after his first major political appointment and was entitled: 'A defence of philosophic doubt', which pleaded for freedom of thought as against the increasing dogmatism of science.

He had first become interested in psychic phenomena and the question of survival in 1882, following an introduction to the matter by Professor Henry Sidgwick - who was then president of the SPR, and married to Balfour's sister.

In 1893, shortly after Balfour's appointment as Leader of the House, he also became president of the British Association. He wrote a series of articles on various related aspects including one notable wartime report in November 1916, described as a 'most constructive presentation of an excellent piece of evidence for survival'.

He continued to serve in various ministerial roles, and worked with Asquith's Great War Coalition Government of 1915 as First Sea Lord. Later he joined the Prime Minister, and another former Manchester-born politician, David Lloyd George, as his Foreign Secretary. In 1917 he made the controversial 'Balfour Declaration', promising Zionists a new and natural home in Palestine. He died in 1930.

As a side issue, and to confirm Balfour's continued interest with James's family after his demise, my grandmother needed to travel to France to visit her husband amidst the chaos of the First World War.

She applied via his office as the local MP, and Secretary of State, for assistance due to problems of travelling within a war-torn country, and Balfour dutifully made suitable temporary arrangements.

I have enclosed a few basic details regarding his intervention, together with facts taken from her application: - my grandmother, Minnie, was just 24 when she applied for this passport in October 1918, and was James's only daughter.

Passport information: Mrs Minnie Stinton (formerly Wood)
Date of birth – Manchester, 9th February 1894. Height: 5' 3".
Forehead: straight. Eyes: Blue. Nose: Grecian. Mouth: Small. Chin:
Round. Colour of hair: Auburn.
Complexion: Fair. Face: Oval. National Status: British subject.
This passport is not valid for the zone of the armies. Military permit stamped in Paris on 18th October 1918. Rated for duration of his leave for 10 days only.

Pass port no 205050:

I, Arthur James Balfour, a Member of His Britannic Majesty's most honourable Privy Council, a Member of the Order of Merit, a Member of Parliament, His Majesty's most principal Secretary of State for Foreign Affairs.

Request and require in the name of His Majesty, all those whom it may concern to allow Mrs Minnie Stinton, to pass freely without let or hindrance and to afford her every assistance and protection of which she may stand in need.

Given at the Foreign Office, London, October 4th 1918.
Signed: James Balfour.

Signed by Balfour
Minnie Stinton's passport, 1918

ALFRED HARMSWORTH – LORD NORTHCLIFFE

Alfred Harmsworth was said to be a genuine Irish charmer. And, like Arthur Balfour, was a popular writer. Harmsworth, however, loved journalism and later became an editor, and an entrepreneur who belatedly became a politician.

He certainly made a major impact on Manchester life and was extremely influential in bringing wealth, prosperity and fame to the region. James came into contact with him on a regular basis around the turn of the century and welcomed the development of his newspaper empire and eccentric promotions.

Harmsworth was born on July 15th, 1865, at Chapelizod, near Dublin. He was the son of a top English barrister. He was a reluctant student however, attending a small private establishment in St John's Wood, London, where he first came into contact with journalism by editing his school magazine.

In later years, he became a full time journalist working on 'Youth' a boys' illustrated magazine, which was then published by the Illustrated London News. In 1886, at the age of twenty-one, he moved to edit 'Bicycling News'.

A couple of years later, Harmsworth joined his brother Harold to produce a rival to the best-selling magazine of its day, 'Tit-Bits'. They called their product 'Answers to Correspondents', and promised to answer by post any questions sent in.

This venture proved a tremendous success, and by 1893 they were selling more than a million copies. This success allowed them to invest in the purchase of other publications, including a children's paper, 'Comic Cuts', and a woman's magazine, 'Forget Me Knots'.

The following year, Alfred decided he wanted to become further involved within the newspaper industry and reports say he bought the struggling Evening News for just £25,000.

He began to drastically change its style and content, producing eye-catching headlines and remarkably, by the end of the year, circulation and profits rose considerably to cap a unique success story.

He then travelled to America to examine production methods, and on his return seemed determined to start another newspaper. This time he opted for a national morning paper, which he called the Daily Mail, and which was first published on May 4th, 1896.

Initially, it was only a small production sheet costing just half a penny, but he used it to try out a number of unusual marketing and editorial ideas, which were later adopted by most other national newspapers.

He encouraged human-interest stories, and made the format much simpler, even including a women's section with features about fashions, cookery, and serialised stories.

The Mail became one of Britain's most popular papers and Harmsworth enjoyed tremendous personal success. However, it seemed a bold move when he decided to print a northern edition in Manchester, helping to promote the region. Later in the same year, he opened new offices on Deansgate, reputedly costing over £1 million.

He encouraged national pride in the Daily Mail, promoting: 'Power, supremacy and the greatness of the British Empire'. Within a short period sales topped 500,000 copies, and he seemed unstoppable.

The following year, he sailed back across the Atlantic to meet with American media mogul, Joseph Pulitzer. For a while, he edited the New York World, and Harmsworth revolutionised the paper, reducing its size under compression to a much smaller 'tabloid' shape.

Harmsworth was an eccentric and flamboyant character, who was always keen to promote new ideas and inventions; and due to his passion for the new motorcar, for a while at least, he even prevented editors publishing details of any road traffic accidents.

He was also a great personal campaigner, promoting healthy eating and a healthier lifestyle. He also introduced the famous 'exclusive' tag, much to the annoyance of rivals, and boasted he had the best reporters in the business.

In later years, he also developed the Daily Mirror and made it an open paper for both sexes, using new photography to great benefit. He encouraged his publications to highlight the lives of the Monarchy, and used 'exclusive' picture specials to promote the lifestyle of the royals to his enthusiastic readers.

James and Alfred Harmsworth came into contact over some incredible national newspaper promotions and challenges, via the Daily Mail in particular.

Some of these included: - offering one hundred guineas to the first person to swim the Channel; £1,000 to the first man to fly the Channel; and the main concern for Manchester police was when he put up a staggering £10,000 prize to the first person to fly from London to Manchester in the Daily Mail Air Race (this latter event is covered in great detail in a following chapter).

During James's royal protection stint, Harmsworth was made a baronet in June 1904, and was said to be the youngest ever peer of the realm. Later, he became known as Lord Northcliffe.

A short time later however, and towards the start of WW1, he fell out of favour with politicians and the general public after his warnings about the German military threats were either ignored or misinterpreted.

He ran a series of hard hitting and critical articles attacking British apathy, and even wrote a book claiming Germany wanted to destroy the Empire. In addition, he also said there were problems with Government policies, equipment and ammunition.

When war finally broke out, he delivered 10,000 copies of his paper to the Western Front, publicising the experiences of front line troops. Lord Kitchener was the constant target for much of his criticism, but the military chief was a very popular public figure at that time, and his plan backfired!

After a long honeymoon period, his campaign finally collapsed and sales dropped alarmingly, with the public protesting at Northcliffe's alleged disloyalty, claiming he was undermining military morale.

He remained a thorn in the side of the Coalition Government until he was offered a compromise, accepting an appointment as the Minister of Information, and working once again with his former Manchester colleague Balfour.

Northcliffe remained a controversial and dominant figure but he is often remembered with great affection. He always welcomed the support of northern readers and was proud of his Manchester base, and when he died in August 1922, the city lost an old friend and a remarkable business associate.

SIR NIGEL GRESLEY

Nigel Gresley was based at Newton Heath locomotive sheds around the turn of the century and came into contact with James on several occasions socially. He was originally employed as an outdoor assistant at the carriage and works department, and in the early 1900's became works manager and then assistant to the works superintendent.

Later, he successfully applied for the post of superintendent of the carriage and works department for the Great Northern Railway, and in 1905 moved to the mighty Doncaster Works as subordinate to the railway superintendent, Henry Ivatt.

Gresley continued his impressive climb and used his skill and experience as chief mechanical engineer to create some of the world's finest, quickest and most powerful steam locomotives including the

'Flying Scotsman' and 'Mallard', the latter engine breaking the world steam record in 1938 with a magnificent speed of 126 mph.

He came to Newton Heath with his wife Ethel, having met and married her whilst working at Blackpool as shed foreman. He was a keen sportsman and probably attended some of Newton Heath Locomotive's football matches (later Manchester United) with James.

Gresley had had an unusual and privileged childhood; born in Edinburgh, and yet brought up in the remote and rural village of Netherseal in Derbyshire.

Sir Nigel Gresley
Pictured with his namesake, one of the famous 'Mallard' type locomotives

Born in 1876, he was the 4th son of the Revd Nigel Gresley and family members expected him to follow in the footsteps of his father and relatives, but he unusually opted for a career as an engineer, initially working as a 'premium apprentice' at Crewe Works for the same firm James had first worked for, the London & North Western Railway Company. He later switched to the drawing office of the Lancashire & Yorkshire Railway at Horwich as a 'pupil' under John Aspinall the chief mechanical engineer before arriving in Newton Heath.

Gresley was a great bear of a man, always interested in community affairs, and shared James's common curiosity for creation, development, sport, law and order.

Secrets of the Royal Detective

FIRE IN THE PARK

It seems quite bizarre, but when I was about two thirds of the way through my inquiries into Victorian policing and relevant social issues of that period, I suddenly came across two very enthusiastic individuals who shared my common interest.

They were Duncan Broady, the curator of the Greater Manchester Police Museum, based at the old police station in Newton Street, and Debbie Freeman, a historical writer of note, who ironically once worked for about a year at the museum as a writer in residence.

I was actually looking for further information about former Detective Superintendent Caminada, when his name suddenly popped up on a website for Stockport-based theatre company, Wise Monkey.

Their company produced a play in 2002, written by Debbie, entitled: 'Fire in the Park'. It mentioned Caminada's police character, and covered a similar period to the one I was already researching.

The information suggested Debbie had studied Caminada's career and that her play portrayed the harsh Victorian age and 'slum life' in Manchester and Salford from around 1885.

After a few emails to Wise Monkey, Debbie got in touch, introduced herself and told me about her time on this project. She also sent me a copy of her fascinating script. It read like a powerful and romantic drama set amidst the problems of that era.

She explained that she had only gone to the Police Museum, in 1998, with the intention of gaining background information to write a play set within a museum.

Her work, however, sparked sufficient interest to obtain a commission from the drama department of the Arts Council and GM Police Museum, where she stayed for several more months to produce this play.

Within the archives, Debbie admitted she discovered material that was quite new and fascinating to her, including the Irish history of Manchester, and the story of a Zulu man recruited by an impresario to come over and play the role of a 'black savage' in one of the famous Belle Vue pyrodramas.

In addition, she found Caminada's biographical books, 'Twenty-Five Years of Detective Life', and said: 'He was an Irish-Italian detective who wrote it all down on his retirement, thereby ensuring himself a role in Fire in the Park.'

Debbie is a third generation descendent of a Jewish-Lithuanian immigrant, and claimed she was now seeing a Manchester her grandparents never saw.

And, within her play, she includes many informative references to life aboard one of the despicable reformatory ships moored off the Wirral, and within a similar girls' reformatory school, where all the harsh realities of the Victorian era are brutally exposed.

Debbie confirmed some further aspects of her work, stating: 'Although Fire in the Park has been intensely researched - this was not academic research. I saw the research first and foremost as a process of curiosity and personal interest. But I tried to remember how I came to the material in the first place – through Greater Manchester Police Museum.

'Certain themes and images of Victorian Manchester cried out to be included. Pyrodramas - spectacular re-enactment of battles, staged beside the lake at Belle Vue, with casts of hundreds - giant collapsible sets and fireworks, seem like the glitz modern Mancunian theatre goers are happy to have left behind.

'Noting how much policing they needed, through Police Watch Committee records, I came to believe they were significant in the lives of my characters.'

Debbie's important personal contact also led to a number of strange coincidences! Some of these included: -

- The fact she made contact about a week before I had already arranged to visit Duncan Broady at the Police Museum.
- My great grandfather was a Detective Sergeant under Caminada.
- Her play was performed at practically the same site and within the same educational facility that I had also studied at many years ago.
- James Wood was Manchester's Explosives Officer during this period.
- He actually took part in many of the South African skirmishes depicted in pyrodramas at Belle Vue.

The reformatory ships were a 'home' of sorts to delinquent boys, with the two establishments officially termed - 'for the re-education of wayward boys and girls'.

The copy indicates boys were very badly treated, flogged and starved for the least thing. Disease too was another major problem onboard, with measles, diphtheria and scarlet fever an ever-present threat.

For the young girls, sheer existence seemed little better. Every morning they would be frog-marched into the hall for exercise, where lines of girls would swing dumb bells and be forced to sing hymns for fitness and recreation purposes.

The children worked long and hard hours in the laundry, gaining sore red hands for their trouble. And part of their task was to clean the clothing of the disease-ridden boat boys, dumping their washing in large, separate vats, under the instructions and guidance of the medical officer.

Debbie praises her research facility and says: 'Little happens in the play – bar the actual plot – and the emotional journeys of the characters that didn't get there through opening a book, an old document, records, or watch committee reports obtained from the Police Museum.'

She added: 'I kept seeing references to the pyrodramas, and requests for more policing. They were open-air re-enactments and used hundreds of enthusiastic extras, and masses of fireworks, not to mention prostitutes, drunks and pick-pockets.'

She says her play is fictitious but is based on factual events from around that period. Caminada is uniquely the only person to retain his true identity, but a couple of other characters are also very loosely based on the lives of real people.

One of these is 'Kumalo', a Zulu man. His role was actually based on the real life of Peter Lobengula, who was recruited to play a 'savage' in the dramas by famous impresario, Pitt-Hardacre in 1893 – and the man behind Wilkie Bard in 1906.

Lobengula, however, was given a very hard time in England, and part of his task was to sit in a raised cage by the lake as a token 'savage' for up to five hours a day - and die when requested, during the re-enactment!

The pyrodramas played an important part in Manchester life. They provided a noisy yet colourful re-enactment of 'Battles from the Empire', and were staged each summer within the Belle Vue grounds.

One of the listed dramas in the summer of 1885 included the re-enactment of the siege of Khartoum, and many years later there was another reference, this time depicting the battle of Rorke's Drift during the Zulu Wars of 1879.

James must have had some sort of input in both the planning and supervision of many of these events for years, as the Government's Explosives Officer for Manchester.

And ironically, using his military experience and memory, he could probably have helped ensure authenticity, as his regiment took part in the Zulu wars and he spent time out in South Africa during several similar skirmishes.

Police records confirm these events became a magnet for pickpockets, thieves and fraudsters of all descriptions. Drunken behaviour too, with brawling and violence, was another major concern, all requiring extensive policing to maintain law and order.

WISE MONKEY THEATRE COMPANY

The chair of Wise Monkey, Guy Holloway, gave an explanation about his company's involvement with this particular project. He said: 'The Wise Monkey Theatre Company began life back in 1997, when three enterprising local writers wrote a short play about a 60's chara (charabanc) trip to Blackpool - won a Guinness award for pub theatre and performed it at the Black Horse on the Crescent.'

He added: 'For several years we staged the work of new "non theatre" voices, tackling various subjects in the history of Salford and its people, and took the work to pubs and clubs, where non-theatregoers would find their own lives depicted on stage.

'From then on it was a gradual development with commissions arriving from local agencies. It became more sophisticated, with issues of quality at the top of the agenda.'

Guy said that in 2001 Debbie Freeman contacted him and said she had a play and was looking for a venue. They met and director Philip Parr read the script and realised that here was a vehicle ideally suited to their new agenda.

Director of Play

Philip Parr, the director of 'Fire in the Park', said this was an enormous challenge of being drawn from factual research, claiming: 'Many of the people you see on stage had real lives and histories about which we know a lot or little.'

He added: 'This demands from us a care and delicacy in treating the characters and situations, because they relate to real people and places which perhaps our audience will know, or have their own relationships with.

'For the Victorian audience, the pyrodramas in Belle Vue Park were a great opportunity for large-scale excitement and thrills.

'Imagine a cast of hundreds, fireworks and explosions on a grand scale, the colour of exotic costumes, because most of the subjects were great exploits from the Empire's farthest regions, and a boisterous happy audience, willing to be thrilled by the spectacle. And health and safety were secondary to the effect!'

He also confirmed: 'The many issues that surrounded the play – race, poverty, crime and the perception of crime, are as relevant today as they were in 1885, when Belle Vue was the exciting, seedy place we saw on stage.'

The play was performed on various dates and times at the Robert Powell Theatre on Frederick Rd, now part of the University of Salford, by members of the Wise Monkey Theatre Co.

It included twelve main characters, with children's voices performed by members of the "SMART" Club at Salford Museum & Art Gallery.

Elite engineer
Sir Nigel Gresley relaxing with his son

CHAPTER 5

The Lost Dog That Saved Manchester United

It seems quite strange by today's modern standards when you consider that Manchester United Football Club may never have come into existence, had it not been for the City Police - and a lost dog!

The curious tale of the dog - excuse the pun - is still a legendary story in the region and dates back to 1902, just before the original Newton Heath LYR (Lancashire & Yorkshire Railway) football team changed their name to Manchester United.

Founded in 1878 from an enthusiastic bunch of young railway workers at the local carriage and wagon works, the club had made tremendous strides since first joining the Football Alliance in 1889/90, and then being elected to the Football League, Division One, in 1892/3.

This progress, however, came at a cost, with a full-time club secretary, professional players' wages to consider and the increased expenses of playing matches up and down the country in a national league.

By early 1902, and following some indifferent results on the pitch, Newton Heath LYC was in severe financial difficulties. Desperate for cash, they held a series of fundraising events, with one staged at the village hall and organised by Heath captain Henry Stafford.

The intention was to raise at least £100 to help stave off bankruptcy from a number of pressing creditors.

Stafford, who was a popular sporting character, attended with his St Bernard dog, Major. And as a publicity stunt, he tied a collecting box around the dog's neck, as if highlighting a definite rescue plea. During the event though, the dog escaped from the packed hall and vanished. The matter was then reported to the local police.

Major was later found, slightly confused and wandering the streets, by a pub landlord. The man was unsure as to exactly what to do with the pet, and unaware as to whom it belonged, so decided to take it back to his pub.

The landlord showed the dog to a local businessman, Mr John Henry Davies, who at that time was the managing director of Manchester Breweries. The dog seemed to take a liking to the man, so Davies paid the landlord for it and went home.

Perhaps guilt eventually got the better of Davies, for he began to make inquiries about the dog, and via the police found it really belonged to the Newton Heath skipper. He contacted the club and invited the player to come and collect 'Major' from his home, whereon Stafford explained the reasons for the dog's disappearance.

The two men formed an immediate bond and Davies took an interest in the club and offered to help financially. Davies later met with a small consortium of friends and local businessmen, who agreed to pay off the debts, on condition they changed the name and put the new management under their control.

All this was quickly agreed. However, deciding on a new name for the club became a major problem in itself and various suggestions were made, including Manchester Celtic and Manchester Central – which some directors said, sounded more like a railway station. Eventually, chief scout Louis Rocco announced: 'Gentleman, we have a Manchester United.'

The name was accepted and adopted, and the rest, as they say, is history. The club then introduced a new playing strip, abandoning the existing colours of white shirts and blue shorts for a new bold kit of red shirts, white shorts and black socks. And it seems that shortly after this, the club also gained the nickname of the 'Reds'.

The club played in various colours during their short life. The first being green and yellow halved shirts, and later white shirts with a deep red V-shape. The old green and yellow kit was later used in more recent times during the 1990s as United's commemorative away strip.

The loss of the name of their local Newton Heath 'Loco' was a bitter blow to regulars, for the 'Heathens,' as they were then commonly known, had fast gained a reputation for skill, flair and style, despite a rather heavy pitch.

Attendances too were fairly healthy, with their first-ever home league match, against Blackburn, attracting over 8,000 spectators. Many other games were equally well attended but the new directors soon realised the bulk of support was not necessarily from locals, but from many others travelling in from far afield.

Much of the 'Heathens' success - and problems - came after they had turned professional in 1885. The club had constantly attracted top players, including several Welsh internationals, because Newton Heath LYC, in addition to paying players' wages, could also provide additional regular employment on the railways.

In just 24 years, this small town band of amateur railway workers had achieved miracles and made unbelievable progress through the leagues. Their first ground was at North Road, close to an old clay pit, where players had to change in the local pub, the 'Three Crowns'.

In later years and following re-organisation, they moved again, this time to a similarly muddy pitch across town at Bank Street, Clayton, where the players at least enjoyed the luxury of their own changing facilities – in a small wooden pavilion – yet had to endure the threat of heavy pollution from an adjacent chemical factory.

The ground was overshadowed and dominated by an enormous chimney, which often belched out black smoke across the pitch halfway through a match, and was surrounded by several daunting high walls.

MOVING TO OLD TRAFFORD

Following the take-over and name change in 1902, the club's directors then launched ambitious plans for future progress and decided to promote the club throughout the North West. Six years later, they made provision to build a brand new, state of the art, and purpose-built football stadium at Old Trafford.

My great grandfather, then as a Chief Inspector of the Manchester City force, was based at the police station at 627 Oldham Road, Newton Heath. He both lived and worked in the area, knew of the missing dog story, and spoke of mixed feelings for the proposed move.

As a resident and sporting man, he had witnessed a period of growth and the introduction of professional standards. He also knew the level of support and realised the potential impact such a move could have on the local community and economy. And yet, much like the town in general, he had helplessly watched many other changes throughout this incredible industrial revolution.

James Wood was a down to earth realist, and as a senior and very experienced police officer, responsible for many other major projects in the city, he was given the joint task of helping to evaluate this latest exciting development.

In 1909, Manchester United won the FA Cup, defeating Bristol City 1-0 at Crystal Palace, and by 1910 the club were in a very strong financial position to expand and were eager to move from their much-criticised Bank Street ground at Clayton to Old Trafford.

Plans had been prepared a year or so before and were based on proposals from Archibald Leitch, a renowned architect and sports fan, who had already been involved with other similar schemes for Tottenham Hotspur FC at White Hart Lane in London, and at both Ibrox Park and Hampden Park in Glasgow.

Old Trafford cost a staggering £60,000 to build in 1910, but now boasted a fine seated and covered main stand, and three other large terraced areas, plus a superb grass pitch!

The fans and directors soon welcomed the move, and everyone understood the need to provide improved facilities, and to cater for the demands of supporters in this rapidly growing spectator sport.

In 1911, their judgement was proven sound when Old Trafford was selected by the Football League for an FA Cup Final replay between Bradford City and Newcastle United. Bradford eventually won the day 1-0, after previously drawing 0-0 at Crystal Palace.

And just four years later, Manchester United staged the 1915 FA Cup Final at this stadium, when Sheffield United beat Chelsea 3-0.

The closure of this successful early chapter in the club's history was recorded a mere eight years after their name change, and confirmed they had finally left the past behind, but remained keen to explore the future – with all its potential opportunities.

I wonder however, what would have happened had it not been for that lost dog? And even more interesting, I am still slightly puzzled as to why there is still little mention of this amazing story in the club's archives, and certainly no memorial or dedication to this extraordinary canine creature's memory?

The move to Old Trafford was indeed quite an occasion. The following words are taken from an extract published in Manchester's Sporting Chronicle, dated February 19th, 1910.

'The most handsome, the most spacious and the most remarkable arena that I have ever seen. As a football ground, it is unrivalled in the world. It is an honour to Manchester, and the home of a team who can do wonders when they are disposed.'

CHAPTER 6

The Old Watchman's Record Book
1825-1833

This chapter contains a host of genuine and fascinating reports covering an eight-year period of operation by Manchester Watchmen between July 18th 1825 and July 30th 1833.

They are all contained within the watchman's record book, which has been carefully preserved and maintained within my family since 1826. It provides a detailed, accurate and compelling account of street life in and around the city several years before Robert Peel's new 'Bobbies' came into being.

The watchmen however, remained the eyes and ears of the city for at least another ten years after Peel's introductions, and it was certainly at least eight years after the last entry in this record book before the police began to patrol the same Manchester patch and suburban streets.

The book not only tells of the daily grind of survival, of constant Watch patrols and criminal incidents, but it also adds some colour and flavour to what life was really like in Manchester at that time – and especially after dark!

For many watchmen, it must have been a stark and lonely existence, particularly in winter, patrolling a tough beat in some desolate slum areas. The chapter reveals something of the constant dangers of the job and makes occasional comment about missing watchmen, drunk and disorderly officers, and others who were constantly absent without leave.

Areas covered include: - New Gorton Road, Hyde Road, Ashton Road, Ashton Lane, Stockport Road, Chancery Lane, The Green, Chapel Street, Ardwick Road, Union Street, Chorlton Row, Pin Mill Brow, and many, many others.

The watchmen mentioned here were obviously based around the Gorton, Longsight, Ardwick and Ancoats areas, and highlight many local pubs, hostelries, and unauthorised drinking establishments, probably long demolished. Some include: - the George & Dragon, Blacksmith's Arms, the General Brick, Ancoats Hall and the Polygon.

There are also details of Wakes activities in the Longsight, Ardwick and Stockport areas.

The record book provides the actual names and addresses of the watchmen employed throughout that period, with comments and remarks about their performances. They are written by several watchmen and their supervisors, and again tell something of the occupations and activities of the inhabitants of the suburbs.

Reports cover incidents at the Lime Kiln Works, Brick Works, Paper Mill, Bake House, Slaughterhouse, farms and orchards. It seems a remarkable contrast within the space of a few miles from heavy-duty industrial working to a rural setting; and it mentions the work of the lamp lighter, and damage caused by strong winds and storms.

The way things were
Line drawing of the Old Smithy door

It was part of the night watchman's duties to ensure lamps were lit and report any damages on the already darkened streets. He was also instructed to check for unfastened window shutters, doors, and gates, with instructions to wake the occupants if found to be un-tethered. This was a particular concern in the summer months and no doubt caused aggravation between the house owners, servants and watchmen.

The entries in the book tell their own story and cover a wide range of unlawful activities, monitored by the officers, who always seemed to come in for extreme criticism – and yet were expected to help keep the peace and satisfy the demands of local businessmen.

Many entries cover people being drunk and disorderly. Others include theft, forgery, highway robbery, horse stealing, sheep stealing, general rustling, and a theft of ducks, apple stripping and vagrancy.

Some of these occurred on a regular basis and the officers certainly needed their wits about them to be able to make arrests. There are also reports of 'ricks' for assistance and mentions of injury and fires, which all had to be dealt with by the watchmen.

There were also many reports of stealing clothing and food in the more poverty-stricken areas, together with shouts of murder, wife beating, aggravated assaults, ferret hunting, threats to shoot, attacks with bricks and stones, poaching and the stealing of whisky.

The incidents covered a varied and wide range of matters and were based on reports from about sixteen watchmen and several supervisors, including many from a distant relative of mine.

One of these men was **James Wood senior**, who was probably my great grandfather's own great grandfather, who was involved as a senior watch supervisor. Many of his entries are clearly shown in the record book and I understand he gave the book to James junior for safe keeping five generations ago!

The actual book has now been donated to Manchester Police Museum, where I am sure the entries can be examined with permission from museum officials. All the entries were neat and hand written, mainly in black ink with the dates and remarks clearly displayed.

* The following reports are taken from genuine extracts from this watchman's record book and were found within private papers of James Wood junior, a former detective & superintendent of Manchester City Police from about 1890-1914.

Record book dates include: -
July 18th, 1825 – Sept 30th, 1825; entries completed by James Wood senior.
October 9th, 1825 – April 24th, 1828; entries completed by Thomas Chantler.

April 30th, 1830 – May 18th, 1830; entries mainly completed by Richard Nicholson, with many others unsigned.

And from August 2nd, 1831 – July 30th, 1833. Many others remained unsigned but one dated **Sept 12th, 1831,** was signed by Alsibrook Sampson.

Names and residence of watchmen: -
No 1. Henry Vaudrey, Coach Alley.
No 2. George Grimshaw, 13 Berry Street.
No 3. James Smith, William Street.
No 4. Joshua Barnes, 56 Loom Street, Newton Lane.
No 5. John Royle, Back William Street.
No 6. Thomas Gardner, Back Chapel, Chancery Lane.

Additional and updated changes: -
No 4. Samuel Woolley, Chapel Street.
No 5. John Parry, No 3 Chandler Street.
No 4. James Foster, Robinson Court, Back Chapel Street.
No 6. John Andrew, Back Chapel Street.
No 3. John Dollaghan, Bench Street.

Other watchmen listed within the reports include: - William Broom, George Kay, William Heywood, Robert Carter, William Jones, John Ryley, and Thomas Pimblott.

START OF WATCHMAN'S RECORD BOOK – FROM JULY 1825

Monday evening, July 18th, 1825
Dist 4. Joshua Barnes absent.

Tuesday morning, July 19th, 1825
ALERT ON THEIR ROUNDS
I visited the watchmen during the night and found them alert on their rounds. No reports.
Tuesday evening, July 19th, 1825
Dist 4. Joshua Barnes absent.

Wednesday morning, July 20th, 1825
CRY OF MURDER
Dist 2. James Smith says that at two o'clock a woman cried out 'murder' near the watch box. He immediately pursued a man who made his escape. He returned back to the place and the woman was gone also.

I visited the watchmen during the night and found them alert and on their rounds.

Thursday morning, July 21st & Friday morning July 22nd, 1825
I visited the watchmen during the night and found them alert and on their rounds. No reports.

Saturday morning, July 23rd, 1825
Dist 5. John Royle says that he found the doors of Mr Shand, King's Head, Chancery Lane, open at three o'clock this morning and all gone to bed.

Sunday morning, July 24th, 1825
DRUNK & DISORDERLY
I visited the watchmen during the night and found them alert and on their rounds. A great number of drunk and disorderly people returning from the New Gorton Road between the hours of one and two o'clock in the morning.
Dist 6. William Broom says that on going his ten o'clock round last night the landlord of the George & Dragon public house insulted him wherein the execution of his duty.

Monday morning, July 25th and Tuesday July 26th, 1825
I visited the watchmen during the night and found them alert on their rounds. No reports.

Wednesday morning, July 27th, 1825
BOYS PUBLICLY WHIPPED
Dist 5. John Royle reports that at six o'clock last night, he saw two boys, Jack Bates and Charlie Hyde, lobbing the garden of Mr Turner. He took them into custody and brought them to the lock-up. The comments in the report book confirmed: They were publicly whipped on the Green and discharged on July 28th.

Thursday morning, July 28th, Friday 29th, and Saturday 30th July, 1825
I visited the watchmen during the night and found them alert on their rounds. No reports.

Sunday morning, July 31st, 1825
STOPPED ON HORSEBACK
Dist 6. William Broom reports that between nine & ten o'clock last night, six men on the Ashton Road attempted to stop two gentlemen on horseback. The first put spurs to his horse and rode to Mr Jakes sign of

General Brick; also, that a horse was found with a saddle and bridle - which was afterwards owned by a Mr Ashton of Blackburn. He stated that he was thrown off at the time of mounting. Broom further stated that he found a strayed cow about half past twelve o'clock on the same road - claimed by Mr Renshaw the following morning.

He also reports that at two o'clock, four men on Ancoats Bridge were breaking the peace and told to go home, but did not. He 'ricked' and they dispersed. Also reports by Joshua Norris, Flag Alley, keeping a disorderly house and at the same time, his wife abusing him and watchman Ryley.

DISORDERLY GANG

Dist 2. James Smith reports that at half past one o'clock, a very disorderly gang of people was assembled on the Green from Chapel Street. That he and Kay went to disperse them and they gave battle – Chorlton Watchmen came to their assistance and one watchman was very much abused. Two were known, James Wright and Elias Gregson with Dan Howard of Chapel Street.

Remarks: Warrant obtained for James Wright and apprehended on Monday and called to answer at Sessions on Tuesday 2nd inst. Elias Gregson left town.

SIX DUCKS IN A SHIRT

I visited the watchmen during the night and found George Kay intoxicated – a great deal of disorderly people at two o'clock and three men on the Stockport Road with six ducks in a shirt. On seeing me the men ran back towards Longsight and I sprung my rattle and they dropped the ducks.

In his remarks, it confirmed: Six ducks were owned by a Mr Deane of Chorlton Road and delivered to his man on Monday morning.

Monday morning, August 1st, 1825

I visited the watchmen during the night and found them alert on their rounds. No reports. Dist 6. William Broom in liquor when going on.

Tuesday morning, August 2nd, 1825

FIGHTING PRISONERS IN LOCK-UP FROM LONGSIGHT WAKES

A great deal of disorderly people through the night returning from Longsight Wakes. At ten o'clock, Mr Hardy brought the prisoners to the lock-ups; one for fighting, and the other for rescuing another. James Murray for fighting, William Mark for rescue.

Dist 2. James Smith reports that at half past ten o'clock, he found a very disorderly set of people in Chapel Street, he took Thomas Howarth into custody.

Remarks: James Murray and William Mark committed for warrant of bail on August 2nd. Thomas Howarth discharged on August 2nd.

Wednesday morning, August 3rd, 1825

BATHING IN ARDWICK POND

At a quarter to ten o'clock, John Bromley of Hooley Hill, Ashton, was bathing in Ardwick Pond. I was under the necessity of sending his clothes to the office before he could be persuaded to come out. George Kay reports he had been in for some time.

When I came up, a great number of disorderly people coming from Longsight watched. Robert Simmons brought to the lock-up by Thomas Hulme for fighting.

Remarks: Bromley discharged on 3rd August. Simmons committed for warrant of bail on August 3rd. He was sent before the Commissioners on same day.

Thursday & Friday, August 4th & 5th August 1825

I visited the watchmen during the night and found them alert on their rounds. No reports.

Saturday morning, August 6th, 1825

STRAYED LAMBS ON ASHTON ROAD

Dist 2. James Smith reports that two men were fighting on his round at twelve o'clock. He took James Nettleton into custody and brought him to the lock-up.

Dist 6. William Broom reports that he found two strayed lambs at three o'clock and left them at Mr Barker's farm opposite the George & Dragon on Ashton Road. They were later claimed by Mr Brogden from near Ancoats Hall on August 7th.

Remarks: Nettleton was discharged on August 6th.

Sunday morning, August 7th, 1825

At twelve o'clock John Royle and William Broom were arguing with a Mr Maskery.

Monday & Tuesday mornings, August 8th & 9th, 1825.

I visited the watchmen during the night and found them alert on their rounds. No reports.

Wednesday morning, August 10th, 1825
DRUNKEN WOMAN TURNED OUT
Dist 4. Joshua Barnes reports that at half past ten o'clock he was called into a house at the Crescent to turn a drunken woman out.

Dist 5. John Royle reports that at half past twelve o'clock some men were in Mr Buchan's garden. On his approaching, they ran through the brick crofts towards Gorton Road.

Thursday, Friday and Saturday mornings, August 11th, 12th and 13th 1825
I visited the watchmen during the night and found them alert on their rounds. No reports.

Sunday morning, August 14th, 1825
ROBBED OF FIVE SOVEREIGNS
Dist 2. James Smith reports that at one o'clock, he found a respectable looking man very drunk near to the box, who stated that he had been robbed of five sovereigns – and later said two sovereigns - by two men. One stopped his mouth. He said he was going to Stockport.

Dist 5. John Royle reports that William Owen, Chancery Lane, has three Saturday nights come home drunk, broke the peace and behaved himself very disorderly at a late hour, and when desired to be quieter, used very improper language to him.

Monday, Tuesday and Wednesday mornings, August 15th, 16th & 17th, 1825
FORGERY CASE AT LANCASTER
I visited the watchmen during the night and found them alert on their rounds. No reports. Remarks: On Wednesday, August 17th, I went to Lancaster to give evidence on a case of forgery on the Mirfield Bank near Huddersfield. Returned Monday, 22nd inst.

Tuesday morning, August 23rd, 1825
1st round from ten till half past eleven. All alert. 2nd round from twelve to a quarter to two. All alert. 3rd round from three to a quarter past four. All alert. George Kay reports that a little before ten o'clock, a man named Tinker who lives in Chapel Street, was very disorderly on the Green.

Wednesday morning, August 24th, 1825
WATCHMAN THREATENED AND BEATEN
I visited the watchmen at the under mentioned times:
1st round from half past ten till one o'clock. John Royle reports that at twelve o'clock a gang of young men were singing and making a great

noise in Chancery Lane. He desired them to be quiet and go away. They then began to threaten and beat him.

2nd round from half past one to half past two o'clock. All alert. 3rd round from three to a quarter part four. All alert. Remarks: Heard before the Commission on Wednesday evening, the 24th inst.

Thursday morning, August 25th, 1825
I visited the watchmen during the night at the under mentioned times:
1st round from ten till twelve o'clock. All alert. 2nd round from twelve till two o'clock. All alert. 3rd round from three till half past four o'clock. All alert.

Friday morning, August 26th, 1825
NEGLECTING HIS ROUNDS
1st round from half past ten to half past twelve o'clock. William Broom neglected to go the upper part of his rounds on the Ashton Road at eleven o'clock; 2nd round, from half past twelve to half past two o'clock. William Broom neglected to go on the upper part of his round on the Ashton Road at ten o'clock and also at two o'clock; 3rd round from half past two to a quarter to five o'clock. No reports on this round.

Saturday morning, August 27th, 1825
STRIPPED OF APPLES
Mr Dean of Chorlton Row says that two men had been larking about his premises and that a tree was stripped of apples. Joshua Barnes chased them across the fields.

Sunday, Monday and Tuesday mornings, August 28th, 29th & 30th August 1825
Round times varied. Monday: James Smith reports that a back door of one of the new buildings in Tipping Street had been broken open during Sunday. No other reports.

From Wednesday morning, August 31st, until Tuesday September 6th, 1825
Round times varied. Remarks: Dist 1. George Kay sick on Sept 5th; and on Sept 6th, reports that between 9-11 o'clock it was very noisy with people returning from Gorton Market.

Wednesday morning, September 7th, 1825
STOLEN SHUTTLE
Remarks: John Mark brought to the lock-up at half past ten o'clock by Mrs Hardie and Mr Thomas Chantler on a charge of stealing a shuttle. He was discharged on Sept 8th by Mr Etholdstone.

Thursday morning, September 8th, 1825

LOCKED UP AS A VAGRANT

Notes confirm round times varied. At eleven o'clock, the under mentioned men were taken to lock-up in custody for fighting at the Blacksmith's Arms. George Lowe, John Young and Robert Kenott. At twelve o'clock, Mary McLennan brought to the lock-ups as a vagrant and for being disorderly on the Ashton Road.

Remarks: Discharged - gave £4. £3 to be distributed to the poor of Ardwick and one for damages. Discharged on Sept 8th by order of Mr Etholdstone.

Friday, Saturday and Sunday, September 9th, 10th & 11th September 1825
Round times varied and no reports.

The old Market Square
Mid 19th century line drawing

Monday morning, September 12th, 1825

LOST HIS CLOTHING

Dist 5. John Royle and Supt William Heywood and I visited the watchmen on the under mentioned hours. Other round times also varied. 1st round, half past nine to a quarter past twelve.

Henry Vaudrey reports when going his ten o'clock round, he found Joshua Oldfield of Hooley Hill, very much in liquor. He stated that he had been drinking at Mr Gee's and that he had been stripped of his small clothing, a hat and pair of shoes and he might have had ten or eleven shillings taken from him by some man who stopped his mouth. He could not describe the person. Remarks: He was brought to the office and kept till morning.

Henry Vaudrey reports that on going his three o'clock round, a number of boards were on fire that had been placed against a brick kiln on Ashton Road. He threw them down and extinguished the fire.

Tuesday morning, September 13th, 1825
Round times varied. Remarks: George Kay sick.

Wednesday morning, September 14th, 1825
Round times varied. Remarks: Henry Vaudrey reports that at half past nine o'clock some person attempted to draw some handkerchiefs through the cotter hole of Mr Renshaw's shop on Ashton Road but was alarmed and made off with parts of two.

Thursday morning, September 15th until Saturday September 17th, 1825
Round times varied. No reports.

Sunday morning, September 18th, 1825
BEATING HIS WIFE
Round times varied. Remarks: At one o'clock, William Haywood brought Thomas Yates to the lock-up for making a disturbance and beating his wife. He was discharged on Sept 19th.

Monday & Tuesday morning, September 19th & 20th, 1825
Round times varied. No reports.

Wednesday morning, September 21st, 1825
Remarks: George Kay in liquor going on duty at nine o'clock.

Thursday morning September 22nd until Friday September 30th, 1825
Round times varied. No reports.
* Final comments from James Wood senior.
Most future reports signed by Thomas Chantler.

Sunday morning October 1st until Saturday October 8th, 1825
Round times varied. No reports.

Sunday morning, October 9th, 1825
WATCHMAN ASLEEP IN HIS BOX
Dist 5. Remarks: William Heywood asleep in his box from eleven till twelve o'clock; and the following day, October 10th; Dist 6, he noted John Wood was not on his rounds from one till four o'clock.

Tuesday morning, October 11th until Friday October 14th, 1825
No reports. Remarks:

Saturday morning, October 15th, 1825
Dist 6. Remarks: William Williams found two men on a brick kiln in Ashton Lane and took them into custody.

Sunday morning, October 16th until Saturday October 22nd, 1825
No reports.

Sunday morning, October 23rd, 1825
Dist 6. William Williams not on his rounds from one till four o'clock.

Monday morning, October 24th, 1825
Dist 6. William Heywood found one man on a brick kiln in Ashton Road and took him into custody.

Tuesday morning, October 25th till Thursday October 27th, 1825
No reports.

Friday morning, October 28th, 1825
Dist 3. Robert Carter sent his coat down at five past nine o'clock; the following day, Saturday, he was reported off-duty.

Sunday morning, October 30th, 1825
Dist 3. Carter off-duty.
Dist 5. Royle sent his coat down by five past nine o'clock.
Dist 6. Mr Heywood says that on going his two o'clock round he saw two men running down Pin Mill Brow. Soon after, he found that an attempt had been made to get into Wilf Ainsworth's kitchen window in Ashton Lane.

Monday morning, October 31st, 1825
WATCHMAN DRUNK AND WITHOUT HAT
Dist 2. Smith found James Beswick drunk and without a hat on the Green.

Tuesday morning, November 1st until Thursday November 3rd, 1825.
No reports

Friday morning, November 4th, 1825
LAMPS OUT OR MISSING
Dist 2. One lamp out at half past nine o'clock.
Dist 3. Two lamps out at by the Green.
Dist 3. One lamp out at Union Street corner.

Saturday morning, November 5th, 1825
Dist 5. Mr Hardy interfered improperly with Royle the watchman while in the discharge of his duty.

Sunday morning, November 6th, 1825
Dist 3. One lamp out at the end of Union Street. Broken by the wind, it being cradled before.

Monday morning, November 7th, 1825
Dist 1. One lamp next to Fothersal's on the Green.
Dist 2. One lamp out on Chapel Street.

Reports then switch from morning to evenings but were still signed by Thomas Chantler.

Tuesday evening, November 8th, 1825
Dist 3. Three lamps out next to Mr Kennedy's on the Green.
Dist 4. Two lamps out at the Polygon and Mrs Wilson's.

Wednesday evening, November 9th, 1825
Dist 1. One lamp out on the Green.
Dist 6. Two lamps on Cotter Lane in Renshaw's shop window on Ashton Lane.

Thursday evening, November 10th, 1825
Dist 1. Lamp out at the Dinnington's.
Dist 2. Lamp out at Chapel on the Green.
Dist 3. Lamp out at Bremner's.
Dist 4. Lamps out. One at end of Hyde Road and one at Polygon.

No reports from May 10th until 22nd, 1825.

Wednesday evening, May 23rd, 1825
Dist 19. Lamps were put up in Ashton Lane, Dark Lane and Hallows Lane.
Dist 6. One lamp broken by a cart in Ashton Lane while it lay on the ground.
Thursday November 24th, 1825
No reports.

Friday evening, November 25th, 1825
Dist 6. Samuel Young struck Vaudrey the watchman while on his duty. Mr Chantler ordered a warrant and had Young taken before magistrates and fined 14 shillings.

Saturday evening, November 26th, 1825
No reports.

Sunday evening, November 27th, 1825
THREATENED TO SHOOT WATCHMEN
Dist 6. Vaudrey saw some men going into Mr Sale's hayloft and informed him. On going towards the loft he became alarmed from someone saying the men had threatened to shoot anyone that came near. Upon which, he 'ricked' and came to me.

When I got there, I found four Ardwick and one Chorlton Row watchmen in Mr Sale's house and Mr Sale serving them drink. I told him they should not do it. I found that the men who had been in the loft were now in the kitchen with a quart of ale before them.

I asked the landlord if he had any charge against them, he said the watchmen made a great stir about nothing. I desired all to go about their business. When we got into the office, Smith the watchman was with Henry Vaudrey. I told him he had better hold his tongue in the street and said if he had anything to say, he should speak in a proper place.

He replied he would speak where he liked. He did not care a damn for any man. Remarks: One lamp broken by Mr Renshaw's cows in Ashton Lane, which he paid for.

No reports from November 28th until December 1st, 1825.

Friday evening, December 2nd, 1825
LAMPS PUT OUT BY WINDY WEATHER
A great many lamps out being on a windy night.

Saturday evening, December 3rd, 1825
Dist 4. One lamp out near Mrs Marshall's between nine and ten o'clock.

Sunday evening, December 4th, 1825
Dist 4. Marshall's lamp out.
Dist 3. Lamp out at end of Hyde Road.
Dist 2. Window loose at Mr Duckray.

Monday evening, December 5th, 1825
One lamp broken at corner of Bingon's works and lamplighter said it was broken before and blamed the frost.
Dist 4. One lamp out at Mass Hall.
Dist 5. One lamp out at corner of Duck Lane.

No reports from December 5th till 14th, 1825.

Thursday morning, December 15th, 1825
Dist 1. One lamp out at Medlock Street.
Dist 2. Two lamps out end of Chapel Street and one at Isaac Gardens.
Dist 3. Eight lamps out from Ardwick Terrace to Chancery Lane.
Dist 4. One lamp out at Polygon.
Dist 5. One lamp out at Brick Street, 3 at Ashton Lane.
Dist 6. Two lamps out at Riverside.
Remarks; Another windy evening.

Friday, December 16th, 1825
Dist 5. Toll House, Shutter Lane at five o'clock.

Saturday, December 17th, 1825
Dist 5. Playing of cards at General Brick at half past twelve on Sunday morning.

No reports on December 18th & 19th, 1825.

Tuesday morning, December 20th, 1825
Dist 5. At half past one this morning, five men were disorderly and were spoken to by Mr Vaudrey after which they ill-used him, Heywood and Royle got him away from them.

No reports from December 21st until 28th.

WATCHMAN'S RECORD BOOK – JANUARY 1826-1828.

Monday January 2nd, 1826
THREAT TO KILL
Dist 5. Watchman Royle off sick.
Dist 6. Vaudrey off and Heywood did their duty. About three o'clock on Tuesday morning, three men came over the edge in Ashton Lane and knocked Grundy down and kicked him, and said if he had been the watchman they would have killed him.

Tuesday January 3rd, 1826
Dist 2. One lamp on Chapel Street and one at Marriott Street.
Dist 5. Two lamps on Ashton Lane.

Wednesday January 4th, 1826
Dist 3. Four lamps out. Two at corner of Chapel Street; one at Mr Buchan's and one at Union Street.

Dist 4. Lamp missing from Stockport Road and found top of Mr Preston's wall. Lamplighter said it was broken.

Thursday January 5th, 1826
Dist 1. Three lamps out. Two at Tipping Street and one at Grove Street.
Dist 2. One lamp out at the Green and one at Manor Street.
Dist 3. Two lamps out at Union Street.

Friday January 6th, 1826
Dist 6. McGee's window uncottered. And John Gee's barrow left out.

Saturday January 7th, 1826
SAME GANG RETURNS
Dist 5. Royle says that at three o'clock this morning, three men came over a gate in Ashton Lane and told him if they did not give it him there, they would before long. He disposes they were part of the same gang that had ill-used him before.

No reports from January 8th until 25th.

Thursday January 26th, 1826
Dist 5. Mr Renshaw's window shutters loose.

Friday January 27th, 1826
Dist 5. Royle says company was turned out of Mr Sales at half past two this morning.

No reports from January 28th until February 4th, 1826.

Sunday February 5th, 1826
Dist 5. Royle reports he found the butcher's shop in Ashton Lane broken into.

Monday February 6th, 1826
Dist 5. Two lamps broken at one o'clock.

No reports from February 7th until March 22nd, 1826.

March 23rd, 1826
Dist 2. Bridge's shop window shutters loose.

March 24th, 1826
Dist 6. Three cotters loose at Gee's.
Dist 5. One loose at Gilbert's and one at Foster's.

March 25th, 1826
Dist 3. Mr Longdon's back door open.
Dist 2. Mr Yates's front door open.

No reports shown from March 26th until April 1st, 1826.

Market Street
As it was in the mid 1800s

April 1st, 1826
Dist 2. Mr Chapman's window open. Mr Hoult's washroom window open.

No reports until April 4th, 1826. Entries then became rather infrequent.

September 1st, 1826
Dist 5. Thomas Smethurst taken from Gillibrand's shop and brought to lock-up as he broke through wall.

September 3rd, 1826
WINDOWS MISSING
Dist 1. Jones says that about one o'clock in the morning, he heard a noise and went to Mrs Butterworth in Downing Street and found the windows taken out but nothing taken away.

No further entries until December 1826.

Sunday morning, December 31st, 1826
Dist 5. Royle absent from his round from one o'clock.
Dist 3. Mr Heywood absent from one o'clock and without returning this morning.

No further entries until June 1827.

Tuesday morning, June 19th, 1827
WATCHMEN IN LIQUOR
Dist 1. William Jones in liquor when coming off duty.

Tuesday morning, June 26th, 1827
Dist 1. William Jones in liquor when coming off duty.

Sunday morning, November 4th, 1827
Districts 5, 4 and 2. Royle, Heywood and George Grimshaw in liquor at two o'clock in the morning. Heywood missed much of his round from two till five o'clock and left his lantern upon Mr Oliver's shop.

Sunday morning, November 11th, 1827
Dist 4. William Heywood in liquor when coming off duty and missed his round between two and five o'clock.

No further entries or reports until April 1828. Most were still signed by Thomas Chantler although Alsibrook Sampson signed one entry in the report book dated August 12th 1831.

April 19th, 1828
ENTICING WATCH DOG
Dist 1. Mr Longden states that the watchman of No I round is in the habit of enticing their watchdog off the premises.

Thursday morning, April 24th, 1828
Dist 1. Jones absent from his round from three till four o'clock.

No further reports or entries until April 1830.

WATCHMEN'S RECORD BOOK – APRIL 1830 ONWARDS

April 2nd, 1830
Dist 1. Henry Vaudrey says that he has had direction from Mr Berry in Tipping Street to inform him when their gates were open, and in telling the servants on Thursday night when going his ten o'clock rounds, he was told they would shut it when they were ready.

* The following reports appear at the back of the watch book and are signed by Richard Nicholson. They run from April 10th 1830 till May 18th 1830.

Saturday night, April 10th, 1830
District 1. Henry Vaudrey brought a woman Mr Duckworth named, Mary Fleming, to lock-up - not appearing, all charged with assaulting, Mr Foster. Discharged Duckworth and created a great hue at New

Bailey, noise was about the printers turnout on the 12th at his works at ten o'clock.

DRUNK, RIOTOUS & FERRETING

District 3. James Smith says that Shelmerdin, back of Club Row, about ten o'clock, was drunk and insulting his wife, but on his going up, he went in the house and was quiet – and also J.H. Cocker, Chancery Lane, about one o'clock was drunk and very riotous but he persuaded him to be quiet and he went home.

He also said a quantity of men were at the back of Mr Gregg's house ferret hunting all night and he disturbed them about three o'clock.

District 6. Thomas Gardner & John Royle dispersed a fight at Gillibrands at 20 minutes past one - they came out of Gillibrands to fight. Richard Nicholson.

Sunday night, April 11th, 1830

Dist 5. John Royle absent.

Dist 1. Henry Vaudrey reports that Gaskin's house window shuts were open when he went on his 10 o'clock rounds.

Monday night, 12th April 1830.

Dist 3. James Smith absent.

WATCHMAN STRUCK BEHIND NECK

Dist 6. Thomas Gardner reports that Pete Murphy followed him down Pin Mill Brow and struck him behind the neck, he 'ricked' and Murphy ran away making a great noise.

Dist 1. Vaudrey found Hollingworth's yard gate open at ten o'clock and he called them up to fasten it. Mr Cooke's back-sash loose at ten and he told them and when he went again at eleven & twelve it was the same. He told them again & they fastened it.

Dist 3. The supernumerary John Donegan, upon going past Jones's house in John's Street, set his dog at him, and Smith says he is always conducting himself very ill and creating a great disturbance.

Tuesday night, 13th April 1830

Dist 3. James Smith reports having found the windows open at No 20 Union Street and no one in the house at ten o'clock and it was eleven before they came in that he could inform them.

Dist 1. Vaudrey found the butcher's window open next to Watson's in Tipping Street and had to knock them up.

Wednesday night, 14th April 1830
COAL HOLE DOOR OPEN
Dist 1. About 2 o'clock Vaudrey found the coal grid lifted up at No 3 next to Holbrook's in Tipping Street and he knocked them up to secure it.

Dist 6. Gardner at ten o'clock found Gee's coalhole door open and he enlisted Mr Gee to secure it.

Friday night, 16th April 1830
BLADDER OF WHISKY FOUND IN HAT
Grimshaw reports that as he and Barnes were going from the office at nine o'clock they met with a man near Mr Willet's house very drunk and upon moving him, his hat dropped off and a bladder which contained whisky came out of it and they examined him and found a measure supposed to be used in selling it off. Nothing else being found they let him go and assisted him on the Stockport cart. The bladder and measure all remain at the office.

Saturday night, 17th April 1830
George Grimshaw was suddenly taken ill on his 11 o'clock rounds. He found Mr Kennedy's back door unbolted after that he was so far bad that he could not go on his rounds and Donegan the supernumerary was sent on his rounds. No report.

No reports for four nights, from Sunday night, April 18th, 1830, until Wednesday night, April 21st, 1830.

Thursday night, 22nd April 1830
PAWNSHOP WINDOWS UNFASTENED
Dist 6. Thomas Gardner found on going on his ten o'clock rounds that Mr Gee's back window shutter without a cotter and he told them and at twelve they took no notice.

Dist 5. John Royle found Mrs Owens's pawnshop windows unfastened at ten o'clock and he informed them of it.

Friday night, April 23rd, 1830
Dist 6. Gardner again found Gee's back window shutter without cotter and he informed them at ten and eleven o'clock, when Mr Gee said they had forgot to get a cotter.

Dist 3. James Smith found Browne's door open at ten o'clock – and them all gone to bed.

Saturday night, 24th April 1830

WATCHMAN ATTACKED BY GROUP OF MEN

Dist 1. Henry Vaudrey reports that at two o'clock he heard a 'rick' in Water Street, Charlton Rows, he went and found there had been a fight. He assisted to take the persons to the Chorlton Rows police office where the captain of the Watch took 2/6 each as security for their appearance at New Bailey on Monday.

Dist 5. Royle reports that on going his 9 o'clock round he heard of watch in William Street, upon going, he found that it was Mr Kenyon calling who stated that he had been attacked by five or six men who took his hat and his spectacles. His hat was found soon after by a neighbour. He states that at eleven o'clock he heard a cry of 'murder' in Ashton Road. He went up and found a woman apparently drunk and her basket with its contents scattered on the ground, which caused him to miss part of his eleven o'clock round.

Sunday night, 25th April 1830

Dist 4. I visited the watchman several times during the night and at twelve o'clock I found that Joshua Barnes was not attending to his duty and I stopped on his round. It was nearly five o'clock that he came about half drunk. I spoke to him about it, when he at first denied being off at ale but he eventually said that he hoped I would not say anything, but he had been at Mr Lees in the Polygon knocking them up at three o'clock. I was informed by a Chorlton Row watchman that he had heard him at that time but although I looked for him diligently, I could neither trace by inquiry, nor find anything of him.

Tuesday night, 27th April 1830

Dist 6. Gardner found Gee's door open at half past one o'clock. They were all gone to bed and he knocked them up.

Dist 1. Vaudrey found Mr Woods' door open at ten o'clock. He was a long time before he could make them hear and at last was answered from the garrett.

Wednesday night, 28th April 1830

Dist 2. Grimshaw found Mr Bunting's window open in Paddock Street and he awoke them.

Thursday night, 29th April 1830

No reports.

Friday night, 30th April 1830
Dist 1. Vaudrey found a window open at eleven o'clock next to Gaskin's and nobody in the house. It was fastened when he saw it again.

Saturday night, 1st May 1830
Dist 6. Thomas Gardner was absent.
Dist 2. Grimshaw found Mr Birch's dining room window open at eleven o'clock and he wakened them to fasten it.

Sunday night, 2nd May 1830
THREW HEAVY STONE AT WATCHMAN
Dist 5. Royle reports that one night this week in Ashton Road, some person threw a heavy stone at him, which hit him on one of his legs. He looked but could not find anyone, and this night another stone was thrown at him but did not hit him and he supposes they are the same parties, which threw on both nights.

Monday night, 3rd May 1830
Dist 6. Gardner says Gee's coalhole door still remaining open although he repeatedly told them and any person may go through the beer house or yard.

Tuesday night, 4th May 1830
'BAD CHARACTER' SEARCHED
Dist 5. Royle reports that at ten o'clock Roe's window shutter was open – on his ten o'clock rounds in Ashton Road, near the General Brick, he met the waiter and another man near the front door. The waiter began to take him with him. He then began to tie the shutters and behind the watering stone he found a ham. He took it with him into the General Brick and asked the landlord if he knew he owned the ham and they went to search the kitchen where they found one more missing. The landlord directed him to search the company and the room but could not find the missing one. He left the ham with the landlord. The company he searched were in the snug and he knew them to be of bad character.
Dist 3. Smith reports that ongoing his twelve o'clock rounds, he was talking with Mr Hewitt at his door when a man came to ask whether Hewitt had lent anybody his handcart. He said he had not. The man went back and Thomas Ireland followed him and overtook the men with the handcart near the top of the Green when they said they had borrowed it knowing different, but he let them go and kept the cart. Smith also following thinking it was suspicious circumstances but did not get near

enough to them to either see them or hear what occurred suspecting the matter. Through this, Smith missed his twelve o'clock round.

No reports from Tuesday night to Saturday morning.

Saturday night, May 8th, 1830
Dist 3. James Smith reports that Parish in Moulds Buildings was creating a great noise about two o'clock in the morning and insulting his wife shamefully. He could do no good with him and he was obliged to bring him to the lock-up – and his wife promised to appear against him. Through this, Vaudrey, who came to Smith's assistance when he 'ricked' him. He and Smith, missed part of their two o'clock rounds.

Sunday & Monday nights - no reports.

Tuesday night, 11th May 1830
FIGHTING IN THE ROAD
Dist 6. Thomas Gardner absent.
Dist 5. At a house in Sharples Buildings, Royle found open at ten o'clock and at eleven o'clock, he found Prickett's smithy broken open but nothing missing when he informed them. Royle at twelve o'clock was also called into the General Brick to turn the customers out and when he went at one o'clock he found them fighting in the road and he dispersed them.
Dist 3. John Caffery was fighting with his wife at 10 o'clock and she cried 'watch' and Smith went out and got them into the house.

Wednesday night, May 12th, 1830
Dist 1. Vaudrey found Mr Booth's distillery of wine door unfastened at eleven o'clock and the shutters too. He informed them of the circumstances when they said they did not know.

Thursday night, May 13th, 1830
STOP THIEF & MURDER
Dist 5. John Royle on going his nine o'clock round heard a cry of 'stop thief' and 'murder,' which caused him to run to beside of Barton's factory, where he found two men carrying a chair, a ring and some clothing. They were charged by an old man with stripping his house, where Royle, with the assistance of Mr George Hall, took them into custody.

Having learned of the occurrence, I overtook them in Union Street, whereupon getting them into the office, I found the old man to be Parish, who was in the lock-ups on Saturday night charged with great cruelty towards his wife, and one of the prisoners his son, who was assisting his mother to carry away her things in consequence of the father's repeated ill usage. The clothing consisted of his mother's - and with the exception of the chair and ring, the old man laid no claim – seeing it was a family affair we discharged the man at the office.

At eleven o'clock, Royle found Barker's window shuts and Schofield's back gate open.

Friday night, 14th May 1830
LAMP TOPS MISSING
Dist 3. Smith reports that during the time he was going his two o'clock round he found that two lamp tops had been taken off in Chancery Lane by some person. He awaited but could see no one stirring he looked for the tops and he found them at three o'clock in Cheslett's Field.

Dist 1. Henry Vaudrey reports that at 3 o'clock he found a large bunch of onions hung at Watson's door. He knocked them up to take them in. He said he had received something hanging before but thought it was only a rag or something that way.

Saturday night, 15th May 1830
Dist 2. George Grimshaw reports that Wilf Yates's back door was open and he desired them to fasten it.

MOB HAD CONGREGATED
Dist 5. Royle reports that at 12 o'clock he and Gardner were called in to the General Brick to assist in turning some company out who had brought a pack of cards with them and the landlord would not allow them to play and took the cards from them, they kicked up a hue and were rowdy. Mr Gill was obliged at first to get Mr Corns and Mr Taylor, who were in the house to assist him and had it not been for the assistance of the watchmen, Mr Gill and the two constables would have been badly ill used as a mob had congregated and collected a quantity of fellows in the street. This caused Garner & Royle to miss the remainder of the twelve o'clock round.

Dist 3. Smith says that the same party came on his round at one o'clock. They went to the King, and he turned them out as through the night on part of his one o'clock round.

Sunday night, 16th May 1830

WOMAN OF THE TOWN

Dist 2. George Grimshaw reports that at nearly one o'clock Wm Heaviside called for him and sent him to search for some person in the house. I went with him and upon getting there, found a woman of the town in Mr H's custody. I searched her, but upon inquiry it turned out that she had been brought into the house by his son James – we of course, sent her about her business. Grimshaw through this, lost part of his one o'clock round.

Dist 1. Vaudrey reports that he found at ten o'clock the house at No 2 Stone Street open, both windows and shutters, and Leake's shop door open.

Monday night, 17th May 1830. No reports.

Tuesday night, 18th May 1830

Dist 1. Vaudrey reports that he found Boulton's front door open at ten o'clock and everybody gone to bed. He waked them and they got up and had to wake Mr Watson to fasten their window shuts at same time.

No further reports or entries until August 1831.

WATCHMEN'S RECORD BOOK – AUGUST 1831 ONWARDS

August 2nd, 1831

Dist 4. Joshua Barnes off his rounds from half past one till half past three.

Dist 5. John Ryley off his rounds from two till four o'clock. He says he was taken very sick at Toll Bar.

Dist 6. Thomas Gardner was off from two till half past three o'clock.

Thursday morning, August 12th, 1831

Barnes was off his round from half past one o'clock till half past three o'clock in the morning. John Ryley from two till four o'clock; and Thomas Gardner from two till half past three o'clock.

James Wood, Thomas Chantler or Richard Nicholson completed most entries during this initial period in the record book - and Alsibrook Sampson made the final entry of that section.

Saturday night, August 20th, 1831
Dist 4. Joshua Barnes absent. Calling his twelve o'clock round at half past one.

Friday morning, August 26th, 1831
Dist 6. Thomas Gardner and John Ryley seen coming from the King public house in Chancery Lane with Sarah Moorcroft at a quarter to one. Landlady refused to fill them drink.

Saturday August 27th, 1831
COACHMAN THREATENED WATCHMAN
Sandy Cheetham, Mr Steele's coachman, threatened to knock Henry Vaudrey down for attempting to stop a foot race at the bottom of the Green.

Wednesday August 31st, 1831
Dist 4. Joshua Barnes. Revd McGibrand's house in Shakespeare Street was broken into and robbed. He complained of neglect on the part of the watchman, not attending to his duty.
On the same night, Mrs Johnson's house at the top of the Green was attempted. The window in the front porch was broken but the entrance was inwards by the inside shutter. The house is included in the Chorlton Row watchman's round, which is taken in lieu of the houses belonging to Chorlton Row on the Ardwick side of the Green - and watched by the Ardwick watchmen.

Tuesday night, 6th September 1831
BULLDOG FLEW AT GARDNER
Dist 5 & 6. John Ryley and Thomas Gardner report that on Monday night about eleven o'clock, they were called into the George & Dragon public house in Ashton Lane to separate fighting at the house. The landlord ceased filling drinks. The men who had before been upstairs then came down and went back into the taproom and persisted in staying there. Notwithstanding, no drinks were allowed. About 1 am the watchmen were again called in, and desired to clear the house, as the company would not otherwise go but continued fighting and disturbing the peace. While the watchmen were clearing the house, a bulldog, which belonged to one of the company, flew at Gardner and bit him. In consequence they missed calling on much of their eleven o'clock & one o'clock rounds. Gardner reported to office that the shop door under his alleyway was open all night.

Saturday morning, September 10th, 1831

BAKE HOUSE & OTHER PROPERTIES ROBBED

Dist 3. James Smith's round. Mr Lee found one Saturday morning when putting out the lights, a coat and three loaves. He afterwards discovered that the bake house belonging to Mr Clarke had been broken open and robbed of the above-mentioned articles. He went with Mr Clarke the baker and Smith, the watchman, in search of the thieves but could hear nothing of them. Mr Clarke's baker found Royle the watchman asleep upon some sheaves. He said when questioned that he was watching the thieves. Smith later said he found two hats and a handkerchief on the opposite side of the road to Mr Clarke's.

Dist 6. Thomas Gardner saw three men from the lime works about eleven o'clock. They had been cutting the rope belonging to the gin. A house was broken open and robbed in Pin Mill Yard of a shirt and some calico.

Dist 2. George Grimshaw. Five men were creating a disturbance by singing and shouting about three o'clock in the morning.

Dist 1. Henry Vaudrey. On Thursday night, the gate and the coach house door belonging to Mr Dawson's house were left open. The watchman locked the coach house doors and returned the key next morning.

Dist 1. Vaudrey. Mrs Dean and lad left the stable door open; the watchman awoke them to fasten it.

Remarks: John Ryley suspended on Sept 10th.

September 18th, 1831

Dist 5. James Smith. Mr Jackson's house in Birch Street was broken open. Theft included a ladies workbox, silk shawl, silver snuffbox, pencil case, bodkin thimble and some rich lace and zip of stiff shoes.

Dist 3. James Smith. On Sunday, a fight in Symes Place about twelve o'clock at night but was dispersed by Sampson, James Smith and George Grimshaw.

Saturday night, September 24th, 1831

Dist 2. George Grimshaw about eleven o'clock found some cloth in Mr Farrington's yard and no one around it.

Thursday October 6th, 1831

PROPERTY GUARDED UNTIL EARLY HOURS

Dist 6. A fight broke out in a stable belonging to John Hebden in Pin

Mill Yard. The watchmen, except Hooley, were detained to guard the property until nearly four o'clock.

Thursday October 13th, 1831
Dist 2. George Grimshaw found Mr Howard's window shutter open about twelve o'clock.

Saturday night, October 15th, 1831
Dist 1. Thomas Gardner found Mr Duckworth's print shop window open in Stone Street.

Sunday night, October 16th, 1831
Dist 2. George Grimshaw found Mr Agnew's front window open on his ten o'clock round. The same night he found Mr Newbury's window half open.

Monday night, October 24th, 1831
Dist 4. James Woolley found Mr Henry McConnell's garden door open at about eleven o'clock.

Saturday night, October 29th, 1831
BONNET & UMBRELLA FOUND ON GREEN
Dist 3. John Dollaghan found Mrs Crowley's front door open about twelve o'clock.
Dist 1. T. Gardner found on Saturday night near Manor Street, upon the Green, a bonnet and an umbrella.

November 14th, 1831
Dist 2. George Grimshaw found Mrs Mawson's window shuts open at about eleven o'clock. On November 18th, he found Mr Birch's dining room window open.

December 5th, 1831
Dist 1. Thomas Gardner found two men at the bottom of Mr E.P. Thompson's cellar. They knocked him down before he was aware and then ran away – he sprang to his 'rick' and Smith came to his assistance but upon examination all was found correct. Mr Thompson later sent up to say his shipping had been robbed.

December 22nd, 1831
George Grimshaw found Mr Mawson's window shutters open.

January 24th, 1832
Thomas Gardner and George Grimshaw said that a stone was thrown

threw Mr Thorpe's window in Manor Street. The following day, Grimshaw found Mr Agnew's and Mr Bateman's back doors open.

February 4th, 1832
Dist 2. George Grimshaw found Mr Birch's dining room window open. He also found Mr Bird's cellar window open all night. He hailed the servant but he did not make it.

March 19th, 1832
Dist 6. Woolley found two foals in Mr Townsend's plant at Polygon at half past one o'clock in the morning.

April 3rd, 1832
Dist 6. Samuel Woolley found drunk on his eleven o'clock round by Joseph Grimshaw and William Ashton and he was ordered to be suspended and that Thomas Harrop be appointed in his place.

WATCHMEN'S RECORD BOOK – APRIL 1832 ONWARDS

April 6th, 1832
WATCH BOX BURNT DOWN
Dist 2. George Grimshaw's watch box was burnt down at half past twelve o'clock on Friday morning while he was going his round.

April 17th, 1832
KICKING AT DOOR FOR MORE BEER
Dist 1. Thomas Gardner found Henry Heaton kicking at William Bradshaw's door and he said that he wanted some more beer. When Mr Bradshaw opened, he tried to knock him down. He would not fill him any more at two o'clock in the morning.

May 10th, 1832
Dist 2. George Grimshaw found Mr Crimson's back door open at eleven o'clock rounds.

May 18th, 1832
SHEEP STOLEN
Dist 2. John Hewitt's shop was broken open at a quarter before ten o'clock at night and four sheep were stolen.

May 21st, 1832
Dist 2. George Grimshaw found Mr Hewitt's stable door unlocked at two o'clock in the morning.

June 14th, 1832
Dist 2. George Grimshaw reports that Cheetham, Steel's coachman, and Hall, a joiner, were fighting on Monday night about four o'clock.

June 15th, 1832
Dist 1. Thomas Gardner found William Toplin's shop door broken into about eleven o'clock at night. Mr Gardner went with him and when he came out he said nothing was stolen.

June 22nd, 1832
RIOT AT LODGINGS
Dist 1. George Grimshaw found Mr Slack's warehouse door open at ten o'clock.
Dist 2. James Smith missed part of his twelve o'clock round through a riot raised by two men and two women at Mr Gee's through being refused lodgings.

June 28th, 1832
Dist 3. John Dollaghan found a man's hat at Summer Place owned by Robert Clarke.

July 7th, 1832
Dist 6. John Parry found three men at Mr Barker's brick kiln.

July 10th, 1832
Dist 5. James Smith found four men at lime kiln at three o'clock in the morning.

July 16th, 1832
Dist 1. George Grimshaw found Mr Leatherbarrow's window shuts loose.

July 24th, 1832
Dist 2. Thomas Gardner found Mr Barlow's window open.

July 25th, 1832
Dist 2. Thomas Gardner found Mr Schofield's parlour window not made fast.

July 28th, 1832
Dist 4. James Foster found three men very drunk in Shakespeare Street.

August 4th, 1832.
Dist 3. John Dollaghan found Robert Ransom very ill drunk at Mrs Shaw's door and he said that he had been robbed of his watch by three

men about a quarter of an hour before.

August 10th, 1832
Dist 6. John Andrews found some men fighting at Mr Gee's door about eleven o'clock at night.

August 14th, 1832
ROBBED OF FOUR SHILLINGS
Dist 5. John Parry found a man in Ashton Road, and that he had been knocked down and robbed of four shillings by four men who ran away.

August 17th, 1832
Dist 4. James Foster says he was going his eleven o'clock round that a man with white hawse and blue jacket got over Mr Watkins's wall into the grounds and opened the kitchen window and then went into the garden and ran away.

August 20th, 1832
Dist 1. George Grimshaw says that he found Mr Leak's window not made at eleven o'clock.

August 25th, 1832
Dist 6. John Andrews says that four men and two women were fighting at the end of Chancery Lane and that he called John Parry for assistance and got them away.

September 4th, 1832
Dist 2. Thomas Gardner found John Hewitt's stable door open at three o'clock in the morning and he went to call them up.

September 10th, 1832
Dist 2. Thomas Gardner found Mr Toplis's blacksmith shop door open at half past 2 in the morning.

September 20th, 1832
Dist 2. Thomas Gardner says that Mr Jones was knocked down and abused.

September 24th, 1832
Dist 3. John Dollaghan says that he was charged by William Murray to assist him to take Ralph Bradley for stealing his hat and that he was brought to the lock-up and sent to the New Bailey.

September 28th, 1832
Dist 3. John Dollaghan brought William Williamson to the lock-ups for striking him on his duty.

October 17th, 1832
Dist 6. John Andrews found John Hebden's mill door open on his two o'clock rounds.

October 24th, 1832
Dist 5. John Parry found Mr George Shatwell's parlour window open on his twelve o'clock rounds.

October 27th, 1832
Dist 4. James Foster found Mr J.B. Clarke's parlour window open.

November 11th, 1832
Dist 2. Thomas Gardner says that he found liquor very nearly out of Mr Thomas Fletcher's parlour window on his twelve o'clock rounds.

Monday November 12th, 1832
Dist 1. George Grimshaw found Mr Duckworth's print works window open at twelve o'clock.

Wednesday November 14th, 1832
Dist 1. George Grimshaw found Mr John Higginton's butcher shop window not made fast on his eleven o'clock rounds.

Wednesday November 15th, 1832
Dist 5. John Parry found John Hewitt's house door open on his twelve o'clock round and them all in bed.

Sunday morning, November 18th, 1832
SHOP ON FIRE & BURNT DOWN
Dist 3. About 2 o'clock. John Dollaghan found Mr Walker's and Moscrap joiners shop on fire - and it was burnt down.

Monday November 19th, 1832
Dist 1. George Grimshaw found Mrs Holmes' garden door open on his eleven o'clock round and Mr Slack's warehouse door open on the same round.

Monday night, November 19th, 1832
Dist 4. James Foster found two very bad looking men lurking about on his round about one o'clock. He watched them for a long time and they went on the Stockport Road.

Tuesday night, November 27th, 1832
Dist 2. Thomas Gardner found Mr P.F. Williams's gates and coach house door open on his eleven o'clock round.

Dist 5. John Parry found Mrs Walker's house door open at twelve o'clock.

Wednesday night, November 28th, 1832
Dist 1. George Grimshaw found Mr Kay's coal grate open on his twelve o'clock round.

Wednesday December 5th, 1832
Dist 4. James Foster said that he heard something in Mr John Barnes garden as if somebody was breaking open a door. When Mr Barnes said that two men had just gone out of the garden they found open the window shuts.

Thursday night, December 20th, 1832
Dist 3. John Dollaghan found Mr Armstrong's window shuts open at half past ten o'clock.

Wednesday December 26th, 1832
SHEEP OUT OF PEN
Dist 1. Thomas Gardner found J Tipping's smithy door open at eleven o'clock. Same night, John Hewitt's sheep pen open and sheep out at half past eleven o'clock.

WATCHMEN'S RECORD BOOK – JANUARY 1833 ONWARDS

Sunday January 6th, 1833
James Foster says that he found four windows open at Mr Schuster's home about eleven o'clock.

Monday January 7th, 1833
John Parry found Joseph Hardy's window shutter open on his eleven o'clock round and them in bed, he called them up to wake them.

Thursday January 17th, 1833
George Grimshaw found Mr S.H. Slack's warehouse shutters open on his ten & eleven o'clock rounds and said they made a practice of leaving them open.

Friday January 18th, 1833
John Dollaghan found John Crowther's window open at half past eleven o'clock.

Saturday January 19th, 1833
Robert Kenyon suspended for being very drunk when coming off his patrol at nine o'clock and Edward McCann appointed on his round at the meeting.

Sunday morning, January 20th, 1833
BEEF & MUTTON STOLEN
John Parry says that Mr Brierley had about 80 lbs of beef and mutton stolen from his lobby in the yard and a single barrel gun from the Garding house.

John Andrews says that he found Mr Gee's window open about two o'clock and his wheelbarrow in the street.

Tuesday January 22nd, 1833
John Parry suspended for being drunk rescuing a person from the constable of Openshaw on the 21st January 1833, and Robert Waite appointed on his round on the meeting night.

February 22nd, 1833
John Dollaghan found George Young trying John Clarke's window shutter and door about two o'clock in the morning. He brought him to the lock-up and went to New Bailey. He was committed for 14 days.

February 26th, 1833
George Grimshaw found Mr Duckworth's stable door open on his eleven o'clock round and Mr Leatherbarrow's window cotters loose on the same round.

February 28th, 1833
George Grimshaw found Mr William Wadsworth's back door open at about eleven o'clock and them all in bed.

Monday morning, March 4th, 1833
FIRE AT NEW HOUSE
Thomas Gardner saw a fire at Mr Johnson's new house in Hyde Road about three o'clock and was got out with little damage.

March 8th, 1833
George Grimshaw reports that he found Mr Higginton's shop open at eleven o'clock and them all in bed.

March 10th, 1833
John Dollaghan found Mr Knight's window open at ten o'clock and them all in bed.

March 11th, 1833
John Andrews found John Hewitt's shop door open and them asleep. At eleven o'clock. James Foster found John Wilkinson's window shuts

open. George Grimshaw found Mr Duckworth's window shuts open on his eleven o'clock round.

March 12th, 1833
George Grimshaw found Mr Hack's back door open on his twelve o'clock round.

March 14th, 1833
CALF FEET TAKEN FROM SLAUGHTERHOUSE
Thomas Gardner found John Hewitt's slaughterhouse window broken open and four calf feet at the outside door on his five o'clock round.

Saturday March 23rd, 1833
George Grimshaw found all John Leatherbarrow's window shutters unfastened about two o'clock in the morning.

Friday March 29th, 1833
Thomas Gardner charged Robert Walton with tricking him on his eleven o'clock round and he was brought to the lock-ups.

Sunday March 31st, 1833
PAPER MILL ON FIRE
George Grimshaw says that he saw William Oliver's paper mill on fire about 5 o'clock in the morning and that he gave alarm to the Manchester watchmen.

Wednesday April 3rd, 1833
INJURED COACHMAN WAS DRUNK
John Andrew found in Hyde Road a sociable and horse thrown over and the horse first and the coachman lying injured at some distance off. They belonged to William Robinson of Stockport. The man was so drunk when they brought him to the lock-up that he could not speak.

Tuesday April 23rd, 1833
Thomas Gardner found John Hewitt's coach house door open about one o'clock in the morning.

Saturday April 27th, 1833
Thomas Gardner found John Hewitt's coach house door open on his two o'clock round.

Monday April 29th, 1833
George Grimshaw found Mr Isherwood's front door open and them all in bed on his eleven o'clock round.

Tuesday April 30th, 1833
COUNTING HOUSE DOOR OPEN
Thomas Pimblott found the counting house open at Lime works on his ten o'clock round. Same night, James Foster found Mr William Clowes' window shuts open on his eleven o'clock round.

Tuesday May 7th, 1833
SERVANT TOLD TO SHUT WINDOWS
John Dollaghan found Mr Armstrong's front window open and he told the servant of it. The same night, James Foster found Mr Schuster's window open and he told the servant but he did not shut them. Same night, Mr Slack's window was open.

Saturday May 7th, 1833
TURNED OUT FOR FIGHTING
John Andrews said that there was fighting at Joseph Shaw at eleven o'clock and him and Pimblott went in to turn them out. Same night, John Andrew found William Renshaw's shop window shutter open on his twelve o'clock round.
Same night, Thomas Gardner found Mr Bargele's new house open with a quantity of lead in it and he went to Mr Egan to tell him and he came to lock the door.

Saturday June 20th, 1833
James Foster reports that seven men stopped Mr Richard Dearman and robbed him of his watch.

Sunday morning, June 30th, 1833
Thomas Pimblott brought Henry Eaton to the lock-up for assaulting and abusing John Steel of Openshaw.

Thursday July 18th, 1833
George Grimshaw found Mr John Higginson's back yard door open about twelve o'clock. Same night, he found John Higginson's slaughterhouse door open about one o'clock - but nothing was missing.

Monday morning, July 29th, 1833
HORSES & GAME FOUND BY BRICKMAKERS
Thomas Pimblott and some brick makers found three horses and game. No account of them at the office but was drunk all day with the brick makers and came at night to the office very drunk to go on his duty. I told that he was very drunk and that he should not go on and he said that

he would go on and thus was not drunk. I suspended him till the next morning and put William Smith on his round.

Tuesday July 30th, 1833
ROBBED OF CLOTHING
James Foster says a person came to him from Stockport and said that he had been robbed of some clothing last night.

Thomas Gardner brought a man to the office with a bundle because he would not give an account of it. When he was at the office, he gave several different accounts of it. At last he admitted that his name was William Howard and that he lives at No 4 Briton Street, Bank Top.

That was the final entry in the old watch book.

MANCHESTER POLICING BOUNDARIES 1839

In 1839, following the creation of a new Manchester Police force, the names and boundaries of the police districts of Manchester were split into fourteen recognised territories, and now included: -

No 1. New Cross District. This was bounded by the New Cross and Great Ancoats Street, Oldham Road, and the River Medlock.

No 2. St Michael's District. Bounded by Oldham Street, Swan Street, Miller Street, part of Long Millgate to Scotland Bridge, and along the River Irk.

No 3. Collegiate Church District. This was bounded by Scotland Bridge and part of Long Millgate, to and through Miler Street, by Shudehill, Hanging Ditch, Cateaton Street, down to Salford Bridge, the River Irwell and the North side of the said Church.

No 4. St Clement's District. Bounded by Great Ancoat's Street, Lever Street and the River Medlock.

No 5. St Paul's District. This area was bounded by Lever Street, New Cross, Swan Street, Shudehill, Nicholas Croft, High Street, Market Street and Piccadilly.

No 6. Exchange District. Bounded by Market Street, St Mary's Gate, Deansgate, Cateaton Street, Hanging Ditch, Withy Grove, Nicholas Croft and High Street.

No 7. Minshull Street. This area was bounded by Piccadilly, London Road, Portland Street, Brook Street and the River Medlock.

No 8. St James's District. Bounded by Piccadilly, Portland Street, Bond Street and Fountain Street.

No 9. St Ann's District. This included St Mary Gate, Market Street, Fountain Street, Brazennose Street, Princess Street and Deansgate.

No 10. Oxford Street District. This area was bounded by Bond Street, Brook Street, Mosley Street and the River Medlock.

No 11. St Peter's District. Bounded by Mosley Street, the River Medlock, Deansgate, Brazennose Street and Princess Street.

No 12. St Mary's District. This area covered Old Bridge Street, Deansgate, Bridge Street and the River Irwell.

No 13. Old Quay District. This was bounded by Bridge Street, Deansgate, Quay Street and the River Irwell.

No 14. St John's District. This area included Quay Street, Deansgate, the Canal, the River Medlock and the River Irwell.

Growth of a modern city
Piccadilly by the end of the century

CHAPTER 7

Robert Peel & The First Policing System

Bury born, Robert Peel was a dedicated, determined, and highly controversial legal reformer, who in his capacity as Home Secretary demanded an urgent review of the criminal code, and a massive shake-up of the country's existing policing system.

The introduction of his Metropolitan Police Act in 1829 had an immediate effect upon policing in London, and although his policies were later adopted nationwide, at first they led to mixed emotions and some drastic action from a sceptical public.

And for some time, Peel, and Tory Prime Minister, the Duke of Wellington, received death threats and became worried about city riots and reprisals - due to the rapid implementation of their severe measures.

Peel however, realised that in the eighty years or so since Henry Fielding had adopted similar reforms and introduced the Bow Street Runners, public demand for law and order had changed and there was now a unique opportunity to co-ordinate all forms of policing.

This included a radical review of the Thames Police, Horse Patrols, Foot Patrols, Parish Constables and Watchmen (Charleys). He also confirmed plans to create a specialised detective office, utilising some revolutionary aspects of new scientific advances and research.

One of his proposals was to try and implement new legislation in order to establish a new force, and to develop a new body of unarmed men, paid and fully equipped to help keep the peace.

At this period in London, crime was again rampant and Peel claimed he had only had a few hundred men to patrol the streets, and just eight magistrates, each responsible for about 8-12 Runners.

Peel said the existing system was 'ineffective and inefficient' and demanded all sections be incorporated within one new organisation of police - and controlled by two new Commissioners of Police.

Peel announced a 'Nine Points of Law' plan: This was to be an integral part of his proposed Police Bill. They included: -

- The basic mission for which the police exist is to prevent crime and disorder.
- The ability of the police to perform their duties is dependent upon public approval of police actions.
- Police must secure the willing co-operation of the public in voluntary observance of the law to be able to secure and maintain the respect of the public.
- The degree of co-operation of the public that can be secured diminishes proportionately to the necessity of the use of physical force.
- Police seek and preserve public favour not by catering to public opinion but by constantly demonstrating absolute impartial service to the law.
- Police use physical force to the extent necessary to secure observance of the law or to restore order only when the exercise of persuasion, advice and warning is found to be insufficient.
- Police, at all times, should maintain a relationship with the public that gives reality to the historic tradition that the police are the public and the public are the police; the police being only members of the public who are paid to give full-time attention to duties which are incumbent on every citizen in the interests of community welfare and existence.
- Police should always direct their action strictly towards their functions and never appear to usurp the powers of the judiciary.
- The test of police efficiency is the absence of crime and disorder, not the visible evidence of police action in dealing with it.

METROPOLITAN POLICE BILL

Peel's new Metropolitan Police Bill was passed on July 19th 1829. And on September 29th, less than two months after the Bill was adopted, his first batch of one thousand men were turned out from Whitehall - in a great long line – for publicity purposes to begin patrolling the streets of London.

Peel celebrated his success with the appointment of two new Police Commissioners, who supervised the massive re-organisation. They included ex-Army officer, Colonel Charles Rowan, and a young barrister, Richard Mayne.

This newly created Metropolitan Police Force only patrolled the London districts, whilst the rest of the country continued much as before with existing policing methods, and in most cases, it was another decade before other authorities introduced their own police forces.

The new London policemen were called 'Bobbies' or 'Peelers' after their founder and their new uniform included top hats and blue tailcoats. This colour distinguished them from red-coated soldiers, and the scarlet waistcoats of the famous Bow Street Runners.

Officers were required to wear their uniforms at all times – both on and off duty, to avoid any potential claims of spying. They also carried rattles and were armed with wooden truncheons. They only received a guinea a week and were allowed just five unpaid days holiday per year.

Many policemen, particularly in rural areas, were desperately short of money and kept livestock to help supplement their income. Some even kept guinea fowl in their station houses but first had to request permission from police headquarters.

Most worked in long shifts and were not allowed to vote in any elections. They even had to seek permission to marry. Church attendance too was considered part of their duties and in most areas, officers had to attend a monthly 'Pay Parade' to claim their wages. It was an unusual tradition that continued for another eighty years!

Despite Peel's pledge that his new force were better trained, better turned out, more efficient and paid, they were certainly not very popular at first with the general public.

And it took another decade before the 'Peelers' were finally accepted. The tide seemed to turn following the murder of a young policeman in Holborn, when residents saddened by such a vicious and unprovoked attack organised a collection for the man's widow and family.

Many authorities, nationwide, waited as long as possible before establishing their own forces, and to a certain extent most waited until they were forced to adopt these radical measures by the introduction of the Municipal Corporation Act in 1835. This ruling insisted that all boroughs and cities outside London should create their own police forces.

MODEL FORCE

The Peelers eventually became the model for all forces, and in some regions a few Chief Constables were appointed from senior London officers, or from experienced Army officers with extensive military experience.

In Manchester, many forces came into operation when towns were first incorporated. This involved the election of councillors, then raising the rates to help pay for the force, and finally a watch committee to supervise the officers.

It was nearly ten years after the Police Act before Manchester and districts formed their own force, but by 1899 all suburban areas had their own systems.

Lancashire and Cheshire Constabularies covered some suburban towns and yet, ironically, one town that decided not to have its own force was Bury, the former hometown of Peel! Bury opted to come under the jurisdiction of the Lancashire force, and remained so until 1974!

Early 'Peelers', 1845

Robert Peel died on July 2nd 1850, following injuries sustained from a fall from his horse a few days earlier on Constitution Hill. He was sixty-two years old. Despite a love-hate relationship with both fellow politicians and the public, the nation mourned for him, and Bury built a rather grand statue to his memory.

Following public subscription, the town also constructed Peel Tower at the top of nearby Holcombe Hill, so that theoretically he could still keep watch over the town, and the rest of the Manchester area.

SCOTLAND YARD, CID, SHERLOCK HOLMES & LIFE

Following Peel's extensive overhaul of the metropolitan police system, he soon set about re-organising and re-locating his detectives to new offices within a centralised location, and took a very keen interest in scientific research.

Initially, he transferred his team of investigators from Bow Street to an old 18th century building within a large area known as Scotland Yards. It seemed a bold move to leave Bow Street and their established police headquarters - and the venue for the Metropolitan Magistrates Court, where most of London's important criminal trials were heard - yet once again Peel triumphed.

The first move included use of the old Market police office in Whitehall Gardens, which had previously been used for army recruitment purposes. And in 1843, the first specialised Criminal Investigation Department (CID) was created.

This was an entirely separate force and consisted of an Inspector and six Constables, who were all dressed in plain clothing! They were primarily appointed to help deal with a specific new threat termed 'terrorism', and related to potential attacks from foreign agents, and from a new Irish-based splinter group, known as the 'Dynamiters', who had begun a series of devastating bombing attacks against prominent targets.

During this period, the country also faced major immigration problems with an influx of unwanted refugees from revolutionary countries.

The detective team also worked closely with a specialised unit at the Post Office Science Crime Laboratory, established in Bell Yard, near Temple Bar. Their brief was to help counter a new scientific war that had developed since the introduction of the penny post, and now involved potential risk from parcel and letter bombs.

By 1850, surprisingly, the detective offices had outgrown this location and offices were hastily constructed at Great Scotland Yard, with the

Metropolitan Police HQ in one section, and the public carriage licensing offices in another.

This building though, and others, became the subject of bombing attacks by terrorist groups, who once exploded a powerful device that practically destroyed the detective office.

Fortunately, it was unoccupied at the time but the explosion demolished a nearby pub, packed with other off-duty policemen, and several members of the public.

Many were badly injured by the blast – two seriously. This proved to be a very lucky escape for the detectives, who over the next few years also had to deal with many other unexpected and similar incidents in the London region.

In 1886, there were massive explosions at both Paddington and Victoria Stations in the heart of the City, and another smaller incident at Ludgate Hill. The attacks continued intermittently, and other notable targets later included large private houses, rail and road bridges, trains, public buildings and even ancient monuments.

One major similar incident of note was an attack on Nelson's Column in Trafalgar Square, on May 30th 1894. Records indicate the police were members of a newly formed anti-terrorist squad, who had been summoned about 9.20 p.m.

The danger apparently came from an unexploded and highly unpredictable package, consisting of sixteen cakes of dynamite - already fused - and tied to the foot of the column. Fortunately, this proved to be one of the few times attackers failed to detonate a device, and the slight delay allowed officers to dismantle the bomb.

This incident though, provided a stark wake up call to the Government, who revised their efforts to try and counter any future attacks and began to employ specialist police officers with military backgrounds and explosives experience.

The Metropolitan Police Headquarters moved on several occasions. The latest seemed to be about 1890, when they relocated to new Scotland Yard offices, situated off Derby Street, close to Whitehall corner.

At this site, they were finally able to boast about having their own crime laboratory, began to deal with the advance of photographic reproduction and witnessed the birth of fingerprinting and the introduction of an extensive criminal records system.

FALSE UNIFORMS – NEW ACT

In early 1894, and shortly before the Nelson's Column incident, the authorities expressed concern over certain individuals fraudulently wearing false military style uniforms. Many were said to be disgruntled ex-soldiers, or down and out civilians, who could regularly be seen begging on the streets and abusing the Queen's uniform.

The Government, worried about 'Trojan horse' style terrorist attacks, and the need to clean up the city streets, quickly introduced the Uniforms Act, which made it a punishable offence for any civilian to wear service apparel, in part or total, or any dress designed to imitate any service uniform.

This new Act also covered the unauthorised wearing of military medals, orders and rank badges. In addition, it also endorsed an instruction given to police officers that they had to wear their uniforms at all times to confirm their role within the community.

SHERLOCK HOLMES

The period shortly before and after the turn of the century coincided with the fictional publications of Sir Arthur Conan Doyle, who depicted his hero as the super sleuth Sherlock Holmes, and his able assistant Dr Watson.

His work was extremely topical and included references to the 'Dynamiters' and 'foreign agents,' and Holmes regularly pitted his wits against the admirable Inspector Lestrade at the new Scotland Yard.

WILKIE BARD & THE MUSICAL WATCHMAN

As I have mentioned earlier, the poor old night watchmen often came in for some 'stick' from a variety of sources. And in particular, were also the butt of many jokes and songs in the ever-popular music hall.

Victorian entertainer Wilkie Bard, who originally hailed from Chorlton-cum-Hardy, was noted for singing a popular monologue about the unfortunate *Manchester Watchmen,* and for using their exploits as part of his famous music hall act.

Heralded as probably one of the great all-time music hall stage performers of his day, Bard was a popular Lancashire singer, and comedian, who told and sang the stories of the day in an amusing style.

His comic timing and rich fruity voice had audiences enthralled, and in 1912 he appeared in the first Royal Command Performance, where it was said he brilliantly performed one of his favourite old time songs about the *Night Watchmen.*

The 1912 report in 'British Music Hall' by Mander & Mitchinson, confirmed:

'Wilkie Bard was put down for "I want to sing in Opera", but for this show he substituted *"The Night Watchmen"*, who mind the drainpipes and other people's business in the funniest way possible.'

It continued: 'In the silent watches of the small hours, he thinks out social problems, and his occupation fosters a natural bent for philosophic reflection.'

THE EARLY DAYS OF MANCHESTER

Manchester, like so many other major cities throughout the country was completely transformed by the Industrial Revolution. It had led to the rapid construction of canals, railways, housing, and scores of factories, with many built close to rivers to make use of waterpower.

The city soon became a magnet for people seeking accommodation and work. And part of this labour force included many Irish immigrants, who started to arrive in great numbers from about 1852, followed by the Italians in 1865.

The unprecedented growth of cotton mills and the increasing demand for additional labour continued to swell the population of Manchester. In 1811, the region's census figures showed a population of 79,459, and by 1838 it had more than doubled to 181,708. It continued to increase, reaching 303,382 just thirteen years later in 1851, and by 1891 the population was estimated to be 563,368.

Manchester became a centre to the cotton trade and merchants travelled with imported goods from Liverpool and other ports to make use of spinners for conversion of products in the factories and cotton mills.

These factories, however, also made extensive use of child labour, with some children as young as six employed for up to fourteen hours a day, six days a week, and earning just 2s 3d for a hard week's work.

Mill owners naturally considered the children to be key workers. They were far more flexible and young girls or very small children were preferred as they were required to climb under or between machines to gather loose cotton. The children were also paid up to ten times less than adults. They earned the nickname of 'Scavengers' but some unfortunately endured rather short and uncomfortable lives, many suffering from broken bones and deformities.

This was a dirty and dangerous occupation and resulted in numerous horrific injuries and many fatal accidents. By 1830 there were five hundred and sixty cotton mills recorded in the area, employing some 110,000 workers.

The dangers at work were not the only hazards. The main everyday killers at that time were tuberculosis, cholera and typhoid. In children, however, diarrhoea was a major cause of death. Many of the health problems at the early part of the century were caused by a lack of hygiene and poor sanitary conditions.

Clean drinking water was almost unheard of, and rivers were still being used for both household water supplies, and the disposal of raw untreated sewerage.

The situation was so bad in Manchester at one time, with cholera and typhoid rife, that the authorities identified certain Manchester suburbs as 'death zones.' They included Ancoats, Ardwick and Chorlton-on-Medlock.

Communal cesspits were also common and often overflowed into rivers and streams when swelled by the winter rains. Stockport too was hit by a severe cholera epidemic in 1832 - and this particular disease was a regular summer visitor to Manchester.

There were numerous other epidemics and in factories too there was a dangerous illness known as 'mill fever,' which led to serious problems of nausea, dizziness, headaches and aching limbs.

Working with cotton lint and dust was deemed to be the main cause, but without any health or safety precautions the disease and fatality rate accelerated unchecked.

It was well into the 19th century before the problems of sewage disposal and the provision of fresh drinking water was successfully addressed. In 1850, the first supplies of fresh water arrived from Longendale Reservoir, using extensive piping into the city.

This supply, however, was not available throughout the region, and many still had to wait for hours on end to collect their small supply in un-hygienic metal buckets.

Two years later the Sanitary Association was formed, and eventually special isolation hospitals were set up to deal with the worst cases of disease. By 1890, additional clean water supplies were being piped to Manchester from the Lake District.

Despite certain advances in household services, most working class people still lived and died in despicable conditions of extreme poverty, where long hours, work dangers and the ever-present threat of serious illness, severely reduced normal life expectancy.

Casually posed...
Peelers take a break in 1850

POLICING & COSTS OF LIVING

The Victorian age was certainly nothing like the 'good old days' often portrayed by television dramas, and was in fact one of distinct contrasts, between people who had everything and others who had absolutely nothing!

It was also a horse dominated world, with the public travelling to work by omnibus or trams, whilst aristocrats, businessmen and their families continued in the main to travel by private coach or carriage, with some employing several coachmen.

Police wages: A police constable in 1900 would earn about £67 per year, which would increase to £80 after ten years service. A sergeant could expect to take home £104 p.a., and a superintendent about £290.

In comparison, general labourers earned £46 p.a., a railwayman about £43, and shop assistant £20. In the higher bracket, a bank manager could expect about £400 p.a., whilst some top earners performed in the music hall for more than £520 p.a.

Rent and rates were high in comparison to wages, and household accounts showed the regular purchase of lamp oil, washing soda, firewood sticks, candles, black lead, and scrubbing brushes.

A loaf of bread was 3d, a pint of milk one and a half pence, pound of cheese 5d, sugar a penny-farthing and a pound of potatoes, half a penny. Coffee was expensive at one shilling, but tea was surprisingly even worse at one shilling and five pence!

A newspaper, dependent upon whether a daily or evening, varied from a half-penny to a penny, and seats at the theatre ranged from six pence to four shillings! Admission to the zoo cost six pence and a ticket for the cinema one shilling.

Transport costs generally included nine pence for a Hackney carriage ride per mile, and tram fares of three pence for a journey from the suburbs into town. Horse tram fares were cheaper but were soon phased out by the introduction of overhead electricity wires.

Many people used a variety of community-based enterprise clubs for boots, clothing and essential supplies, and families somehow survived on a very mediocre diet.

Restaurants: In London, a respected quality restaurant was the Globe in Coventry Street, where a first class luncheon could cost anything from two shillings. A five-course meal however, would have set you back about three shillings and sixpence!

If you preferred a cheaper alternative, Previtali's Hotel in Arundel Place offered a very wide choice from the menu from just eight pence - and one unusual facility offered at that establishment was a foreign guide for non-English speaking visitors.

With specific Italian connections, it was extremely popular with continental visitors to London, but due to the political and economic problems overseas it often remained under police surveillance - and provided some very interesting customers!

CHAPTER 8

Detective Superintendent Jerome Caminada

Jerome Caminada was said to be one of Manchester's most successful thief-takers. A former engineer, born of mixed race parentage, with an Irish mother and an Italian father, he joined the city police force in February 1868 - and enjoyed a highly successful thirty-one year career, becoming the first Superintendent of Detectives.

My great grandfather worked with him on many occasions over several years until Caminada retired in 1899. James served under him, first as a detective constable, then as a detective sergeant. They were based in the same office.

Caminada was born in the very poor Deansgate area of the city in 1844. His father Francesco came to England from the Lombardy region during a time of political unrest in his home country. He was just one of many thousands who took a similar journey from northern Italy, seeking a peaceful life, with new opportunities for their families.

Many bizarrely settled in the Ancoats area - which quickly gained the nickname of 'Little Italy', where despite exchanging the lush rolling hills and mountains of their native lands for the dark, satanic mills, and tall dirty black, smoke-stacks and belching chimneys of east Manchester, many immigrants saw this as a vast improvement to their earlier basic way of life.

Most readily moved into a number of one hundred year old former mill houses, which although needing extensive renovation and repairs to protect against the cold winter weather, still offered exceptional accommodation with living rooms, bedrooms and outside toilets.

The Italian immigrants soon introduced Catholic Whitsun walks and homemade ice cream to the city, and gradually began to import other specialist food products from their native regions and helped establish a unique and highly successful business empire.

These new settlers, however, did not always have everything their own way, and from the initial arrivals in 1865, until the latter immigrants of around 1900, often clashed with rival English and Irish inhabitants and neighbours.

Fortunately, this 'Little Italy' soon established its own identity, and quickly brought welcome colour, vitality and prosperity to the area.

Caminada was a staunch Roman Catholic and was just twenty-four years old when he first joined the Manchester force as a constable. At that time, the police were only about eight hundred strong, and had to deal with a population of 350,000.

On his first night of duty, Caminada had to deal with an incident of a serious wounding in which a well-known local drunkard, 'Fat Martha', was attacked and stabbed in the stomach.

The rookie officer had to first help sober her up before she could be treated. This was, of course, at a time long before any emergency services, and he soon realised that it was part of a policeman's lot to care for the sick and injured and take them, if necessary, to the nearest infirmary.

In some cases, this meant a hike of several miles aided by fellow officers, and carrying the casualty on a handcart or stretcher.

Three years after joining the force, he gained promotion to sergeant and was introduced to the newly created Detectives' Office. It was here he gained an enviable reputation as an exceptional 'thief-taker', claiming several cash awards for the successful detection, arrest and subsequent conviction of many dangerous and habitual criminals.

Caminada was said to have imprisoned 1,125 people during his career, for a whole variety of crimes. He worked with a vast network of informants, and it was said he met many at his local St Mary's Church in Mulberry Street.

He was a rough, tough, and often ruthless individual, who was extremely ambitious and was afraid of nothing and no one. He became much feared within the criminal fraternity. He established a mean reputation for being able to defend himself, and was never concerned about using his fists, a gun, or another weapon, in order to secure the arrest of a supposedly dangerous villain.

In 1888, he was promoted again, this time to detective inspector, and helped introduce the use of photography and 'mug-shots' to help catch and deter criminals.

He was also known as a master of disguise and sometimes acted undercover to secure arrests and convictions. He once hid in a piano case, and in another example posed as a patient to expose a quack doctor.

His powers of detection became legendary following an investigation into a mysterious hackney carriage murder. In trying to establish whether the victim had been deliberately drugged or poisoned before being robbed, he persuaded the surgeon to send away an organ from the victim for scientific testing in the new crime laboratory. He later caught the killer at home with some of the victim's possessions.

Despite his bullish attitude, Caminada bizarrely tried to help the families of criminals that he had put away and was determined to tackle many social issues, including an attempt to reduce the problems relating to re-offenders.

He also received many worrying threats and attacks during service and one experienced villain, Robert Horridge, vowed he would kill him. The man fired two shots at fellow officers in an effort to escape justice, but Caminada tracked him down, and used his pistol to make the arrest.

Jerome Caminada in 1901

Caminada and many other detectives carried firearms. He had cause to use his own gun on numerous occasions. His personal favourite was a Colt 38 calibre double-action revolver, made from blue steel, with a chequered walnut handle.

Other guns were supplied through the Army at Pall Mall, London, and most were made of nickel or chromium plated to prevent rust. James Wood had his own army service revolver and I understand that, due to his military experience, he was allowed use of this as and when required. He also gave instruction to other officers in the use of firearms.

In addition to crime investigation matters, Caminada also took a tough stance on the unlawful sale of alcohol and lewd entertainment. He claimed to have helped to close over four hundred public and beer houses around the city. He prosecuted many landlords for selling illegal ale, or serving customers cheaper poisonous substitutes.

115

He retired from the police force in 1899, and the supervisory Manchester Watch Committee rewarded him with a 'handsome pension'. In later years, he worked as an estate agent, and private investigator before taking an interest in local politics, where he later stood as a city councillor.

Records indicate that, unfortunately, Jerome Caminada only enjoyed less than fifteen years of retirement. He was apparently involved in a road traffic accident in North Wales sometime during 1913, and later died from the results of his injuries the following year at his home in Moss Side. He was seventy years of age.

TWENTY-FIVE YEARS OF DETECTIVE LIFE

In 1895, and just a few years before his retirement, Caminada published the first of two comprehensive volumes about his work with Manchester Police.

It was entitled: 'Twenty Five Years of Detective Life', and published by John Heywood of Deansgate & Ridgefield, Manchester. He dedicated the book to the Chief Constable, Charles Malcolm Wood.

In the preface to volume I of his book, he surprisingly made a general criticism against the few fictional crime writers of the day, claiming: 'Unlike so many so-called stories of detectives, these are founded on facts, and are from first to last, in all their details, truthful histories of the crimes they purport to describe, and of the detectives and punishment to the criminals.'

He explained that the work consisted of fifty stories dealing with all manner of crime and criminals. He stated: 'The methods of quack doctors are exposed and the credulity of their victims revealed; the practices of swindlers and impostors of all kinds laid bare, including exploiters of sham registry offices, bogus agencies of various kinds, next of kin frauds, insurance and other swindles; begging letter writers are exposed and the modus operandi of burglars, pickpockets, watch snatchers, racecourse thieves etc., are described and dealt with.'

He added: 'In compiling the experiences, I have guarded myself against giving to individuals unnecessary offence or pain. I have endeavoured also, when dealing occasionally with subjects of a delicate or risky nature, to do so in language free from offence that may be read alike by old and young of both sexes.'

Caminada also explained that at a time when he joined the police force, the area and character of what he called 'Criminal Manchester,' was very different from what it was then (1895).

'Both sides of Deansgate, then a narrow street or lane fringed with property of the lowest class, were hotbeds of crime. The widening of Deansgate, the early closing of public houses and the building of Central Station did much to break up the Deansgate colony, whilst a better supervision of the police tended to keep down crime in other parts of the city.'

Caminada also claimed within his introduction that: 'Manchester with all its great moral, religious and political associations, its commercial enterprise recognised in every part of the world, and its corresponding wealth, still has its dark spots.

'Within an arrow's flight of the princely grandeur of the Town Hall may be seen many dreary dwellings of misery and wretchedness.

'Twenty-seven years ago however, things were much worse! Then in Charter Street and Angel Meadow, not so much of a meadow now, and in the vicious streets around to which my thoughts are at the same time directed, "the wicked never ceased from troubling, nor were the weary ever at rest", for the fitful midnight slumbers gave place, as daylight broke, to the restlessness of evil.'

THE STREETS AND SLUMS OF MANCHESTER

Caminada continued to give a highly graphic and most vivid description of life on the dark, dangerous city streets and within the grotesque slums of Manchester from 1868 onwards.

In some extracts from his book, he claimed: 'The exterior of one of these houses to which I propose to carry the mind of the reader will be a fair specimen of the rest. It present a dingy face of crumbling brick, begrimed by the soot of years.

'The elevation consists of three storeys; the first two are lighted by windows which denote unmistakable antiquity, and multifarious are the methods employed to refuse wind and rain admittance.

'Tattered garments, crowns of old hats, brown paper, and paper rendered brown by exposure, are all pressed into the service of stopping a hole; and so varied are the contrivances utilised for this purpose, that the several windows are more suggestive of a rag merchant's establishment than a dwelling house of Christian England in the 19th century.

'On entering, we proceed along a lobby until we come to a room whence issues a babel of tongues, and in which a scene as extraordinary as can be conceived presents itself. The apartment is full of men and women, though the former predominate.

'Some are seated on broken backed chairs, or upon dilapidated stools ranged round a filthy table, most of the occupants eagerly devouring various kinds of messes, washed down by tea, coffee or beer. Others again, are on their knees before the fire – one broiling a red herring; another a slice of fat bacon.

'Some appear to have just left their beds, or, as is more probable, being obliged to quit them, have descended to the common room in a state of dishabille, and are proceeding to attach their tattered rags to their persons in the best way they can.

'Some of the women are patching garments, the primitive colour of which has long since vanished; others are endeavouring to make a stocking perform its duty one day more. And crouched on each side of the fire, such as it is, sit two thinly clad creatures, whose bruised and disfigured faces are eloquent examples of the "bully's" brutal treatment, which many of Eve's fallen and forlorn daughters have to endure.

'Running along one side of the room is a dirty bench on which a large number of men are smoking and drinking. The furniture is of the most meagre description, and consists of one table, some half-dozen broken backed chairs, two stools and a bench.

'The walls are dotted with gaudily coloured prints, the subjects of which are mostly of a licentious nature. A few common ornaments are on the mantelpiece, the principal one being a large blue earthenware dog with a brown tail. The room reeks; the whole scene is squalid and cheerless; yet no sense of shame is visible on the countenances of the motley occupants.

'The ribaldry of one black-browed fellow is equalled only by the dreadful oaths of the young girl by his side, and the grossness of the mere child is applauded by a hoary-headed wretch whose condemnatory substantives are the familiar flowers of his speech.

'Then look at the object of pity, once a bright-eyed girl, on whose lap lies an infant with scarcely a shred to cover its delicate little form. One cannot help wondering what sort of life is in store for this blameless infant. A happy one it cannot be. For what chance will it have in future years of escaping the sinful surroundings of its birth?

'Let the reader still follow me in imagination to view the scene upstairs. The passages are narrow, the plaster broken in many places, the stairs weak and yielding to our footsteps. The room we enter contains four dirty rickety beds, mere pallets, the threadbare and ragged covering of which fails to conceal the creaking bedsteads and dirty straw mattresses beneath.

'The boards of the floor seem to have had no contact with the scrubbing brush for years, and we note the absence of all arrangements for personal cleanliness. On those beds rest, or rather restlessly lie, men and women of various types and ages, from the frowning confirmed felon to the innocent bastard babe.

Dingy faces of crumbling brick...
Angel Street, Rochdale Road

'There lie old and young – grey headed convict, wizened wig, infant and child of tender years – presenting a sickening picture of moral depravity; the atmosphere being nothing but a foetid composition of pestilential vapour emitted from filthy beds, dirty clothing, foul breath, and worse than all, the presence of offensive matter in the room.

'Before we enter, out step is heard upon the stairs, and the wretches, who have learned from experience the necessity of watchfulness, are awake and on the alert. The word "D's", detectives, runs around the room as we enter and commence to inspect the inmates of the different beds.

'"Now then! Sit up! Let's look at your phizzogs!" and men, women and children instantly obey, passive as lambs, with the remark, "Oh, is it you Mr Jerome?"

119

'The inspection over, and none of them being wanted, they sink once more into a morbid slumber until the sorrowful daylight enters, and the unhallowed repose gives place to trouble, sin and debauchery.

'Doubtless, the sad fate of most of these wretches is attributable to their own persistence in criminal and wayward folly. Yea, they may not only have shaped their own crooked paths, but have willingly paced them until hardened in heart and reckless in consequence.'

Jerome Caminada makes mention of some of the general behaviour, crimes and activities performed daily by many slum dwellers.

He explained: 'Occasionally, we come across men, woman and children, who followed no regular callings, and yet were not members of the criminal class, but whose daily familiarity with hideous aspects of crime and debauchery, with fallen women and professional thieves, could scarcely fail in their ultimate evil effects, especially when honest work became scarce.

'The occupants of such houses chiefly graduated from "snow-droppers" (strippers of clothes lines), to "cracksmen" (burglars), and fallen women. The latter were often seen parading along Market Street in their characteristic blue gowns and jacket make-up of factory lasses.

'On some of the principal thoroughfares at midday, we find the sham "sailors" and "colliers" begging along the streets with legs and arms professedly crippled, and although they had never been to sea, or down a coal mine, drawling out in doleful voice fearful tales of shipwreck and coal mine explosions, and of their miraculous escapes from death with the loss of an arm or leg.

'Visit them in their lodgings, or in their well known beer house rendezvous, and you would find they can use their disabled limbs in a very nimble manner.

'Another class of impostors, that I might call "land sharks", street tradesmen in a small way, known also as "dry land sailors". They could be seen parading Shudehill or lounging at street corners, or in public houses in quest of their prey.

'The majority of their victims were country rustics whom they plausibly decoyed into some quiet back street or alleyway, under the pretence they had some smuggled articles, which they could sell them very cheap.

'They usually consisted of remnants of cloth, or silk, and sometimes tobacco, or cigars, all of them damaged goods, and purchased from another tradesman, but by wearing the typical sailor dress and chewing tobacco in seaman fashion, they found little difficulty in disposing of their wares at twice or three times their value to unsuspecting simpletons.'

Caminada went on to describe certain other parts of the city that were notorious for specialised crimes. He again emphasised the neighbourhood of Deansgate and claimed this was the rendezvous of thieves and a hotbed of social iniquity and vice.

He confirmed: 'The women of the locality were of the most degraded class, and their chief victims were drunken men, collier lads and country "flats" whom they picked up and rifled with impunity.

'Wood Street, Spinning Field, Hardman Street, Dolefield and the adjacent courts and alleys on the one side, and Fleet Street, Lombard Street, Lad Lane and Bootle Street on the other side of Deansgate, were the worst haunts of vice.

'Such places as the "Dog & Rat", the "Red, White & Blue", the "Old Ship", the "Pat McCarthy", and the "Green Man" and other notorious places, were then in full swing as licensed beer houses. Passing along, the pedestrian's ear would be arrested by the sound of music proceeding from mechanical organs, accompanied sometime by drums or tambourines. On entering, you would find a number of youths and girls assembled in a room furnished with a few wooden forms and tables.

'The women generally lived upon the premises, the proprietor of the den adding to his income by the proceeds of their shame. Some rude attempt would be made to sing at an indecent song by a half drunken girl for the edification of some collier lads, who were the chief victims of these haunts, but her voice would be drowned by the incessant quarrelling and obscene language of her companions.'

He confirmed that many of these places had no licence whatever for the sale of intoxicating liquors, and explained there were other well known beer houses which did nearly all their trade during prohibited hours - selling all sorts of poisonous stuff to the public under the guise of beer and spirits.

PRIZE FIGHTING, DOG & BADGER FIGHTS

Deansgate was also a noted place for prize fighting. In several of the garrets there were regular rings of stakes and ropes. When the battles were stopped, the fights took place in kitchens, stables, cellars, or in any other place the police were not likely to put in an appearance.

Many of the garrets were also fitted up for dog fights and drawing the badger, and 'Swells', who did not mind paying for the spectacle, used to turn up, sometimes through their own misfortune of losing a watch or another article of value.

Other areas of particular concern for the police in Victorian times included the neighbourhoods of Canal Street, Minshull Street, Richmond Street and back of Piccadilly.

The detective agreed: 'These plague spots were terrible agencies for recruiting year by year the ranks of dangerous society from our middle class population, and many a clerk and other respectable young men have begun their a criminal career by becoming a secret pilferer from the till to obtain the means of gratifying his appetite in such haunts of sin.'

Caminada also gave numerous other examples of common crime, and highlighted the role of 'bullies' or 'coshers' who preyed upon the community. They managed to grab some girl and compelled her to lead a loose life, and when she had accosted and decoyed her victim to some convenient place, allowed the 'cosher' to rob him of all the valuables he possessed.

FLOGGING AND BIRCHING OF FIRST OFFENDERS

The detective also made bizarre reference to some common punishments, including a 'healthy flogging', and 'birching' of a first offender.

Caminada confirmed the facts from such cases of note, stating: 'One of Her Majesty's Judges of Assize in a case of robbery with violence, at the trial of prisoners charged with the offence, and who were found guilty by the jury, proceeded to pass sentence.

'He informed the prisoners, who were aged from sixteen to twenty years of age, that they were charged with a very serious offence and very properly were found guilty by the jury. Also to send them to penal servitude would be considerable expense to the community.

'As they had applied great violence to the prosecutor, he would only give them a short sentence of a few months imprisonment, but each would receive twenty lashes of the cat-o'-nine-tails. The gang referred to were similar to the Manchester Scuttlers.'

Caminada added that: 'After lash no 5, I have never known a case where prisoners have come for a second dose of this sort.'

THE FIRST OFFENDERS ACT: BIRCHING

'A boy was charged with stealing postage stamps and money from the drawer of a till in the cashier's office of the place where he was employed.

'After being detected, he was sentenced by the Stipendiary Magistrate to receive twelve strokes with the birch rod. Before a juvenile is birched, a police surgeon examines him; he is then strapped to the horse, his wrists and ankles are strapped, and a body belt goes over his back.

'These preliminaries are worse than the birching. The little fellow, not knowing what will really take place, shouts and screams during the strapping process, making it painful to be within hearing.

'The birching itself is not severe, but the effect is very deterrent, and has prevented many juveniles from having to be sent to prison. The police surgeon and a police inspector had to be present in every case of birching.'

Jerome Caminada's volume II book was published in his own name from No 2, Mount Street, Bernard, Whitworth Park, Manchester, during 1900. This was about a year after his retirement. And once again, he reported a selection of fascinating true-life accounts of his work, offering a similar number of stories to that of his first volume.

It included amongst many others: - a typical Saturday night in Deansgate; great coal frauds; how insurance companies were robbed; the Fenian Conspiracy; The Cronin Murder; prison mysteries; juvenile criminals; and reports of burglary and arson.

In his second book he also gave details of a review for the Manchester Police force. He said: 'The police force of every large town is regarded generally by the people as a kind of civil army of quiet occupation, a gentle force pertaining to the community for their defence and for co-operation with all the respectable members of it, but never for aggression.

'The members of it move about almost unarmed, and are welcomed as the visible embodiments of law and order, confirming the safety and security of all who recognise those chief two elements of social and communal life, and checking the erratic tendencies of those who fail to recognise the advantages of civilisation, and who fret under the restraints and limitations alike of labour and poverty.

Street traders in Rochdale Road, 1900

'The feeling that exists between the police and the people is, undoubtedly, of the most friendly and often confiding nature. By the young folks generally they are looked upon with mingled awe and admiration, and by those of them whose consciences are clear, a sense of safety is enjoyed so long as one remains in sight; they feel within reach of omnipotence.

'By children of a larger growth and much riper age they are regarded as men of encyclopaedic knowledge, and as peripatetic directories of the names, addresses, and marked characteristics of all the people resident on their respective beats.

'This has recently been attested by the wide acceptance of the assurance, sealed by all the principal music hall authorities, and now almost crystallised into a proverb of the century, that when you are worried by uncertainty, even as to the time, you "only have to ask a policemen."

'These remarks may. At a casual glance, appear somewhat wide of the mark, but as a matter of fact, they are concerned with the root of the whole business, and touch the first causes that rendered the formation of what we call the force necessary.'

Caminada also made reference to the fact that many city police stations were situated very close together. He urged reforms and reviews of the number of officers employed and wondered whether the use of so many stations was really necessary.

He was asked to submit about a dozen reports to the Watch Committee between 1897-1899, and claimed he had demonstrated by hard facts how re-arrangements could be effected, antiquated and useless customs abrogated, small abuses abolished, and surplus men supplied with something to do.

Caminada claimed that in most cases the men themselves cordially received his suggestions, which he said were never hidden from the individuals concerned.

He cited that police stations at Park Place, Knott Mill, Albert Street, and the Town Hall were just a few hundred yards apart from each other; as were the Police Courts to Fairfield St, Fairfield St to Newton St, Newton St to Goulden St. He said additional stations at Lowe St, Cannel St, Brook St, Openshaw, Fairfield St, Police Court and Belle Vue Street were also equally close together.

Caminada proposed that if a re-arrangement of the police divisions were made and a central police station formed for each, it would be found that a great reduction of police stations could be effected.

He also claimed the City Police Courts had access for hundreds of prisoners and yet occupied a most expensive area of ground, and were only to a small extent occupied. He suggested that if they were utilised, a central lock up for prisoners and a great saving could be affected. He claimed this arrangement would enable the Goulden Street police station to be dispensed with and prisoners transferred to the nearest station.

He believed this arrangement would materially reduce the cost of conveyance of prisoners from police stations to police courts because only one van would be required, rather than four at that time.

In the conclusion within his second book, Jerome Caminada, said he believed: 'The intelligent detective agent is not long in discovering that the lines of demarcation between different classes of criminals are most distinctly marked.

'And having obtained an intimate acquaintance with the members of such circles, he is not infrequently able to find a clue to a robbery, or other daring offence, the perpetrator of which has apparently left no trace by which he could be inculpated.

'Courage and fixed determination must ever be among the most distinguishing characteristics of the detector of crime, and woe to him if he should once show the "white feather". I ascribe no small part of the good fortune, which attended me during my long connection with Manchester police to the fact that I always stood my ground, even when confronted by overpowering odds.

'At the same time, I declare with equal confidence that I have never taken a mean or cowardly advantage of a prisoner. I have met men as they emerged from gaol, and done my best, by advice and assistance, to encourage their return to the path of honest labour; and have frequently had the pleasure of helping them on that path, by finding the employment their unaided efforts would have failed to obtain.'

Two signed copies of the original volumes of Jerome Caminada's work were personally autographed and handed to my great grandfather in recognition of his assistance and friendship.

Following James' death, the books were later handed down to his only daughter Minnie and eventually on to her husband, Thomas Stinton. In later years, they were given to my mother, and their only daughter Doreen. The books have remained within our family archives ever since.

THE MANCHESTER ANARCHISTS

The Manchester Anarchists gained much adverse publicity from Caminada's initial archive recollections of 1899. And as previously explained, the two volumes of his work were both published to popular acclaim around the turn of the century.

The anarchists were a radical group who campaigned for free speech, yet soon became unfairly branded by the authorities as 'irresponsible young men'. Normally, they held their meetings at Ardwick Green, and their ranks included large numbers drawn from both working class men and women.

Many of the more dramatic events appear in police records around September 1893, and include claims that they were responsible for 'criticising and abusing members of the royal family'. Caminada reported his personal involvement with this group.

No doubt under pressure from Government sources, Manchester's Chief Constable, Charles Malcolm Wood, claimed the anarchists were a 'serious nuisance', and demanded his officers put an immediate stop to their activities.

He proposed a number of desperate and determined measures, including the infiltration and disruption of their meetings. And he even tried to persuade the group to move from Ardwick Green to another much quieter site at Stevenson Square.

This location, however, was considered too remote by the organisers, who demanded that the public should see and hear their controversial proposals.

When his offer was refused and the meetings continued at the original site, the Chief Constable insisted on much tougher, immediate action, ordering his officers to prevent anyone from speaking, claiming they caused an obstruction.

The press reported that on several occasions, police clashed with both demonstrators and supporters, and in one scuffle, when the main speaker was arrested, Detective Caminada admitted breaking his umbrella by attacking the man - and yet claimed compensation for criminal damage!

Many of these so-called anarchists were charged and imprisoned.

Caminada's actions, later however, came back to both haunt and taunt him, when he became the subject of ridicule during a popular music hall song, often used on the thriving national entertainment circuit. Entitled: 'The scamp who broke his gamp at Ardwick Green', this was generally performed to the tune of 'The Man from Monte Carlo', and to a certain extent allowed this vigorous campaigning group to claim a rather belated moral victory.

The lengthy and descriptive verses in the song, and subsequent brutal actions, only tended to highlight the stupidity and ineptitude of the authorities at that time, and their remarkable determination to ban free speech.

Heart of the Beat
The Detectives' Office, home of the 'Ds'

CHAPTER 9

A Royal Bodyguard, Foreign Agents & Agitators

One of the undoubted highlights of my great grandfather's career was a temporary, although highly prestigious, appointment as Manchester's first official royal bodyguard during the spring of 1902.

The position involved a vital role as an armed police protection officer based within the royal household for the visit to the city by the Prince and Princess of Wales, Princess Louise, and her husband the Duke of Argyll.

The facts indeed remained so secret that the press were only told about his unique involvement sometime after the visit, with most details remaining under lock and key for several generations later.

James Wood was a respected detective sergeant in the Manchester City Police force. And for this particular visit, he worked with a senior colleague, Chief Detective Inspector Corden, to help ensure the safety of the royal party during their extensive three-day visit to the region.

The city arrangements - all personally approved by the Prince - primarily included a ceremonial procession of thirteen open-topped, and horse-drawn carriages through the streets of Manchester to Owens College for the opening of the new Whitworth Hall; returning later to Manchester Cathedral for the unveiling of a statue of the late Queen Victoria.

The initial part of James's duties included travelling as an escort with the Royal train from London Euston to Huyton Station, situated on the outskirts of Liverpool. Upon arrival, he then accompanied the party to nearby Knowsley Hall, where he mingled unobtrusively with distinguished guests of the Earl and Countess of Derby.

The following day, most of the group then continued by train to Victoria Station, to commence their official engagements, before returning to Knowsley Hall, and later back to London.

It was quite an historic event for Manchester. It commemorated the very first visit in state by the Prince and Princess of Wales and 'Heir Apparent', and obviously involved a tremendous amount of detailed planning and preparation by anxious Corporation officials.

Victoria Station concourse on a normal Edwardian day

They hoped it would also lift the spirits of the city and nation, following the end of Queen Victoria's incredible sixty-four year reign, just fourteen months earlier; and believed it could help introduce some of the next generation of royals to an enthusiastic, yet curious public.

At this particular time, the Prince's father, the uncrowned king, Edward VII, and fondly known as Bertie, was still some five months away from his coronation at Westminster Abbey. Born in 1841, he had had to wait until his fifty-ninth year before finally inheriting the throne.

A most popular royal, Edward had married Princess Alexandra of Denmark in 1863, but unfortunately his reign, in stark contrast to his mother, eventually became rather short-lived.

The Manchester visit was an early and unexpected opportunity for Prince 'George of Wales' to both meet and greet the North West public.

George, the Prince of Wales, became genially known as the 'Sailor Prince' and was a professional naval officer until 1892. He was in fact the second son of King Edward VII and Queen Alexandra, but inherited the title of 'Heir Apparent' following the sudden death of his elder brother Prince Albert Victor.

He later met, and in May 1893, married his late brother's fiancée, Mary of Teck, and in subsequent years, they had four sons and a daughter.

This royal visit, however, rang many potential alarm bells and came at a rather difficult and dangerous period for the Monarchy.

Since his grandmother, Queen Victoria's, extremely volatile jubilee year of 1897, several threats had been made to certain members of the royal family, by what the Government very loosely termed as 'foreign agents and agitators'.

This period also marked an uncertain and controversial time, when the country, if not the world, seemed to be in turmoil.

It also noted and highlighted a series of unprecedented attacks, bombings and threats of terrorism by Irish nationalist groups - and other militants - and witnessed a time of growing unrest, social change and mass demonstrations from unemployed workers, and from disgruntled railway, dockyard and mine workers.

In addition, there was trouble brewing within many of the unpredictable Balkan States and this country was struggling to cope with an influx of immigrants from many revolutionary countries. Meanwhile, the British Army faced many unpopular and expensive overseas conflicts.

According to the official records, James was extremely excited about his unusual task, and like his colleague, felt able to deal with any contingency.

He had served in the King's Own Royal Lancaster Regiment, and with the 4th Regiment of Foot, which provided a personal guard to the Sovereign.

My recent inquiries suggest the Prince of Wales had a strong affiliation to this particular unit, and at one stage, he may even have served as their Colonel in Chief.

James was thirty-four years of age, just three years younger than the Prince, and had achieved military promotion to the rank of regimental sergeant during his term of service.

He was known for his prowess with weapons, explosives and self-defence. The notes also confirm he was very tactful in delicate situations and therefore was perhaps seen as the ideal candidate for this extraordinary duty.

With the help of James's own exclusive cuttings book, personal notes, police records, photographs and newspaper archives, I have hopefully managed to reconstruct a fairly accurate account of this exceptional and spectacular visit.

It now recalls a time of preparation before, during and after the event, when the centre of Manchester came to a standstill in typically drizzly conditions.

It certainly seems to have been a tremendously colourful, and very splendid occasion, supported by thousands upon thousands of spectators, who eagerly packed the city streets and makeshift grandstands just to catch a fleeting glimpse of the royal party.

Ironically, the record of James's special duties meant a remarkable return to Victoria Station, the place where he worked, some twenty-two years earlier, as a railway clerk!

Tuesday March 11th, 1902
THE ROYAL VISIT
Preparations in the City

Manchester is today busily preparing itself for the great event of tomorrow, when their Royal Highnesses, the Prince and Princess of Wales, will for the first time visit the city together in state.

The citizens have roused themselves to the occasion, and although workshops and warehouses will be open as usual, business out of doors will be in a great extent suspended.

To many people, the city presents a most attractive aspect when its streets are full of businessmen and the hum of commerce is the only music to be heard. Tomorrow however, it will look well in a totally different aspect – that of festivity.

Already, the thoroughfares, and more particularly, those which the royal party will ride through, are putting on their festive garb. The Corporation have done their full share, and the tradesmen are not likely to fail in their display of loyalty and bunting.

The Venetian masts dotted about the royal route now bear their banners and streamers boldly aloft. Tomorrow, the flower garlands and other beautiful decorations will be added at an early hour to make the scheme complete.

Helped out by the displays of the tradesmen of loyal mottoes and crests, they will probably make up a show sufficiently attractive to prove the heartiness of the city's welcome to the Heir Apparent and his Princess.

OWENS COLLEGE

Rapid progress is being made with the arrangements at Owens College, and there is now little fear that everything will be in order some time before the hour fixed for tomorrow's ceremony arrives. As to the ceremony itself, many of the distinguished guests will arrive in the city today.

The following is a list of congratulatory addresses, which have been received from the universities, and learned societies, which will not be personally represented: -

France: College of France.

Germany: University of Berlin; Acadima dei Lincel; University of Eilangan; University of Freiburg in Baden; University of Giessen; University of Halle; University of Heidelberg; University of Kiel; University of Strasbourg; Royal Academy of Sciences at Berlin; Royal Academy of Sciences at Leipzeg.

Austria: University of Vienna; Bohemian University of Prague; University of Pesth; Imperial Academy of Sciences at Vienna.

Prussia: Royal Academy of Munich.

Holland: University of Amsterdam; University of Leyden; University of Utrecht.

Switzerland: University of Berne; University of Basel; University of Zurich.

Belgium: University of Liege.

Russia: University of Helsingfors.

Denmark: University of Copenhagen.

Norway: University of Christiana.

Sweden: University of Lund; University of Upsala.

Greece: University of Athens.

United States of America: University of Columbia; Cornell University; John Hopkins University; University of Pennsylvania; University of Princeton.

THE TOWN HALL

Flowers and foliage are still arriving at the Town Hall to decorate the interior, and today a small army of men are engaged in arranging the lavish display about the building.

An idea of the work, which the Town Hall staffs has now to cope with, may be gathered from the statement that no fewer than 320 guests will take luncheon with the royal visitors and the Lord Mayor.

MUSIC IN ALBERT SQUARE

The crowds in Albert Square waiting for the arrival of their Royal Highnesses will be able to listen to the music of the Manchester City Police Band. Commencing at one o'clock, the band will provide a number of selections (15 varied examples were given including the Festal March by Cornelius, The Waltz by *Tendres Baisers* and *Gallop* with the Earl of Chester).

THE CEREMONY AT THE CATHEDRAL

The ceremony of unveiling the statue of the late Queen Victoria in the west porch of the cathedral, which will be the last engagement of their Royal Highnesses in the city, will be necessarily very brief.

In addition to the Prince and Princess of Wales and suite, the Lord Mayor and Lady Mayoress; the Earl and Countess of Derby; the Duke and Duchess of Devonshire; the Earl and Countess Spencer; Lord James of Hereford and Miss James; will alight from their carriages, and the royal visitors will be received by the Very Revd the Dean, the Canons, Archdeacons, Hon Canons, and other clergy of the Cathedral.

Much curiosity exists as to the statue, which is the work and gift of the Princess Louise, Duchess of Argyll. So far, the work has been kept well covered, practically none of the workers having seen it, and until the statue is unveiled in the niche reserved for it no description of it can be given.

The band of the Manchester Volunteer Battalion of the Royal Medical Staff Corps will play at the cathedral on the occasion.

TRADESMEN & THE MEDICAL CHARITIES

The happily conceived idea of letting business premises to view the royal procession and giving the proceeds to medical charities, has been taken up by a number of traders besides those who originated the scheme. This is probably due to the approval expressed by the Lord Mayor to the deputation, which waited upon him early last week.

No doubt a much larger response would have been received had not the proprietors of many establishments already promised their windows to friends and customers. Some of these however, expressed their approval of the movement and instead of making a charge for the use of the window, intend to make a collection for the Hospital Sunday and Saturday Fund. It is hoped that many more will follow this example.

LATEST DETAILS: -

A supplementary programme has been issued to members of the Manchester Corporation for their use in connection with the visit, in which it is explained that the Lord Mayor and Lady Mayoress, the reception committee, the Recorder, and the Town Clerk, will be in attendance and will leave the Town Hall in carriages for Victoria Station, Manchester (London & North Western platform) with police escort at 10.15 a.m.

The guard of honour at Victoria Station will consist of three officers and 100 non-commissioned officers and men of the 1st Battalion, Manchester Regiment.

Their Royal Highnesses, the Prince and Princess of Wales, arrive by special train at Victoria Station from Knowsley at 10.50 a.m. The Lord Mayor and Lady Mayoress will be presented to their Royal Highnesses by the Earl of Derby upon the station platform.

The Lord Mayor will then make the following presentations: -
Alderman Briggs (deputy Lord Mayor) and Mrs Briggs.
Alderman Rushworth (chairman of the Town Hall Committee).
Alderman Gibson (ex Lord Mayor).
Alderman Rawson (chairman of the Watch Committee).
Councillor Vaudrey (ex Lord Mayor).
Councillor Shann (deputy chairman of the Town Hall Committee) and Alderman Joseph Thompson (chairman of the Council and treasurer of the Owens College).
The Recorder, Sir Joseph F. Leese, K.C. MP.
The Town Clerk, Mr Talbot.
The Chief Constable, Mr Robert Peacock.

The procession to Owens College will proceed by way of Market Street, Downing Street, Ardwick Green, Brunswick Street, Upper Brook Street, and Dover Street.

The proceedings at Owens College will occupy somewhat less than two hours. The procession will return to the Town Hall by way of Oxford Street, Peter Street, Mount Street and Albert Square, and after the presentation of an address and the luncheon fixed to take place at 2.15 p.m., the royal visitors will proceed to Victoria Station by way of

Cross Street, St Ann's Square, Victoria Street to the cathedral, where the unveiling of the statue of Queen Victoria by the Princess Louise will take place. Their Royal Highnesses leave Victoria Station for Knowsley at four o'clock.

Manchester came to a standstill in typically drizzly conditions

RAILWAY ARRANGEMENTS

The London & North Western Railway Company (upon whose line their Royal Highnesses will travel to and from Manchester) have made very complete arrangements to meet the occasion.

In conjunction with the Lancashire & Yorkshire Railway Company, who are joint owners of Hunt's Bank, they have carried out an elaborate scheme of decoration, in which garlands of evergreens play an important part.

The old Victoria Station, belonging to the London & North Western Company, has also been given a new coat of bright paint, and there is a profusion of bunting overhead.

In order that the little ceremonies at the station may be carried out under cover, the outside bay, upon which Lord Roberts's train ran into the station, has been built over, and the royal train will run straight into the next bay, and will be flush with the new platform.

By this arrangement, the platform has been converted from stone to wood, and a carpet of bright new canvass lends a nice finish to the scheme.

THE ROYAL TRAIN

The train in which their Royal Highnesses will travel, will consist of an engine and tender of the best London & North Western type, a brake carriage, two saloons, the royal saloon and a brake composite carriage.

Following the brake carriage will be a family saloon for the Earl and Countess of Derby, and the second saloon will be occupied by other guests from Knowsley. Then will follow the saloon, which is reserved by the company for members of the royal family, and which on this occasion will be occupied by their Royal Highnesses, the Prince and Princess of Wales.

Colonel Fred Harrison, the general manager of the company will travel by the royal train from London to Huyton today, and from Huyton to Manchester tomorrow. Mr Henry Linaker, district superintendent, will have charge of the arrangements at the old Victoria Station, and will return with the royal train to Huyton, when the ceremonies of the day have been concluded.

THE PRINCE AND PRINCESS OF WALES LEAVE TODAY

The Prince and Princess of Wales left York House at noon today to catch the 12.15 train from Euston to pay their visit to Lancashire, where they are to be the guests of the Earl and Countess of Derby at Knowsley Hall.

Their Royal Highnesses were accompanied by Princess Louise (Duchess of Argyll), the Duke of Argyll, the Countess of Airlie, and the Hon Derek Keppel. On arriving at Euston, they were met by Mr Harrison, general manager of the line, and entered the train in waiting for them.

The royal party are expected to arrive at Huyton at five o'clock this afternoon. Tomorrow, the Prince and Princess of Wales leave Huyton at 10.20 for Manchester, and will return to London on Thursday, arriving at Euston at 3.30 p.m.

* The Prince and Princess of Wales passed through Crewe at 3.55 this afternoon.

Evening News, Wednesday March 12th, 1902

ARRIVAL OF THE PRINCE AND PRINCESS

The Prince and Princess of Wales after their reception in the streets of Manchester today, will have no doubts in their own minds as to the loyalty of Lancashire folk.

The weather was not at first of the brightest, and the thousands of spectators who lined the streets to catch a glimpse of the royal visitors more than once found use for their umbrellas. The slight fall of rain an hour or so before their arrival had no depressing effect.

The street decorations, at any rate, in the centre of the city, were a credit alike to the corporation committee entrusted with the work and the tradesmen and business people along the line of the route.

Businesses were suspended for the day and the citizens made holiday as heartily as is their custom on occasions like this. The principal function of the day was of course, the opening of the new Whitworth Hall at Owens College, and the brilliant gathering within the college precincts was worthy of its best traditions at the County Palatine.

In addition to distinguished visitors from the seats of learning in the United Kingdom, representatives were present from many foreign universities.

The graduates of Owens were present in large force, and the present students of the college made a brave show. The welcome they gave to the Prince and Princess was an indication of their appreciation of the honour paid to Owens College and Manchester in thus taking the leading part in an event of such interest and importance to the city and neighbourhood.

Nothing better managed, or in every way more successful could be imagined, or indeed desired than the proceedings within the beautiful Whitworth Hall of Owens College, which, with the golden key, the Prince was supposed to open.

The programme was both well arranged and admirably carried out and, happily, nothing but pleasant recollections of the occasion can arise. The royal visitors, the distinguished guests, senate, council, and staff, all did exactly what was expected of them in precisely the right way.

Probably the surprise of the occasion to those who had not carefully followed the story of the Prince of Wales adventures during the 'Grand Tour,' was the admirable self-possession and tact with which he faced and fulfilled the responsibilities of the occasion. Surrounded as he was by statesmen and public men practised in oratory, he more than held his own.

Certain it is, that not a single word of his address was lost, and so excellent and yet so natural was his elocution that it was quite impossible to misunderstand or hesitate about the meaning of any point.

The Princess's share in the proceedings did not, of course, include any speechmaking. It was her contribution to the joy of what is undoubtedly a historical occasion to look charming and pleasant, and all that she does apparently without effort.

From this, as well as from every other point of view, the visit was entirely successful.

EVENTS OF THE DAY

People who did not know the by-ways had much difficulty in reaching Victoria and Exchange stations this morning. The footpaths on the ordinary routes were blocked by thousands of people, and forces of soldiers and police kept the roadways clear.

Having overcome the difficulties, and having reached, by way of Hunt's Bank, that portion of Victoria Station which forms the connection to Exchange Station, even those most familiar with the structure hardly knew where they were.

A marvellous transformation had taken place, The dingy old platform had gone; a siding in which wagons, designed more for utility than ornament are usually found, was invisible. In its place was a broad and spacious platform, carpeted in red, while above and around were gaily-coloured flags and pretty devices.

Considerable charm was added to the scheme of decoration adopted by the London & North Western Railway Company, the owners of this part of the station, by the co-operation of the Lancashire & Yorkshire Railway Company, whose extensive suite of offices on the opposite side of Hunt's Bank was very brightly ornamented.

The space all round the approaches was filled with picturesque groups of the Duke of Lancaster's Imperial Yeomanry, waiting to form the second escort of the royal party.

139

The favoured people who were on the arrival platform spent the hour, which elapsed before the arrival of the royal train, in admiring the completeness of the arrangements. Under the personal direction of Mr Henry Linaker, the district superintendent, everything worked perfectly.

It became known that the ordinary Liverpool to Manchester express leaving the former city at ten o'clock, would play the role of the pilot train, and that after it had passed the line from Huyton to Manchester was kept clear, all points being locked, and nothing being allowed to approach the main line.

Shortly after 10.30, one hundred men of the 1st Volunteer Battalion of the Manchester Regiment took their positions on the platform. Their black uniforms looking more business-like than pretty.

A moment or two later, the Lord Mayor of Manchester and the members of the reception committee, who had accompanied him from the Town Hall, arrived. The carriages were placed in position, and soon everyone was eagerly looking forward for the signal, which would announce the arrival of the Prince and Princess.

About five minutes to eleven the train steamed into the station and the first to alight from the royal saloon was the Earl of Derby, the picture of a smiling and genial host. The distinguished visitors quickly alighted, while the guard of honour stood at the salute.

The Prince who was looking much stronger and much more robust than on his former visit to Manchester, was attired in the ordinary garb of an English gentlemen. A thick overcoat protecting him from the coldness of the morning. Her Royal Highness was attired in a handsome dress of heliotrope, with sable collar and sable muff, and wore a hat with violets.

The Earl of Derby at once presented the Lord Mayor and Lady Mayoress, with whom the Prince and Princess shook hands. A similar recognition was given to a host of other civic officials and dignitaries (including Manchester City Police Chief Constable Robert Peacock).

This ceremony over, the ladies and gentlemen who had accompanied the royal party entered the carriages in waiting. The Princess, meanwhile, continued in conversation with the Lord Mayor, and the Prince inspecting the Guard of Honour.

When he had walked along the two files of men, he rejoined the Princess and they entered the open carriage in waiting, drawn by four splendid bays with two outriders in the handsome livery of the Earl of Derby.

Before her Highness took her seat, an attendant handed her a sable cape lined with ermine, which she wore during the drive, then amid the loud cheers of those at the station, taken up with alacrity by those outside, the procession started on the two-mile route to Owens College.

The official order of the procession was as follows: -
Mounted Manchester city police.
Duke of Lancaster's Imperial Yeomanry.
The Chief Constable.
Mounted police.
1st carriage – The Duke of Devonshire, the Duchess of Devonshire, and Alderman Thompson.
2nd carriage – Colonel Courtenay, Major Oxley and Captain Mansfield Clarke.
3rd carriage – Councillors Shann and Vaudrey.
4th carriage – Aldermen Rushworth and Gibson.
5th carriage – Alderman and Mrs Briggs and Alderman Rawson.
6th carriage – The Recorder and Town Clerk.
7th carriage – Lord Stanley, Lady Stanley, Lady Alice Stanley, and the Hon William Walsh.
8th carriage – Lord James of Hereford and Miss James.
9th carriage – The Earl and Countess Spencer.
10th carriage – The Earl and Countess of Derby.
11th carriage – The Lord Mayor and Lady Mayoress of Manchester (with mace).
Advance Guard.
12th carriage – The Countess of Airlie, Sir Arthur Bigge, and General Swaine.
Escort, the Duke of Lancaster's Imperial Yeomanry.
Main royal carriage – The Prince and Princess of Wales.
Escort of the Duke of Lancaster's Imperial Yeomanry.

JOURNEY TO OWENS COLLEGE
An abundance of incidents – policeman lost his helmet
The spectacle between Hunt's Bank and the Victoria Hotel was of a memorable character. The route between these two points was thickly lined and it was evident from the character of the crowd that thousands upon thousands had come into the city for the purpose of witnessing the royal procession.

The time of waiting was passed pleasantly and there was an abundance of incidents. As the cathedral was passed, one or two of the bells were rung, it being evident that the ringers had either been misinformed as to the time of arrival of the royal train or that they were testing the bells.

Loyal address by the Mayor at Manchester Town Hall
A perfect setting for a grand civic ceremony

The assemblage of so many brilliant and striking uniforms made the scene one which will live in the memory of those who witnessed it.

The spectators assembled about Hunt's Bank whiled their time away by the singing of loyal and patriotic songs, the first favourite being 'God Bless the Prince of Wales', with 'Rule Britannia' ranking next in the order of popularity.

At length, a sound of escaping steam intimated to those nearest the station that the Prince and Princess had arrived. About this time, someone apparently in the neighbourhood of Victoria Station, fired a gun or let off a fog signal as a sort of royal salute. The explosion startled a flock of pigeons.

Immediately afterwards, the procession made its appearance, and the singing of the spectators was then exchanged for cheers, which were taken up and along the entire length of the route.

142

An incident, which caused some uneasiness just when the start from Hunt's Bank was being made, was due to the acclamations of the populace. The team of four dappled greys, which was drawing the open carriage conveying the Lord Mayor, became restive, and the near hind wheeler began to plunge.

The coachman kept the horse under restraint admirably but his example seemed likely to be imitated by the horses of the yeomanry and the mounted infantry. A horse ridden by a policeman also became restive and dashed down Hunt's Bank, the rider losing his helmet in his efforts to bring the animal to a standstill.

Past the cathedral and the Victoria Hotel and then around the corner into Market Street, the cheering was again and again renewed. The thoroughfare presented a wonderful sight. Behind the barricades, the spectators were five and six deep, all the windows were occupied, and even the roofs were taken advantage of as well.

Passing the big hotels in Piccadilly, it was noticed that the servants had taken possession of the top windows, and some of the women were on the roofs in most dangerous positions.

At the corner of the Queen's Hotel there were banks of people who cheered as the procession passed. The most striking incident en route was observed near the London Road Station, the scene being the site of the new chief fire station at the corner of Whitworth Street.

Here, a stand had been erected for the accommodation of school children, something like fifty-feet high, and providing space for thousands. At the foot of the stands were bands, which played the national anthem and 'God Save the Prince of Wales'.

The airs were taken up by the children with great vigour, and at the same time they waved their handkerchiefs. Nothing more noticeable in the shape of a royal demonstration has been witnessed in the history of Manchester.

Evening News, March 12th, 1902
THE ROYAL VISIT
Magnificent Reception of the Prince and Princess of Wales
Ceremony at Owens College - speech by the Prince
Manchester is today honoured by a visit from their Royal Highnesses, the Prince and Princess of Wales, who come to take the leading part in the ceremony of opening the new Whitworth Hall at Owens College.

The co-operation of the municipal authorities with the college governors enabled the time at the disposal of the royal couple to be used to the fullest advantage, and their Royal Highnesses approved a programme, which would occupy them for the whole of the day.

Last evening, three members of the royal house of England – the Prince and Princess of Wales, and Princess Louise, the latter accompanied by her husband, the Duke of Argyll, arrived at Knowsley to accept the hospitality of the Earl and Countess of Derby.

The house party also included, in addition to their Royal Highnesses' suite, the Duke and Duchess of Devonshire, Lord James of Hereford and Miss James, Earl and Countess Spencer, Lady Battersea, Lady Sophia McNamara, the Marchioness of Downshire, Lady Alice Stanley, the Hon Derek Keppel, General Swain, Captain Mansfield Clarke, Mr Russell Stephenson, and the Hon William Walsh.

Today, whilst the Princess Louise, with her husband, the Duke of Argyll, visited Liverpool to open a bazaar, the Princess of Wales entrained at Huyton for Manchester, where the citizens were preparing to give them a royal reception.

The morning broke disappointingly around Manchester. In the early hours, there were the slightest possible falls of rain – hardly more than a mist – and when these ceased the prospect overhead was still a depressing one. A grey and murky sky gave no promise of future brightness, and for a time, between nine and ten o'clock, there was a reinception of the thin drizzle of the early morning.

Though this ceased shortly, the haziness of the sky remained to throw doubt over the minds of those thousands of spectators who had already made their way into the city.

For a few hours before the royal visitors were timed to arrive, visitors poured into the city, spending the time of waiting in inspection of the decorations. It could not be said that the judgement was generally favourable. Great expectations had been formed and were not realised.

Still, there was a profuse display of bunting, and if the street decoration possibly failed to impress the Prince and Princess of Wales after the beautiful scenes presented to their eyes during their grand colonial tour, they could not but be gratified by the enthusiastic reception accorded to them by the immense crowds lining the route.

THE ROYAL ROUTE – The decorations

Though doubtless gratified by the many manifestations of loyalty to be seen on every side, the royal visitors could hardly have been struck with the wealth of decoration, or with the character of the general scheme.

In brief, this was composed of Venetian masts connected with festoons of streamers, and adorned with trophies and plants. Wherever possible, the electric tramway standards were utilised and converted into a tolerably good representation of Venetian masts, whilst here and there the scheme was elaborated by the use of evergreens and artificial flowers.

For the most part, the general public contented themselves by hanging out flags and banners, and of these there were enough to demonstrate to their Highnesses, that whatever may have been the defects of the decorations from an artistic point of view, there was nothing lacking in the outward signs of loyalty.

Passing the mother church, the first glimpse was unquestionably a pleasing one, for along Victoria Street there was a charming vista of waving colour. At the top of this thoroughfare, the very large electric standard in the centre of the crossing had been completely transformed by the liberal use of decorative material.

Surmounting it was a large crown of yellow flowers and radiating from it were long festoons of artificial flowers, forming a sort of triumphal canopy.

MARKET STREET TRANSFORMED

Manchester's busiest and richest thoroughfare, Market Street, invariably rises to such an occasion, and thanks to the combined efforts of the tradesmen, it presented quite an imposing appearance. A thousand and one flags of infinite variety hung limply in the sluggish breeze, and away at the top of the street, where Messrs Lewis's had lavished a wealth of colour on their handsome premises, the grey clouds were almost shut out from view by the lines of fluttering streamers and the more stately flags.

In some instances, elaborate decorative work had been done, in others there was an apology in the shape of a coloured covering for a dirty window ledge, with an occasional artificial flower thrown in.

Everybody had done something however, and in the face of such dismal weather, every available bit of colour was needed to relieve the gloom.

In Piccadilly, the general effect was also good, though more imposing than anything else was the vast assemblage on Manchester's only esplanade. The electric standards are placed in the centre of the rails at this part of the route, and these were made full use of, being entwined with artificial flowers.

The branches were also decorated in the same way, the whole being surmounted with trophies of flags. For the most part there was a striking absence of loyal greetings, but two were observable in Piccadilly. On the front of the Queen's Hotel were the words: 'Welcome to the Prince and Princess of Wales', on a background of crimson cloth fringed with gold.

Police and yeomanry share crowd control on the misty royal route

HUMBLE EFFORTS

The moment London Road Station was passed, their Royal Highnesses saw the less imposing side of Manchester, but even there, a modest effort, and indeed more than this, had been made to lighten up this somewhat dingy district.

The site, however, no doubt designed to most greatly impress the distinguished visitors was the great stand at the junction of London Road and Fairfield Street, erected for the accommodation of school children.

Some of the attempts at decoration were pathetic in their simplicity, and these were not confined to the thoroughfare. Ardwick Green opened out to a much better prospect. There was not so much colour, but there was plenty of life, thousands of board school children having been given places on the broad footpath adjoining the Green.

In Brunswick Street, the lines of streamers had been arched and this plan was not so nearly effective as the general one.

OXFORD STREET & PETER STREET

It cannot be said that the trades people on the return line of route from Owens College to the Town Hall had made any general response to the mayoral suggestion that they should decorate the fronts of their premises, and only here and there was there any attempt to assist the efforts of the municipal authorities towards enlivening the appearance of Oxford Street and Peter Street.

Lines of streamers suspended from Venetian mast to mast, themselves relieved with banners and trophies of shields and flags, were the principal feature of the display, and so far as they went, they were by no means ineffective, it must be confessed that there was nothing very striking or novel about them.

Garlands of artificial flowers were thrown across the roadway in the immediate neighbourhood of the college, and foliage and flowering plants were interspersed here and there. Grandstands were erected in Dover Street, on some private grounds along Oxford Street, facing Coupland Street, and in front of the Wesleyan chapel.

The fixed barricades, so noticeable along the route from the station to the college, were almost entirely dispensed with on this, the second stage of the journey. They were however, brought into requisition in places where there was reason to believe that the crush would be exceptionally severe.

The least interesting stretch of roadway was undoubtedly that between All Saints Church and the railway arch, in which section there was practically no attempt whatever at decorating the fronts of the buildings. From the latter point onwards to St Peter's Church, where another grandstand had been erected, a brighter state of affairs prevailed, and large flags were freely displayed at various points.

MOUNT STREET & ALBERT SQUARE

Turning into Mount Street, one noticed that the decorations provided by the corporation were on a more elaborate scale than hitherto, and there was quite a profusion of real and artificial flowers as well as evergreens and foliage plants.

No attempt was made to decorate the front of the Town Hall itself, except that an immense royal standard with Union Jacks on either side floated from the upper storeys of the building. The square however, was bright with colour and the general scheme was undoubtedly very effective.

ST ANN'S SQUARE

There were no festoons or streamers in St Ann's Square, but elegant floral designs were worked around the Venetian masts and gave quite a charming appearance to the surroundings.

With nothing else to remark upon as far as effects this stage of the journey to be traversed by the royal party on the way from the Town Hall to the cathedral at the conclusion of the luncheon proceedings, it must be frankly admitted that it was impossible to avoid a feeling of disappointment that the decorations, taken generally, were not more worthy of this occasion.

THE FLORAL DECORATIONS IN THE TOWN HALL

The interior of the Town Hall, beginning just outside the principal entrance, then up the grand staircase to the grand corridor above, was elaborately and beautifully decorated with flowers and foliage plants.

The scheme also included the staterooms, the large hall and a suite of rooms above the staterooms. When Mr R. Lumb, the superintendent of the parks, had, with the co-operation of Mr Mason of Victoria Street, seen the completion of his work. He was quite justifiably pleased with the transformation he had produced.

Confirmation of James's involvement in this major event were outlined within several newspaper reports, police records, and by other personal notes and cuttings from the day in question.

National newspaper report, March 12th, 1902
VISIT OF THE PRINCE OF WALES
Compliment to the Chief Constable

The police arrangements appear to have given satisfaction to all concerned, and at the close of the day's work, Mr Robert Peacock, the Chief Constable, received at Victoria Station, Manchester, an expression of approval from their Royal Highnesses.

The Prince of Wales beckoned to the Chief Constable and personally expressed his appreciation of the manner in which the police had done their duty.

The Princess of Wales acquiesced in the remarks of the Prince, and remained for a few moments in conversation with Mr Peacock.

A North West welcome
Massed crowds at the Town Hall greet the royal visitors

The fact probably passed unnoticed yesterday by the crowd that the royal visitors were personally attended by two Manchester detectives.

Unfortunately, it is necessary that members of the royal house in England, as well as rulers of continental nations, shall be protected from the possibility of attack by some madman or other, and with this object, **Chief Detective Inspector Corden and Detective Sergeant Wood** were included for the time amongst the members of the royal suite.

In the procession, they travelled immediately behind the royal carriage, and indeed, were never far from their Royal Highnesses during the whole period of their stay.

Pomp and ceremony
The royal procession

CHAPTER 10

Obscene Publications
& City Police Courts

This next section covers a period when James was under strict instruction from the Chief Constable, Robert Peacock, to clamp down on a number of key issues affecting the Manchester City authorities.

In particular, they included several alleged breaches of juvenile performances in theatres; numerous bogus registrations of servants; and a necessity to tackle an unusual and unexpected influx of unsavoury material - including objectionable postcards - that were rapidly flooding seaside and tourist areas in particular.

He was also required to act quickly upon other serious reports of so-called 'scandalous' publications that were becoming readily available in Manchester and North West city centres.

The following stories and newspaper cuttings reflect a sample of some of the many cases and convictions during this period: -

1905 ONWARDS

Evening News. January 30th, 1905
JUVENILE PERFORMANCES
The result of a breach of the Act

A music hall turn or theatrical performance of any kind by juveniles is nowadays subject to certain conditions, which are imposed on the parents or guardians under the Employment of Children's Act in the interests of the young performers.

A breach of the Act leads to police court proceedings, and a case of this kind was considered today by the City Stipendiary.

The defendant was Lachie Thompson, whose two sons, one under fourteen, were billed last December at the Metropole Theatre, Ashton Old Road, to give a boxing and wrestling performance.

151

The charges against Thompson were (1) with conducing to the commission of an offence by allowing his son to be employed on the stage at 9.35 p.m. on the 28th December without having obtained a licence, and (2) with falsely representing the boy to be over fourteen years of age, whereby he obtained employment for him.

Evidence was given by Inspectors R Dorricott, Wood and Ogdon, of the performance of 'Lachie Thompson's Topweights' having taken place.

The offence was practically admitted by the defendant, who, however, pointed out that the lads were strong and healthy and the training had done them much good physically.

The manager of the Metropole stated there was a growing dislike amongst the artistes to take out licences owing to the great disparity in the charges made in different towns, ranging from a shilling to seven and sixpence.

A fine of 10s and costs in each of the two cases – amounting altogether to £2 7s 6d – was imposed.

Evening News. January 30th, 1905
A LICENCE FOR CHILD ACROBATS

An application for a licence for the public performance of 'The Butterflies', two child acrobats, at the Manchester Hippodrome this week, was made today at the City Police Court.

The children are too young to perform without a licence, and Inspector Wood objected to this permission being given unless with the condition that a net be provided. The applicant consented to this condition and the licence was granted.

Evening News. Monday April 17th, 1905
A BOGUS REGISTRY OFFICE
Fraud at Chorlton-cum-Hardy

Mr Edgar Brierley, second stipendiary, was occupied for some time at the City Police Court this afternoon, investigating a series of charges of obtaining money by false pretences against Lizzie Clarke, a married woman at present living in Bury New Road, Bolton.

The allegations against the prisoner were that through the medium of a servants' registry office, which she had conducted in Warwick Road,

Chorlton-cum-Hardy, she had obtained various small sums from persons who required servants and from servants requiring situations.

In the cases under consideration, she had not carried out the undertakings in these respects, and evidence was given by the persons concerned as to the falsity of her representations to those from whom she had obtained money.

The offences were brought home to her as the result of investigations by Detective Inspector Wood and Detective Sergeant Dorricott.

Mr Brierley said there was no doubt that the prisoner had been carrying on a fraudulent registry office. In 1902, she was convicted of fraudulently obtaining alms from charitable people, but was allowed to go.

Inspector Wood said a number of complaints had been received by the police in regard to the prisoner's conduct. Mr Brierley said he could not look over the offence, and prisoner would have to go to gaol for six weeks with hard labour.

Evening News. April 26th, 1905
GOSSIP FROM 'TRUTH'

At Manchester the other day, a Mrs Clarke was sentenced to six weeks' imprisonment for obtaining money from various persons by false pretences in connection with a servants' registry office.

Mrs Clarke merited her punishment but she may well be puzzled to understand why she is sent to gaol when so many other swindlers in the same line remain at large.

Certainly if she had set up her fraudulent registry office in London, she might have carried it on for years without any such disagreeable sequel in a police court.

Daily Dispatch. August 19th, 1905
OBJECTIONABLE POSTCARDS
Blackpool & New Brighton compared with Manchester

'Blackpool is not the only seaside resort where visitors are offended by the sight of indecent postcards,' said Mr E Jones Davies, the district secretary of the National Vigilance Association, to a Daily Dispatch representative.

Mr Davies added that New Brighton was also afflicted with the product of prurient foreign minds. He was doing what he could to suppress the sale and exhibition of such postcards.

Two complaints lately received about the state of affairs in Blackpool were, together with copies of the 'Daily Dispatch' containing the letters of complaint from its readers, being forwarded to the chief of Blackpool police.

Mr Davies hoped this action would be sufficient to check the pernicious practice. The same means were adopted in Manchester some time ago with excellent results.

Thousands of cards had been destroyed by order of the police. One wholesaler dealer, after prosecution, had gone round to his customers warning them against selling or exposing any of the objectionable pictures.

'Manchester is more free from this form of evil than it has been since the picture postcard vogue began,' said Mr Davies. 'Indeed, it is impossible for us to lay hands on a single card that is bad enough to warrant prosecution with hope of conviction.

'The dealers are very careful not to run risks nowadays and I know that many of them make a practice of submitting samples of new cards for approval before offering them to the public.'

Indecency was, of course, largely a matter of opinion, said Mr Davies, and he was careful not to take proceedings except on pictures that must appear to any sane person as improper.

The Blackpool cards, he added, were not only indelicate; many of them were disgusting.

Manchester Guardian. September 2nd, 1905
BALZAC'S 'DROLL STORIES'

The seizure by the Manchester police of certain cheap translations of Balzac's works on Friday was followed on Saturday by the confiscation of a large number of copies of a penny edition of the 'Droll Stories', together with the type from which they had been printed.

It is said to be impossible now to purchase a copy of the English translation of Balzac's 'Droll Stories' in Manchester, except by ordering it through a bookseller.

Hitherto, it appears, Balzac's works have been sold in Manchester both in French and in English without hindrance. Probably no one would have interfered with their sale now had it not come to the knowledge of the authorities that thousands of a cheap reprint of the least desirable of Balzac's 'Droll Stories' were being printed and offered for sale.

Many complaints were made of the circulation of this reprint. The Chief Constable thereupon directed Detective Inspector Wood to make inquiries, and the result was that 15,000 copies of the work were seized on Friday and Saturday – not merely the penny reprint but other editions, ranging in price from one penny to three shillings, and in a few instances, even more.

It seems that the seizure of the offending books was accomplished on Friday with dramatic suddenness. Inspector Wood arranged that officers entrusted with the business should appear simultaneously at the place suspected of having books on sale.

In three or four instances, the booksellers tried to warn their neighbours of the police descent, but when their messengers arrived on the scene they found the police already there. Divining the object of the messengers, the police told them they were too late.

The further seizure made by the police on Saturday, led to proceedings before the city justices at Minshull Street Court on Saturday. The defendant, Mr James Miller, of Palace Street, Market Street, was summoned to show cause why a large number of copies of a certain book found on his premises and intended for publication should not be destroyed.

Detective Thomson said that on Friday afternoon, in company with Detective Sergeant Bloomfield, he visited the defendant's printing establishment. The defendant, when informed of the purpose of the visit, at once said that he had in his possession, copies of Balzac's 'Droll Stories' which he had printed and was quite willing to give them up if they were held to be indecent.

He led them to a room in the building and handed over 9,000 copies of the 'Droll Stories' which were removed to the Town Hall. The type from which the books were printed was subsequently taken possession of.

Mr Adams, solicitor (who represented the defendant), said: We may take it that Mr Miller gave you every assistance?

Detective Thomson: Every assistance. He told us that he was ignorant of the character of the book that he had not read it at all, and simply printed it to order.

A JUSTIFIABLE SEIZURE

Replying to Magistrates' Clerk (Mr Heywood), Mr Adams said that he did not contest the matter. Mr Miller was merely the printer of this work, which had been sold in many large establishments all over the country, just as he had printed other and perfectly innocent publications relating to wrestling, boxing and other games.

This one he (Mr Adams) was bound to admit had been justifiably seized. The book was an abridgement of a well known classic – popular in the past, but not now admissible for public sale, particularly in penny editions and it might do a certain amount of harm.

With the consent not only of the printer but also of the publishers, he submitted to an order for the destruction of the entire stock. Only one thing he asked was that the defendant might have his type restored to him.

Mr Miller promised to exercise more care in the future and see that nothing was printed at his establishment that was of a questionable character. An order was made for the destruction of the books; the defendant's type to be returned to him.

Mr Adams wished, on the part of the publisher, to express regret that this had happened. He would take care that it did not happen again.

A DISCLAIMER

In Saturday's 'Manchester Guardian', it was stated that one of the shops visited by the police was in Cannon Street. Mr C E Smith, of 4 Cannon Street, writes to say that it is incorrect. He is the only bookseller in that street, and he has not sold any of the books to which exception is taken.

We understand that the shop in which some of the objectionable books were seized is in New Cannon Street.

Letter to the editor...THE 'CONTES DROLATIQUES'
To the editor of the Manchester Guardian

Sir, It was with much surprise I read the account in Saturday evening's paper of the raid by the Manchester police on the printing establishments. From the talk indulged in at court one is led to believe that Balzac's 'Droll Stories' is a piece of very indecent literature, and that the book is not fit to be placed in the hands of any person.

This is far from true. 'Droll Stories' is a volume written with a motive, and when well read and understood will prove a strong weapon in the hands of the moralist.

It is clean from cover to cover, and can only serve the turn of 'filth' in the hands of the filthy-minded. '*Virtus rectorem ducemque desiderat*' (virtue requires the aid of a governor and director); vices are learned without a teacher.

Balzac in his works is a governor and director of virtues. Such is the opinion of yours & co. Marcus Duddleston, Pendlebury, September 2nd, 1905.

Evening Chronicle. November 10th, 1905
COUNCILLOR AND POSTCARDS

The 'housing' councillor for New Cross, Mr Marr, was asked last night, in the course of discussion on 'The Man in the Street', what he thought should be done to deal with objectionable postcards displayed in shop windows.

Councillor Marr said his advice would be that the public should leave them severely alone. They got very little further forward in dealing with these things if they set up a policy merely of suppressing them.

Suppress them by all means if possible, but the policy of suppression was after all, a poor one, and he preferred to deal with the aspirations of 'the man in the street'.

If by their public policy they could elevate his tastes, then it would become extremely difficult to sell objectionable picture postcards with the ordinary business result.

Letter to the editor of the Manchester Evening News
PICTURE POSTCARDS

Sir, Referring to your correspondent's remarks in yesterday's issue upon the display of indecent picture postcards in shops in Manchester, I should be obliged, with your permission, if I may inform the writer that if he will report anything of indecent character to Mr E Jones Davies, local secretary to the National Vigilance Association, 56 Peter Street, City, it will have his immediate attention.

The chairman of this Manchester branch was our noble citizen, the late Mr Herbert Philips, and this was one of the many institutions for moral purity, which had his support, and his lamentable death will be an untold loss.

I have reason to know that the authorities are very diligent in supporting anything of the above character coming to their notice.
Yours etc.

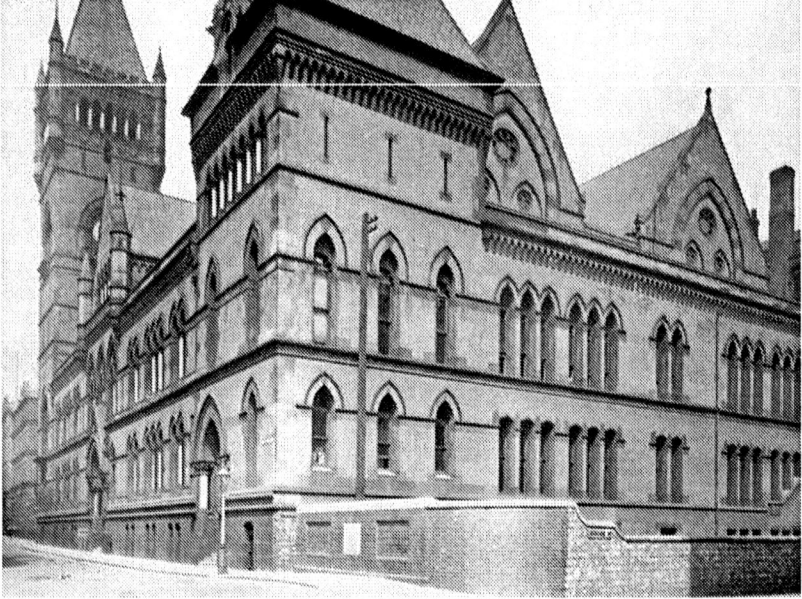

Impressive symbol of civil power
The City Police Courts, Minshull Street, in 1906

Evening News. November 29th, 1905
PICTURE POSTCARD CRAZE
Large numbers condemned by the Police

The Manchester police have lately been turning their attention to the sale of picture postcards of an offensive kind, and Inspector Wood, and other officers, have during the last ten days seized a large number of cards of various designs, together, in some instances, with the printing blocks.

Of the number of postcards seized, no fewer than 3,332 have been condemned as unfit for public sale. Over 1,000 of these were from one design, and they have been collected by the police from 46 shops in the city.

The procedure is to inquire of the shopkeepers whether they have any objection to giving the cards up, and in nearly every case their consent was obtained. Arthur Kay, a shopkeeper, of Ashton Old Road, was fined 5s and costs at the City Police Court today for selling an offensive picture postcard to Detective Dorricott.

INDECENT POSTCARDS
Over 3,000 seized in Manchester

The campaign in Manchester against indecent picture postcards, headed by Detective Inspector Wood, is going apace.

During the past ten days, no fewer than 3,332 condemned postcards of various designs have been seized - and in some cases, the blocks also. Of one particular design, over 1,300 have been impounded from forty-six places.

It is only fair to the shopkeepers of Manchester to say that almost invariably, when requested, they have raised no objections to giving up the offending postcards.

But Arthur Kay, of Ashton old Road, point-blank refused to let Detective Sergeant Richard Dorricott have the specimen which he had displayed in the street showcase, and at the City Police Court today, he failed to see anything objectionable in it. The Stipendiary (Mr Brierley) thought otherwise, and fined him 5s and costs.

1906

Memo dated: 15th January 1906
List of applicants for vacant superintendency

Eight candidates were shown to have applied for the vacant post of superintendent.
They included: -
Thomas Edwards (48), Length of service 27 years, 11 months.
William Kearney (51), served 25 years, 4 months.
Frederick Knott (50), served 24 years, 11 months.
William Walker (45), served 23 years, 6 months.
Walter Roome (47), served 23 years, 1 month.
William A. Wilkes (40), served 18 years, 7 months.
Thomas Harper (38), served 17 years, 10 months.
James Wood (38), served 15 years, 2 months.

The records showed that there were no serious reports against any of the applicants. James Wood was shown to be the youngest and an inspector with the least number of years service.

The position was eventually awarded to William Walker, who had served 5 years and 2 months as an inspector. James Wood had only served 2 years and 2 months in the same position. It was to be another five years before he finally gained promotion to superintendent.

1907 ONWARDS

COPY OF LETTER FROM HOME OFFICE. 24th April 1907
HM Inspector of Explosives,
Home Office,
Whitehall, SW.

This is to certify that before Chief Inspector James Wood was appointed Inspector of Explosives for Manchester the 'stores' and registered premises in that borough were in a very indifferent condition.

Owing to his exertions however, I was able to report in the year 1903 that their condition was 'good' and in the year 1904 'very good' – the highest term of commendation we use.

I may add that Inspector Wood gave me the impression that he is a man who would make every effort to perform in the most efficient manner any duties that he may undertake.

Signed: Major A. Cooper-Keys,
HM Inspector of Explosives.

IN COMMAND OF CITY POLICE COURTS

The police records at the Manchester Police Museum and information taken from James' personal notes confirm that he was officially appointed Officer in Charge of the Manchester City Police Courts in the spring of 1907.

This latest promotion was granted following unprecedented success with other supervisory roles in key areas of the city's development. In particular, these included his success with committees and with overseeing the Street Trading and Licensing of Theatrical Children departments in addition to ensuring compliance with the 1875 Explosives Act, where he was an appointed government inspector.

The previous three years had seen an unprecedented and rapid rise through the ranks with a series of worthy promotions.

Coupled with the burden of additional responsibilities, James had quickly and successfully progressed from senior constable to sergeant, detective sergeant and then inspector.

During this period he also collected many small cash awards and recommendations for meritorious service and conduct. This latest move to supervise the important City Police Courts was to lead to a period of stability and consolidation in his life and became one of the most enjoyable of his short but distinguished career.

And once again, from what I can determine from his personal records, both he and other potentially high-flying fast-track type officers seeking promotion, were given a trial period of working in order that both sides could assess the situation. This confirmed that on many occasions, he was afforded the acting rank of sergeant, detective sergeant, inspector and later chief inspector.

This appeared to be many months ahead of the official rank confirmation by the Watch Committee in some instances - and often re-iterated by certain newspaper cuttings, telling of his various exploits.

It may well be the case that in June 1907, James, who was already a fully-fledged and very experienced inspector following promotion to the rank in January 1903, was already working as an acting chief inspector.

Certainly this new rank was noted, if not confirmed, in a Home Office letter of April 24th that year, which certified 'that Chief Inspector James Wood was the Inspector of Explosives for Manchester'. It could also have meant he was the Chief Inspector of Explosives.

It is highly likely he received this new 'chief' rank following his appointment as Commander to the Court, and equally likely that he was required to carry out additional duties and deal with many other varied commitments away from that area at times of need.

These notably included dealing with the organisation and supervision of large public gatherings, and where assessment on the protection of prominent citizens was required; coupled with regular safety and security inspections of events for spectators and supporters.

James always had the welfare of his staff at heart. Shortly after arriving at the City Courts, he was asked to evaluate the overall situation, and with the permission of his Chief Constable Mr R. Peacock, prepared a detailed summary of his findings and proposals.

SPECIAL REPORT OF PARTICULAR OCCURRENCES
E. Division. Dated: 14th June 1907

Inspector Wood respectfully begs to draw the attention of the Chief Constable to the business of the City Police Courts.

There are always three courts open daily, in two of which inspectors are in charge, and the third, a sergeant in charge. Very frequently it has happened that two or three extra courts have had to be opened in order to complete the day's work.

The staff of officers consists of two inspectors and seven sergeants; two inspectors and three sergeants only are available for court duty, and three sergeants are permanently employed in the records, summons and property offices respectively. There is at present a vacancy for a sergeant.

As it is necessary to have an officer in charge of each court, the staff of officers should be increased by the addition of one sergeant, whose services could be utilised for court duty and in taking charge of the vans used in collecting prisoners and their property each morning from several police stations and conveying prisoners and their property to gaol.

During the past twelve months there have been 15,863 summonses issued and 19,925 prisoners dealt with. As each prisoner is examined in order to obtain information for the guidance of the Justices, the records, His Majesty's Judges and the Governors of the Prisons, it will be seen that the work of the records office is very important and considerable, and requires very careful and experienced officers to perform the work in connection therewith in order that an injustice shall not be done to a prisoner.

Other forces too, are continually asking for information respecting prisoners in their custody and of persons wanted by them.

The inspector respectfully begs to suggest that the application for promotion to the rank of sergeant made by E PC Daniel Sweeney and E PC John McCreash be granted. Both constables have been on the court staff for several years and are well versed in court routine and the work of the records office.

They are painstaking, obliging and courteous officers and in the event of their being promoted, PC Sweeney would be appointed to carry out the duties mentioned in the forepart of this report and PC McCreash would remain in the records office.

Mr Robson, Clerk to the Justices, had been spoken to by the inspector and he states that it is very essential to the dignity of a court and to good order and discipline that an officer shall at all times be in charge of a court and he therefore supports the inspector in his application for an additional officer.

Signed: James Wood. Signature of the Police Officer making the report.

PROMOTION TO SUPERINTENDENT

James officially remained in command of the City Courts from June 1907 until July 1911, although it seems that once again, he had began to oversee his court duties from midway through 1906. On leaving, he gained further promotion to the rank of superintendent in command of the city's B Division based at Newton Heath.

His latest promotion was confirmed by a Watch Committee report of 6th July 1911 and also meant that at 44 years of age, he was the youngest superintendent on record at that time to hold this senior post.

He gained promotion following a series of interviews with 21 other applicants. His army service and vast experience in dangerous matters including firearms and explosives probably helped fast-track his career, and judging from his notes and the press cuttings, it was obvious that he was constantly involved in a wide variety of challenging tasks.

Indeed, he was one of only a handful of promising young officers, who had worked their way through all departments of the police force from uniform to the detective office and was known as a master of clerical duties and officialdom. He also became known as an 'expert in regulations with connections to the government'.

National newspapers, July 6th, 1911
NEW POLICE SUPERINTENDENT
Appointment in Manchester

The Manchester Watch Committee, at their meeting today appointed a superintendent to the vacancy caused by the retirement through ill health of Superintendent Corden.

There were 21 applications for the position and six inspectors of the city force were invited to meet the committee today. The successful applicant was Inspector Wood, who for the past five years has had charge of the City Police Courts.

He joined the force in 1890, and since has been in almost every department of the police service. He has passed through the uniform, detective and clerical branches, and has had charge of the street trading, servants' registry, explosive, and theatrical children's licensing departments.

A popular officer, Superintendent Wood has made many friends whilst holding the responsible position at the City Courts, and he has earned the respect of the bench and his police colleagues, as well as of the other habitués of the courts.

Possibly Manchester Guardian, July 6th, 1911
APPOINTMENT OF NEW POLICE SUPERINTENDENT

At the meeting of the Manchester Watch Committee this morning, Inspector Wood was appointed to the vacancy in the ranks of the superintendents, which arose through the resignation of Supt Corden on account of ill health.

A popular officer, Mr Wood is very well known to the legal fraternity and the public by reason of the prominent offices he has held. For the past five years, he has been in charge of the City Police Court staff.

Prior to that, he had control of the Street Trading and Theatrical Children Licensing Department, and of the Explosives Department. Joining the force in 1890, Mr Wood has passed through all the uniform, detective and clerical branches of the services.

Proud muster
Inspection parade, 1912. Superintendent James Wood, in the left foreground wearing his ceremonial helmet, escorts civic officials

CHAPTER 11

When The Mail's Flying Machine Came To Town

I can still recall on several occasions many years ago, my grandmother Minnie, and my own mother Doreen (Minnie's only daughter) telling me slightly different versions of the same story.

It concerned a major event in the spring of 1910, when the pilot of the first long-distance flying machine landed in Burnage, Manchester, after making a hazardous journey from London to win the Daily Mail air race - and collect a cheque for £10,000.

My grandmother's memory naturally became a little bit hazy as the years rolled by, and later the story was perhaps enhanced, and may even have been unintentionally exaggerated in parts by 'mum'. However, the essential nucleus of the story remained valid and encouraged further investigation. My later findings supported many of their claims and added credibility to decades of family uncertainty.

My notes therefore, have not just been based on family paperwork and newspaper cuttings kept by my great grandfather, but include the results of further research from many other reliable archive sources.

In April 1910, and after more than four years of prompting by the public and press; two intrepid flyers, an Englishman Claude Grahame-White, and a French rival, Louis Paulhan, fuelled the country's enthusiasm for aviation racing by taking part in an exciting challenge, flying from London to Manchester in an attempt to win an incredible £10,000 prize offered by Daily Mail newspaper proprietor Lord Northcliffe.

My grandmother, Minnie, who was just sixteen years of age when the race took place, explained that she had once been taken by a policeman during the early hours of the morning, to a wet and soggy field on the outskirts of Manchester to witness the arrival of a small biplane piloted by a young Frenchman.

'Grannie' recalled that despite the early hour, thousands of spectators packed the field, and described a vast sea of faces and cheering people present to witness this momentous occasion. She also told me that at first she thought the pilot had been Bleriot, the recent champion of the Channel crossing, and that the location might have been Platt Fields, before confirming her other knowledge of this remarkable landing.

Platt Fields had certainly been the centre for numerous public events and a host of other activities involving Manchester City Police; therefore, I can quite understand her slight confusion. Following further inquiries though, I was able to confirm the exact time, date, venue and details of her amazing sighting.

The landing site was not Platt Fields but a grassy field close to Mr Bracegirdle's Farm at Burnage. And the pilot was not Louis Bleriot, but a Louis Paulhan, another notable young French pilot, who had just completed the 185-mile journey from London via Lichfield, to win this extraordinary competition.

The memorable date in question was Thursday, April 28th 1910, and the early hours start, vividly remembered by her, was due to Paulhan's unorthodox arrival at 5.30 a.m.

My own recollections of her precise story, as a child and at the time of later discussion on this same issue, are also a bit fuzzy now, therefore I was delighted to be able to clarify matters and confirm the details from additional sources.

I certainly remember my grandmother claiming that her father, James, who was then a chief inspector of police with the city force, had arranged a special treat for her at the landing site, but remained uncertain as to the precise time of arrival.

Due to his rank, he had managed to secure Minnie a 'bird's eye' view of the landing strip from the top of a police cart, where apparently she remained quite close to the plane.

From later conversations over the years, I seriously doubt whether James's wife (my great grandmother), was aware of her daughter's presence in that muddy field; and I am equally certain she would not have approved. In addition, I remain convinced Letitia would have also prevented her from attending had she realised the other potential dangers involved with this bizarre episode.

Minnie was a very bright, attractive, and popular young student, who spoke a little French. She may even have conversed with Paulhan. I cannot remember that part. She certainly claimed she heard him speak

166

briefly to the crowd and to his assistants, amidst a great roar and the sound of constant cheering from the thousands of spectators.

The plane of course by then, was surrounded for public safety by a vast cordon of police officers, keeping the public at bay. 'Grannie' meanwhile enjoyed the magical moment, and said that she waved to the flyer in sheer delight from her privileged position, perched high above the ground.

She certainly explained that within minutes of the pilot departing under police escort towards the railway station, the heaven's opened and everyone was thoroughly drenched to the skin. The field became a quagmire and she said they experienced great difficulty in removing the machine to a place of safety.

In later years, my mother believed this soaking eventually led to my great grandfather's bout of pneumonia and forced a rapid deterioration of his health. She also suggested other VIP guests suffered a similar fate.

Louis Paulhan and Claude Grahame-White were in direct competition in this particular race. The previous afternoon, and very late in the day, they had begun a mad-dash attempt to reach Manchester, flying high over the exposed tracks of the London & North Western Railway Company, closely following the route to the North West.

Although a 24-hour race, the flyers were forced to land due to the darkness of the hour, and both had arisen early the next day, determined to be the first to reach their magnificent goal.

Huge crowds greeted the pilots at the beginning and throughout their journeys. The constant publicity and a remarkable sense of achievement soon fired the imagination of the general public, with constant news of their progress quickly forwarded along the telegraph wires and via railway signal boxes en-route.

Paulhan even had his own special train, which followed the plane. Amongst the passengers were his wife, together with invited guests, railway officials and his own maintenance crew. The train also carried aviation fuel and spare parts.

I wonder how much of this dangerous equipment and sheer haste would have been allowed by today's standards?

The whole debacle proved a great worry for Manchester police, who had no real idea of what to expect. It was certainly an occasion that had never happened before; although some city officials had been given a brief taste of the dangers of aeroplanes, following a series of trials in the suburbs a year or so before.

This however, was now the very first time that two flying machines competed in an exciting head to head cross-country endurance event for a major cash prize. Whatever the outcome, the public realised this race was certain to break all national and international records - and a great crowd was guaranteed at the designated landing site.

EARLY TRIALS IN HEATON PARK

Some trials by early pioneers were staged in Heaton Park, with others held on Salford Racecourse during 1909. Here, the actions of the participants were monitored and controlled, and yet despite the tranquil settings at secluded sites, several trials resulted in damage and severe personal injury.

Transport, old and new
Police maintain order as thousands gather at Burnage to witness the arrival of Paulhan's flying machine

This latest race escapade was a huge risk, especially with potentially thousands of spectators present, and coupled with the obvious dangers of transporting highly inflammable fuel by both air and rail. It also presented an uncertainty of the great unknown.

'Flying machines', as these early aeroplanes were called, were noisy, smelly, dirty, unreliable and highly unpredictable. This is all the more reason that I wonder why my grandmother was permitted to attend.

Personal knowledge however, suggests she had both a strong desire and an absolute determination to be present on this grand occasion.

Details of the challenge were first published in 1906. At that time, very few flying machines were available and Lord Northcliffe, formerly Alfred Harmsworth, and a former associate of James, probably thought it was a safe bet offering a staggering sum of money, £10,000 to the winner. This of course represented an absolute fortune at that time, with average wages for white-collar workers around £100 per year, and general tradesmen only earning about half that amount.

Manchester Police had been on standby several times over recent years in case of any other attempts, and remained concerned with problems such a cash prize might attract.

Many officers also remained on alert from Englishman Grahame-White's aborted solo attempt just five days earlier. They quickly realised that his failure had sparked at least one other pilot into action and eagerly awaited confirmation from their London based colleagues of any other attempts.

What could the police expect? How many people were likely to attend the landing site? Would the landing site be where they envisaged? What emergency procedures were in hand? These were just some of the many imponderables worrying James and his police colleagues in the days immediately prior to this latest race.

They knew Grahame-White would go again quite soon, and had made preparations for his departure the following day, Thursday. Yet, the sudden and unexpected ascent of his French rival the night before, and again very early that morning, kept every available policeman on his toes throughout the night. It also ensured the duties of senior colleagues remained flexible in order to cope with any possible contingency.

The only definite fact known about these new machines – which did little to settle the nerves – was that they were definitely unpredictable, with both the pilot and engines exposed to the elements, and were consequently extremely vulnerable.

There were numerous basic problems to consider and James, in his capacity as the city's appointed explosives and regulations expert, constantly found his guidance sought and tested by a desperately worried Watch Committee.

The air race posed many unique problems, not just by the thought of a potentially flying bomb, with gallons of petrol strapped to the fuselage in straddle tanks, but also by trying to maintain law and order, and public safety from an excitable crowd within a confined and untested area.

For my great-grandfather, I am sure he relished this exceptional challenge and was thrilled at the prospect of helping to supervise the safe landing and celebration of Manchester's first ever flying-machine in some muddy field.

Perhaps he thought that in later years, it might be something he could even tell his grand- or even great grandchildren about!

LAUNCH OF THE AIR-RACE COMPETITION IN 1906

It was on November 17th 1906, that newspaper chief, Lord Northcliffe, first announced details of a substantial cash prize to the first flyer to travel from a distance of five miles from the London headquarters of the Daily Mail, to alight within a similar distance from their Manchester office.

The rules insisted that not more than two landings were permitted within a 24-hour journey and that the prize would be allocated for journeys in either direction.

An additional incentive was offered by Adams Manufacturing Company, who proposed an extra sum of £2,000 to the successful winner, if they flew an all-British machine. An additional sponsor, Autocar, also suggested a prize of £400 to the maker of the winning engine – provided again, that it was of British manufacture.

At the time of launching this prize challenge, the majority of people claimed it was 'mission impossible' and 'totally unobtainable'. It meant a flight of nearly two hundred miles cross-country between two great cities by inexperienced pilots in rather primitive, untried and unreliable machines.

Nothing of note had been achieved at that particular time by early flyers, and aviation development was still slow, risky and badly under-funded.

To support this astonishing theory, and to highlight the magnitude of the undertaking, Punch magazine offered the exact same prize money to the first man to swim the Atlantic – and also to the first person to reach Mars and back within a week!

Such was the agreed scepticism of the time that even intrepid novice flyers Alberto Santos Dumont, Henri Farman and Wilbur Wright were struggling to reach any great height or distance with their own delicate contraptions.

Indeed, in 1909, three years after the race launch, Wilbur Wright established a remarkable feat in flying for just over two hours in the United States, shortly before a daring Frenchman, Louis Bleriot, crossed the English Channel to claim a £1,000 prize.

Bleriot went on to claim other additional cash prizes with a series of daredevil performances both at home and abroad.

Manchester was fast developing as an industrial and commercial centre with many national newspapers now opening offices in the city. This race was seen as a perfect opportunity to promote the area and enhance the pioneering spirit of the North West.

Despite the publicity of a London to Manchester race, Doncaster and Blackpool also tried to muscle in on the aviation act with specific meetings and attractions, offering large cash prizes to other prospective young flyers.

Many machines were now being designed and developed by motor engineers based in Manchester. Charles Fletcher of Rusholme, who used his Stockport Road factory to produce cars and the first motor ambulance for Salford, began to take a keen interest in flying. He joined forces with Norman Crosland and William Arnold and encouraged a talented young apprentice John Alcock (later of Alcock & Brown fame), to share his enthusiasm for aviation matters.

Fletcher built a single seat monoplane, and utilised his own manufacturing facilities to develop new ideas based on French designs and powered by five-cylinder rotary engines. His trial flights, though, were not without mishap and confirmed several obvious dangers.

On October 20th 1909, Fletcher travelled about thirty yards in Heaton Park. He managed a few more similar attempts before coming to grief with the park's bandstand. Much of his progress was featured in the 'Aero' magazine and highlighted the fact he made numerous seventy-five to one-hundred yard long jumps, and confirmed that in January 1910, a strong wind caused his plane to collide heavily with a clump of trees.

A couple of months later, and shortly before the London to Manchester race, Fletcher built another monoplane using parts from the wreck of his earlier plane, and exhibited his machine at White City.

He continued with the testing and development of a new engine and biplane, but after further mishaps – where he even landed in the River

Irwell in Salford – he opted to move to Brooklands in Surrey with Alcock, to work on new aviation projects with other like-minded pioneers.

Fletcher was one of Manchester's first flyers and without doubt this early work encouraged a lot of other local men to follow in his example. The cost of production though often put flying out of the reach of many individuals, until certain parties began to pool their resources to help develop skills.

Some enthusiasts opted to form a new aviators' club, which later became known as the Manchester Aero Club, and on August 25th 1909, prospective members attended a preliminary meeting at the Douglas Hotel on Corporation Street.

On September 9th a further meeting was arranged at Manchester's Midland Hotel, which was attended by more than three hundred prospective members. It was here that new club chairman William Bailey also discussed the possibility of an aerodrome at Trafford Park.

The club was supported by a host of experienced international flyers including Claude Grahame-White, Louis Bleriot, William Cody and A.V. Roe, who were each invited to become honorary members.

A month before the Manchester air race in April 1910, Manchester's Lord Mayor opened a special club exhibition of model planes at White City.

PILOTS WERE SELF-TAUGHT AND HIGHLY AMBITIOUS

The two main participants for the Daily Mail air race of 1910 were Claude Grahame-White and his more experienced French rival, Louis Paulhan. Both were self-taught and highly ambitious.

Grahame-White was called an 'exhibition flyer' and was said to be constantly fascinated by aviation. He was always full of enthusiasm for the sport. The son of a wealthy businessman from a highly respected English family, he studied engineering at university and successfully ran a vibrant motor dealership in London's plush Mayfair district – at exactly the same time as Bleriot flew across the English Channel.

He became entranced by the prospect of flying and examined Bleriot's machine when it was displayed in Selfridge's London store. The following month, he travelled across to Rheims in France, telling all his friends and staff that, surprisingly, he might even return with a new plane.

Grahame-White was a highly confident young man and a popular self-publicist. He introduced himself to many of the top pilots of the day, including Bleriot, Henri Farman, Curtiss, and Esnault-Pelterie.

He carefully examined all the machines and finally agreed to purchase one of Bleriot's new planes, a Bleriot XII. He stayed at the French factory for about two months during the construction and began testing the machine on a nearby runway, practising his techniques with a series of long hops before eventually taking off.

Later, he claimed that after sharing the advice, experience and techniques of his tutor Bleriot, he had learned to fly in about twenty minutes!

Grahame-White became obsessed with aviation and in an attempt to continue with his new passion, he started a flying school in southwest France using several of Bleriot's latest machines.

By the spring of 1910, he had many regular pupils but said he intended to return at the first opportunity to compete in the Daily Mail Air Race. He claimed the £10,000 prize money would provide the perfect opportunity to help launch a new flying school in England.

To achieve his ambition he purchased a new Henri Farman biplane and arranged for it to be shipped across the Channel, so that he could begin training for the main event.

The British challenger
Claude Grahame-White

Although most of his limited flying experience had been achieved in Bleriot machines, he believed the London to Manchester race was not possible in that type of plane with only two landings allowed. He believed his Farman designed machine offered greater speed and flexibility.

Farman, a Frenchman born to English parents, lived in Paris. He was a former cycling champion who had turned first to motor sport, and then

173

to aviation. He had much in common with the English flyer and like many other pioneers of that era, he too was a self-taught pilot.

Although he won a major national aviation title in 1908, Farman's speciality was in flying at high altitude rather than at speed. He preferred designing and building the machines to actually flying them and concentrated his efforts in the manufacturing side of the business, but continued to help a number of pilots achieve their own personal ambitions.

Farman and his team of mechanics volunteered to help Grahame-White in his attempt to win the £10,000 prize, and even travelled to England with him on the ferry, complete with his newly crated biplane.

Grahame-White was one of the most popular British flyers of the first decade of the early 1900's. He was not however, the first flyer to state his intention to win this prestigious race.

That particular honour was reserved for George Davidson, who began by designing an ambitious one hundred-seater air car. He submitted a race entry in the autumn of 1909, but regrettably had to drop out of contention through a lack of funds.

Other potential cross-country flying champions included Edgar Wilson, Eugene Gratz and another ambitious young Frenchman M. Dubonnet. The latter pilot, however, was not in a position to make a serious challenge until after the prize had been claimed.

International aviator Samuel Cody was another worthy contender and claimed he made the first powered flight in Britain. Cody visited the North West and even selected a route in reverse from Manchester to London. Ingeniously, he also prepared for a series of smoke signals to be used en-route to assist with navigation.

About the same time of Cody's visit, another challenger, the ruthlessly determined Frenchman Louis Paulhan, suddenly appeared on the scene and carefully surveyed the route, taking a peculiar interest in the London & North Western railway line, which ran directly from London Euston to Manchester.

As Paulhan considered his options, Cody also re-assessed his journey plans and decided to take the more conventional route from London. And, similar to Davidson, he planned to challenge for the prize in the autumn of 1909. His attempt though also failed when he was forced to withdraw after several hours following the seizure of his engine.

Claude Grahame-White studied the efforts of all these competitors and was fascinated and delighted by the amount of publicity each attempt received. He too visited the Manchester area and inspected potential landing sites at Urmston and Chorlton cum Hardy. After much consideration, he finally selected another preferred site in a field adjacent to the railway station at Fog Lane, Burnage. A fact also duly noted by Louis Paulhan.

Grahame-White even managed to persuade the L & NWR to assist his efforts by agreeing to colour certain sections of track with whitewash, for several one hundred yard stretches at major junctions.

Due to the oncoming winter weather though, he postponed any attempt to win the prize until the following spring, believing no one else could better his preparations. The freezing temperatures, though, restricted his regular practice, and it was to be another six months before he decided to make any serious challenge.

APRIL 23RD, 1910. GRAHAME-WHITE'S FIRST ATTEMPT

Greeted by his friend and associate, Henri Farman, and a large supportive crowd, together with members of the Aero Club, Claude Grahame-White first set off for Manchester on April 23rd, 1910.

This was to be his inaugural attempt. He took off in near darkness from Park Royal in favourable weather conditions. His immediate target was a gasholder at Wormwood Scrubs, where an official waited to confirm the time, and ensured his start was within five miles of the Daily Mail's London offices. He then carefully followed the train tracks towards Manchester.

Crowds waited all along the route and cheered him on. They packed railway bridges and every possible vantage point. Many supporters also followed his journey in motorcars but were unable to keep pace with his efforts. At Kilsby, near Northampton, one car, said to be hurrying along, and carrying some of his mechanics overturned, injuring several passengers.

Grahame-White was totally oblivious to the confusion and excitement on the ground. His own race programme seemed to be running to plan until he reached his pre-arranged landing site near Rugby, where despite a relatively smooth landing, he broke a strut on his undercarriage. He was glad to descend though as he was numb with cold and could be seen visibly shaking when he alighted at 7.20 a.m..

During his journey he achieved a new British record, covering a distance of 75 miles. He told friends he had been wretchedly cold all the way and said his eyes suffered and fingers were numbed.

He was taken by car to nearby Gellings Farm for a brief snack and hot drink whilst his assistants re-fuelled his machine. By 8.15 a.m. he was off again, this time heading towards Crewe. The wind had now increased and his machine suffered severe buffeting and turbulence which forced him to land again at Hademore near Lichfield.

At this point, his colleague Henri Farman warned that conditions were too dangerous to continue. They waited all day for a break in the weather but at 7 p.m., with the light fading, Grahame-White decided to abandon any further attempt that day.

He considered that if he made a 3 a.m. start early the next morning, he believed he could still win the prize – allowing just over two hours to reach Manchester within the 24-hour limit.

At the appointed time the wind and storms continued, if not worsened, and the flyer told the waiting crowd that unfortunately, he would have to abandon his quest.

He planned to fly onto Manchester to continue the attempt in reverse but his assistants failed to secure his plane to the ground with stakes and ropes, and it was later overturned and damaged by several strong gusts.

The victor
Louis Paulhan

His plane suffered a badly torn canvas with several broken struts. Bitterly disappointed, he immediately decided to return to London for repairs and said he hoped to make another attempt when the weather improved a couple of days later.

Meanwhile, Grahame-White's main Continental rival Louis Paulhan, who was in Cologne watching German military aviation trials at the time of the failed attempt, celebrated the news. He immediately made plans to travel to Britain and notified the race organisers of his intention to compete for the prize. Paulhan hoped to take-off before the British flyer repaired his own machine. He knew time was against him and travelled directly to London.

Paulhan was a very experienced flyer in comparison to Grahame-White. He had won many cash prizes at several influential meetings. Like Henri Farman, Paulhan was also a high-flyer, preferring to travel at high altitude, and enjoyed endurance events.

This competition seemed ideal for a man of his capabilities and later during 1910, he won another substantial cash prize of £5,000 for the greatest number of competitive flights.

Paulhan was also interested in training future pilots and in designing new aircraft including tri-planes for the French military. He also intended helping to develop a revolutionary new flying boat or sea plane in conjunction with Glen Curtiss, a fellow aviator and former colleague of Grahame-White's.

Paulhan's racing plane was another Henri Farman designed biplane but was totally different in style to his English rival's. Paulhan's plane had two rear rudders in a box shape within the tail-plane. Grahame-White's had only one central rudder and it was built with slightly lower wings for increased speed and mobility.

The Englishman knew of Paulhan's expected challenge and worked solidly to repair his machine but remained hampered by strong winds. Paulhan too was having serious problems. His crated plane was sent after him by boat to Folkestone but had to travel by road to London, as it was too wide for the railway tunnels en route.

Despite a close association with both flyers, Henri Farman and his team of mechanics spent all Wednesday morning (April 27th), preparing Grahame-White's plane for readiness. When the work was completed, the pilot still considered it was too windy to leave and decided to retire and make an early start the following day.

Paulhan, however, quickly assembled his machine that same afternoon and without any adequate testing decided to make an immediate attempt, lifting off from near Hendon at 5.31 p.m., in order to gain a slight advantage over the Englishman.

This was a brilliant tactical move on his part, and obviously took his opponent completely by surprise. Grahame-White had to be awoken in his bed just before 6 p.m. to be told of this news. Without hesitation, he ordered his machine to be withdrawn from the hangar and brought to readiness while he dressed.

His friends claimed he remained 'perfectly cool' and yet 'frustrated and vexed' by this manoeuvre. He was soon ready for take-off and departed without having had any time to eat or drink. Grahame-White was airborne within half an hour of being woken, and yet at 6.29 p.m., was still practically an hour behind his rival.

Paulhan continued flying at a high altitude for 117 miles until he descended near Lichfield due to the failing light. Grahame-White, though, flew at low altitude and paid the price, constantly struggling against the buffeting wind and rain before descending at Roade, near Northampton, some 61 miles from London.

This head to head challenge certainly caught the imagination of the nation and every radio broadcast, newspaper and railway station buzzed with the latest news of this exceptional adventure. This next day was certain to be a day to remember...

EMOTIONAL DRAMA & HIGH EXPECTATIONS

This was the background to the sheer drama and emotion of the fateful day on April 28th, 1910, and helps explain the anticipation of my (then) teenage grandmother, who somehow persuaded her police commander father to allow her to witness this epic landing – along with thousands of other spectators.

It was certainly a momentous event of high expectation. Who was actually in charge still remains a mystery. Certainly the Chief Constable, Robert Peacock, would have had overall responsibility, and an Inspector Dickenson is mentioned in news reports as being in charge at the landing site. And we know that a large contingent of police officers was delegated for the purposes of public order and protection.

My great grandfather certainly played some sort of supervisory role prior to and during the event as an experienced senior officer and as a high-ranking chief inspector.

For several days, since the initial attempt a few days earlier by Grahame-White, many officers from the Manchester force had remained on standby in case of need for what eventually proved to be a momentous occasion.

The following newspaper cuttings and general reports help provide further explanation and evidence of the build up to this historic event.

They also re-affirm and confirm the dedication and determination of two very ambitious flyers.

The air race became a major talking point in most households for several decades and raised the obvious question of 'were you there when the first aeroplane arrived in Manchester in 1910?'

Manchester City Council eventually commemorated the event in 1976 – some 66 years after the Daily Mail air race – by naming a road after the winner. It marked the completion of a new council estate that covered the original landing site in a former muddy field near Mr Bracegirdle's Farm at Burnage.

The start
Claude Grahame-White takes off from Park Royal, London

CHAPTER 12

News Reports Of London To Manchester Air Race

The *Manchester Evening News* of Thursday April 28th 1910, and the *London Times* of Friday April 29th, 1910, both carried extensive coverage of the race. I have reproduced some extracts from this copy and from some other unknown publications to highlight the importance of this prestigious Manchester event.

Certain times and facts contained within these old cuttings may differ slightly from my own findings but were included within official reports at the time.

The Evening News featured a comprehensive report of the air race and spread several photographs over three news pages. The pictures on one particular news page depicted three varied scenes at Mr Bracegirdle's Farm at Burnage, where the plane successfully landed in the early hours at 5.30 a.m.

Evening News. Thursday April 28th, 1910
PAULHAN'S TRIUMPH - Wins £10,000 flying prize – A MAGNIFICENT PERFORMANCE... Full details of journey...

The rival aviators started, last evening, their attempts to fly from London to Manchester for the £10,000 prize. The contest began dramatically and became a race with Mr Grahame-White an hour behind.

M. Paulhan, after working hard on his machine all day to get it ready, rose from Hendon at 5.22 p.m. and flying 116 miles without a stop, descended at Trent Valley Station, near Lichfield at 8.10 p.m.

Mr Grahame-White had given up the idea of starting at all yesterday and was asleep at a hotel near Wormwood Scrubs hangar when he was roused by the news that M. Paulhan was off. Hastily turning out his machine, Mr White set out at 6.29 p.m. He descended at 7.55 p.m. at Roade, five miles south of Northampton and 61 miles from London.

181

In both cases, the flights were suspended owing to the failing light and the difficulty in seeing the way. A correspondent states that Mr White found just before he descended that he had mistaken the track and had to turn back a short distance. The average speed of both aviators was over 40 miles per hour.

Subsequently, Paulhan set off again and landed safely at Didsbury at 5.30 a.m. this morning, his banking account thereby being increased by £10,000.

Paulhan's journey... thousands of people witness the start

Paulhan started on his attempt at twenty-two minutes past five o'clock last evening from Hendon, his preparations being completed shortly before five o'clock.

About twenty minutes to five he took his seat on the machine. There still remained some final touches to be given and the engine had to be tested. M. Paulhan then left his seat again, and accompanied by his wife, entered the shed. A quarter of an hour later, he emerged and after he had kissed his wife, and Monsieur Henri Farman, the huge aeroplane was wheeled in to the centre of the field ready for the start.

The aviator once more took his seat and in conversation said that he intended to start in good order. The aeroplane ran along the ground for about one hundred yards and then rose gracefully into the air to a height of about a hundred feet.

Paulhan make a complete circuit of the field and after heading in the direction of Hampstead cemetery went off towards his goal – being quickly out of sight.

The start was witnessed by a crowd of about 8,000 people and the daring aviator was cheered frantically by the spectators. Immediately after the start, the officials motored to Willesden to join the special train in waiting there to accompany M. Paulhan en route.

Aviator's intention

The aviator had a map of the route suspended from his neck and announced his intention of trying to get to Manchester without a stop, having 16 gallons of petrol in his tank.

At 5.40 p.m., Paulhan passed over Harrow, flying splendidly. The passage of the aeroplane was watched by large crowds, who observed the plucky Frenchman frantically. He was flying at about a height of 200 feet and travelling at a rate of about 35 mph.

Going along finely, Paulhan passed over Watford at a height of over 700 feet, and at 6.20 p.m. passed over Leighton Buzzard, crossing Bletchley, 47 miles from the starting point, at 6.27 p.m. He was flying splendidly, his speed now being nearly 50 mph.

A special train was following the aviator and thousands of people gathered along the route. Paulhan next passed over Roade, five miles south of Northampton at 6.40 p.m. He appeared to be going smoothly and well, and his flight was witnessed by a large crowd.

The aviator was within a hundred yards of the course taken by White in the last flight. After leaving Roade, he veered to the left and appeared to leave Northampton about two miles to the right and was keeping low.

Steady progress

Continuing to make steady progress, he passed over Rugby at 7.20 p.m. He was now keeping high in the air and still appeared to be travelling at a great rate. M. Paulhan's time at Nuneaton was 7.40 p.m., and at Tamworth eight o'clock precisely.

At the latter place, the special train was a minute behind the aviator. Hailing along swiftly with darkness coming on, Paulhan reached Lichfield at 8.10 p.m., and then dropped safely at Trent Valley Station, from which point he started off again at daybreak.

Ready to go
Preparing Paulhan's flying machine

Descent at Lichfield

A Lichfield correspondent telegraphed that Paulhan had dropped safely at Trent Valley Station at ten minutes past eight. He was travelling well but could not see to go any further. The descent was perfect, Paulhan making a wide sweep and alighting without the slightest injury, clear of all obstacles.

A large crowd witnessed his arrival and there were scenes of wild enthusiasm, round after round of cheering being raised. To Mrs Clarke of Freeford, who conversed with the aviator in French, M. Paulhan said he had had a good voyage and was quite well but quite cold and slightly numbed.

The special train, which had followed him from Willesden, arrived at 8.17 p.m. with Madame Paulhan, M. Farman, railway officials and others. The aviator and his friends immediately proceeded to the hotel where Mr Grahame-White had made his headquarters last Saturday.

Having warmed himself and partaken of refreshments, Paulhan proceeded to rest.

The aeroplane was taken charge of by railway officials, who placed a guard around it and had it staked down for protection against any sudden rise of the wind, and thus it was left for the night.

Lichfield was thronged with visitors who had come in all manner of vehicles and intense excitement prevailed.

A perfectly clean ascent – numbed with the cold

M. Paulhan came down because of the darkness. He made a perfectly clean descent. The Lichfield correspondent telegraphed that he saw the aeroplane coming from the direction of Tamworth over towards Fulfen Wood and making almost directly for Trent Valley Station, which is about two miles out of Lichfield on the road towards Burton-on-Trent and Derby.

He seemed to resolve quite suddenly upon making a descent before he reached the belt of trees near a meadow near the station. The machine described a graceful curve, missing by about a couple of yards, the dozen telegraph wires beside the highway, and alighted gently like a great gull, running only three or four yards along the sloping turf.

The aviator stepped from his seat seeming stiff and numbed from the cold. To the few people who had watched him come down, he seemed somewhat excited, and after a few minutes was talking with Mrs Clarke of Freeford Hall, a Spanish lady who with her husband had motored to the spot as soon as the aeroplane was sighted in the dark sky.

Mrs Clarke speaks French fluently and M. Paulhan explained to her that he had had a good voyage and that his machine and his engine had behaved well all the while.

Although he was very cold, he would certainly have continued his journey had it not been for the darkness of the moonless night, rendered the denser by a large expanse of cloud.

He could no longer see with any great certainty what obstacles he had to avoid, and he thought it better to descend with a view to continuing his flight at dawn.

Journey resumed

Paulhan ascended and flew from Lichfield at 4 a.m. this morning. He left the George Hotel at 3 a.m. with Madame Paulhan for the field where the aeroplane was secured.

When they arrived, the engineers were putting the finishing touches to the preparations and Madame Paulhan herself assisted in raising the machine while a strong stay was added to the tail plane.

Great excitement was caused by a report coming from the railway that Mr Grahame-White was on the way and was then between Nuneaton and Atherstone. The field in which Paulhan had alighted was a small one, and between his aeroplane and the hedge, there was a distance of only about forty yards.

As the aviator mounted his seat, Madame Paulhan came forward and embraced him, whereupon the crowd took up a cry of 'Vive Paulhan' and 'Vive la France'. M. Paulhan smiled and acknowledged the compliment.

It took more than five minutes to start the engine and when it was going Paulhan walked for a while to see that it was running smoothly before giving the order to start. This he did by raising his left hand.

The machine rose from the ground halfway down the field. It seemed to skim the hedge and never rose very high as long as it was within sight. Paulhan brought his craft round in a fine long sweep and started away north, the crowd cheering him enthusiastically as he passed above them. The special train that was accompanying the aviator left at the same time.

Over Crewe

Paulhan's progress after leaving Lichfield was resolved at Crewe every few minutes and despite the early hour of the morning, thousands turned out on cycles and in motors to greet him. He was first sighted at 5 a.m. emerging from a dull sky, west of the Staffordshire hills.

He kept to the railway lines and in less than three minutes was soaring over Basford Hall sidings, south of Crewe. He seemed to alter his course, leaving the railway and cuttings as though making a beeline for North Staffordshire.

The pilot engine gave three loud shrill whistles and then the aviator who had travelled some distance along the North Staffordshire line, curved round again, and went straight across Lord Crewe's park, leaving Crewe town on the west.

He made straight for Sandbach, where he again joined the railway ahead of the pilot engine. He might have known every inch of the road the way he manipulated his machine.

Alderley Edge

At Alderley Edge, a few dozen people assembled on the railway bridge, and soon after five o'clock a message came along the line that Paulhan was close at hand. A minute or two later, he passed smoothly on his way at a terrific rate. He had the railway on his left hand and he was very low down for Paulhan.

A motor car containing Manchester people who had gone to get an early morning glimpse of him was turned when they heard the news at Alderley, but Paulhan's speed was so great that although the car travelled at a great rate, which must have alarmed the policemen on the road, he soon dropped out of sight.

The progress of the aeroplane was delightfully smooth. The wind was favourable and the wings during the last portion of the journey appeared to remain perfectly horizontal.

A magnificent drop

There was a strong easterly wind blowing over Burnage and district at daybreak and it seemed doubtful to the large crowds awaiting the arrival of the flying-man in Mr Bracegirdle's field, off Fog Lane, whether it would be possible for either of them to complete the long journey, and so win the £10,000 prize.

However, by five o'clock, word was passed round that Paulhan was well on his way and might be expected at any minute.

Excitement naturally ran high, and there was tremendous enthusiasm when, a few minutes before half-past five, the daring Frenchman was seen steering his graceful biplane high over Fog Lane.

Instead of dropping straight into the field, which skirts the railway within a few yards of the new Burnage station on the London & North Western Railway Company's Styal line, Paulhan flew on for another quarter of a mile or so in the direction of Ladybarn, and then, making a wide circle, came down exactly at half-past five with a gentle swoop right on the appointed spot, without the slightest mishap.

The motor was stopped the second the machine reached earth and Paulhan was enthusiastically cheered as he stepped from his seat to the ground.

A fine aviator

Disappointed as the immense crowd naturally knew that Grahame-White had not succeeded in winning the great prize, it was too sportsmanlike to allow this fact to distract from the heartiness of the welcome accorded to the victor, and Paulhan was enthusiastically cheered as he steeped from his seat to the ground.

FINISH OF A HISTORIC FLIGHT.
Paulhan Sweeping over the Railway at Burnage Station, at the End of His Dash to Manchester.

The finish
Newspaper photograph of Paulhan's arrival at Burnage

Paulhan finds it cold

There were loud cries for a speech but Paulhan simply remarked that it had been very cold, could not be prevailed upon to accede to the demand, and accompanied by those of his friends who by this time had gathered round, and followed by the cheering crowd, he made his way to Burnage Station, where a special train was now in waiting to convey him to Manchester.

This train had been in attendance upon him throughout his journey, the route of which was practically identical to that of the London & North Western Railway. Travelling with it was Mr Frank Lee, general manager of the London & North Western Railway Company; Mr R. Turnbull, superintendent of the line; Mr Trench, chief engineer; Mr Walker, assistant superintendent; Mr C. Lowndes, district superintendent at Euston; and Mr S.B. Carter, district superintendent at Manchester.

On the station platform Paulhan was the subject of a friendly mobbing, everyone being anxious to shake hands with the man who had accomplished so great a task, and there were again calls for a speech.

Still the Frenchman was not to be drawn, though he repeatedly acknowledged with bows and smiles and ejaculations of the word 'merci' the compliments showered upon him.

Husband and wife

The meeting of Paulhan and his wife at the station was a very touching spectacle. Madame Paulhan threw her arms around her husband's neck and kissed him repeatedly.

The aviator and his party, including M. Farman, then boarded the train and within 30 minutes from the time the aeroplane landed, Paulhan, his wife and friends were on their way to London Road Station.

Sending the news to friends

It was after six o'clock when M. Paulhan and his group of companions reached the Queen's Hotel. His arrival did not go unnoticed and there was such a crowd of people at the hotel that the doors had to be closed.

The aviator's first thought was appropriately for his friends. Though utterly worn out, and in great need of sleep, he at once seized a bundle of telegraph forms and asked his interpreter to send messages to friends and the air authorities in England and France, announcing his success.

This work occupied M. Paulhan and his wife for some time, and it was seven o'clock when, after having a hot bath, he at last got to bed.

The aeroplane admired

In the meantime, the aeroplane remained in the field, the object of loudly expressed admiration from the spectators. The weather up to this point had worsened and light rain began to fall. In spite of this however, the crowd remained in the hope that Grahame-White, who it was understood was at Crewe, would complete the journey, even though he knew the prize had been snatched from his grasp.

Monsieur Henri Farman at Burnage

The designer of both Grahame-White and the winner Louis Paulhan's machines, Henri Farman, appeared on the scene at Burnage having left Paulhan at his hotel in Manchester. He made an inspection of the machine and afterwards interviewed Messrs Hans Renold and Co., whose works are in the neighbourhood, with a view to the storage of the biplane, until M. Paulhan's future actions were to be decided upon.

Paulhan reunited with his family

Dismantling the machine

Arrangements having been completed for the temporary storage of the aeroplane at Messrs Hans Renold's works on Burnage Lane, the work of dismantling it was at once undertaken under the presence of superintendent M. Farman and was rapidly proceeded with.

By this time, the crowd had gathered to between 1,000 and 4,000 persons, and amongst those present were the Count of Abbans, Consul General of France for the West of England, M. Robert Kersanon (a friend of Paulhan), Mr Holt Thomas of London, Mr W.E. Rowcliffe (of the Manchester Aero), Mr S.W. Royce, Mr W. Tattersall, Mr W. Clayton, Mr P.B. Murray, and other representative men.

A narrow escape

A rainstorm, almost tropical in severity, passed over Burnage shortly after ten o'clock and considerably impeded the work of dismantling the aeroplane. Indeed, a sudden gust of wind at a critical moment almost overturned the undercarriage, which had been detached from the rest of the machine. One of the straps was broken, but fortunately the damage was not serious, and the work proceeded with without further incident.

The thousands of people, however, who had gathered round by this time were drenched to the skin, and the growing crop of clover upon which M. Paulhan had descended was in a sorry plight.

For many yards circumference round the machine, it was trodden into an undistinguishable mess and the damage thus done must be very great. In spite of the weather the crowd waited hoping to be present at Mr White's descent should it be at the spot.

A well-behaved crowd

Rain continued to fall heavily, and information on the whereabouts of Mr Grahame-White being unobtainable, the crowd at last disappeared and a mere handful of spectators remained on the ground.

It is right to say that the behaviour of the public throughout had been admirable, and the police who were in attendance, under the direction of Inspector Dickenson, had very little work to do in the maintenance of order, or preventing damage to the aeroplane.

Verification of the race

Before Louis Paulhan can ask the Daily Mail to hand him its cheque for £10,000 he will have to obtain from the Royal Aero Club their certificate that in accomplishing the flight he complied with all the conditions of the race.

Though the Daily Mail defined quite clearly the terms on which the prize was offered, the race was under the control of the Aero Club, whose observers said that the departure and the arrival were within the prescribed limits and took the necessary observations as to the times.

Victory lunch at the Aero Club
Louis Paulhan receives his prize

CHAPTER 13

British Challenger's Gallant Attempt

London Times. April 29th, 1910

When Mr Claude Grahame-White descended at Roade on Wednesday evening it was his intention to start on the second stage of his journey at dawn next morning. The news that Paulhan had landed safely near Lichfield however, led him to make an alteration in his plans, and at one o'clock it was stated he had decided to resume his journey as soon as the moon rose – that is to say about two o'clock.

He fully realised that Paulhan, nearly 60 miles further on the route, had gained a lead that would be difficult to overtake. His only chance therefore was to start from Roade so early as to be able to reach, or pass, Lichfield before Paulhan resumed his flight towards Manchester.

Daring as this project would have been in the most favourable circumstances, the weather proved to be anything but propitious for a start before daylight. At two o'clock, the sky was obscured by heavy masses of dark clouds through which only fitful gleams of a watery moon were visible.

The breeze too, though light, had an unmistakable promise of increasing strength and carried with it occasional sheets of fine rain. Mr Grahame-White had pledged himself to a hazardous undertaking. The field in which his machine lay was by no means large, and was bounded on three sides by hedges and trees, while on the fourth, the railway cutting with its bridge and telegraph lines supplied an obstacle which might well have made an aviator with far longer experience hesitate.

In spite of these dangers, which were increased greatly by the darkness, Grahame-White declared that he would go up, and arrived on the field with his mother and sister, about two o'clock.

By this time, a considerable crowd from the neighbouring villages had collected, and the road, which skirted the field, was lined by a long string of motorcars, most of them in readiness to follow the flight.

The crowd which had gathered on the field behaved well, and there was no trouble whatever in getting a clear space for the run of the machine. Lamps were placed at each end of the field to mark the limits between which a safe descent was possible if the aviator should decide to come down again.

The machine was then drawn up to the railway line boundary, from which the longest 'take-off' run might be obtained. At the sight of these preparations, the crowd cheered loudly, and at the same moment the moon broke through the clouds, shedding a pale but very welcome light on the scene.

Mr Grahame-White took his seat and the engine was started. For ten or fifteen seconds he waited; then in response to his signal, the assistants released their hold and the aeroplane leaped swiftly over the shadowed field. It was a sight which will remain fixed in the memories of those who saw it.

The frail machine, its diaphanous planes faintly luminous above the sable ground, speeding, as it seemed to almost certain destruction; the closely grouped spectators, their cheering silenced on common anxiety as they watched the aeroplane draw nearer and nearer the ominous belt of trees at the far end of the field, and then the sudden roar 'He's up!'

Away over the black tree tops he rose, and, making a wide sweep over the railway line, for a brief space, the machine was visible silhouetted against the green cloud-rifts before it was swallowed up in the darkness as the pilot set his face towards Manchester.

In an instant, the road below sprang into hurried life as car after car sped away in pursuit. To the man in the air above, if he looked down, they must have appeared as so many black specks speeding along the broad path of light made by their headlamps. The official time of Mr Grahame-White's ascent from Roade was 2.48 a.m.

Three quarters of an hour later, he was seen in the moonlight sky at Rugby, being then 34 miles from Lichfield. He was travelling at a good speed and at a great height, and it seemed as if he might reach Lichfield before his rival had started.

There were crowds of people in the streets of Rugby, but the aviator was too high above them to hear the cries of encouragement. At

Nuneaton, Grahame-White appeared to be going well, but misfortune soon overtook him.

The breeze had strengthened into a strong wind, which rocked the biplane and seemed to threaten it with disaster. At Grendon, near Polesworth, when about 10 miles from Lichfield and 40 from Roade, and about the same moment that Paulhan was setting out on the last stage of his journey, he had to descend in a rather rough field about four o'clock.

He was soon joined by friends who had followed his flight by motorcar, and to them he said that he had been obliged to come down owing to the wind. 'It turned me round completely three times,' he said. 'And I thought it was no use trying to go on as I could make no headway.'

Soon afterwards came the news that Paulhan had started for Manchester from Lichfield. 'The wind doesn't seem to bother him very much,' Mr Grahame-White remarked. A bystander pointed out that M. Paulhan flew at a considerably greater altitude than him. 'Just so,' was Grahame-White's reply.

'But you must remember that M. Paulhan was an experienced aviator before I had begun to think about aeroplanes.'

He declared that he would make another ascent as soon as possible. But the strength of the wind increased so greatly that he was obliged to abandon any idea of flying during the morning.

When the news came that Paulhan had descended safely in Manchester, Mr Grahame-White was so disappointed at his own failure, but with characteristic sportsmanship, he climbed on the seat of a motorcar and announced his rival's victory to the crowd assembled in the field.

He called for three cheers for M. Paulhan, whom he described as the 'finest aviator the world has ever seen,' adding, 'compared with him, I am only a novice.'

Towards 4 o'clock the wind moderated, and Mr Grahame-White announced that he would try to complete the flight to Manchester in the stipulated time. He made a successful ascent and had soon reached a good altitude. He passed over Tamworth quickly but rather low down, and on reaching the Hademore crossing, he descended practically at the same spot on which he alighted on Saturday morning.

He encountered a rainstorm, which loosened the canvas, and he was unable to go on further. The storm abated soon afterwards and he made another ascent. Circling round Lichfield he finally came to ground at the

Trent Valley Station about three fields from that which M. Paulhan had started that morning.

It was now ten minutes past six o'clock and Mr Grahame-White decided to abandon the flight. He gave instructions for his machine to be dismantled and sent back to London.

Mr Grahame-White is to leave England either today or tomorrow to take part in the aviation meeting at Barcelona on Sunday.

Shortly after his retirement from the Manchester air race, Grahame-White, who owned one of the first gasoline-driven motorcars in England, was charged by the police for running beyond the speed limit in his automobile and summoned to the police court at Woking, where he was fined £10 with costs.

Grahame-White was one of Britain's top aviators

Throughout his turbulent career, Claude Grahame-White continued to attract both controversy and notoriety as one of Britain's top aviators and exhibition flyers, achieving mixed fortunes.

And during one practice session in Lancashire, he landed unexpectedly on Southport beach – where he made a surprise descent next to the pier – much to the amazement and obvious delight of the large crowd.

He later went on to win the lucrative Gordon Bennett Trophy at the Belmont air meet in America during October 1910, and gained further success in the Los Angeles air meet and Brighton Beach air meetings of 1911.

National newspapers, April 29th, 1910

PAULHAN'S ARRIVAL IN MANCHESTER

The news that neither aviator could finish the journey on Wednesday night did not satisfy the large crowd that had assembled at Bracegirdle's Farm, New Burnage. They were not sure that a surprise was not in store for them. Some stayed at a neighbouring inn and slept on chairs, for it was realized that Mr Grahame-White must make a very early start if he was to make up lost time.

At four o'clock there may have been a hundred persons present, and among these were several ladies. Some had come on foot and some on bicycles. At half-past four there were less than a thousand, but at five o'clock, there were three or four thousand people.

Conflicting messages arrived, one to the effect that Mr Grahame-White had started at three o'clock, another saying that both competitors were flying, and that one was only 25 miles behind the other.

At 5.15 a.m., the official time-taker of the Royal Aero Club walked out to the centre of the field in which a white sheet lay on the ground. The sheet however, was not unrolled, for it was known that both aviators would recognise the field, and in an emergency, signals could be made.

At 5.25 a.m., a report arrived by telephone at the signal box at the station that a flying machine was approaching, and that it had been seen from a point about five miles to the south. Not until that moment had the crowd fully realised the marvellous nature of the feat, of which they were now to see the completion but that pregnant message stopped the babel of voices, and the great crowd stood silently expectant.

Along the road to the south of the field the houses were fronted by a double row of motorcars. The public paths at the sides and through the field were marked by thick lines of people; the platform of the high-level station to the east was thronged.

Every eye was directed towards the skyline of the houses and the trees in the south. The western horizon was crimson with the light of a threatening sunrise; overhead the sky was dull grey, and a light cold drizzle was driving along on a south westerly wind, which at times blew at 15 mph.

The first sight of the aeroplane

Suddenly there was a scattered volley of exclamations: 'Here he is! Paulhan is coming!' Over the tops of the trees he appeared, small and faint at first, but rapidly increasing in size, the now familiar outline of an aeroplane.

From the crowd there arose cheer after cheer. No one cared then whether the aviator was Frenchman or Englishman. It was enough that he was a hero of the air. The manner of his coming, too, was prophetic of so much yet to be achieved that international and sporting rivalries seemed to be forgotten for the moment.

197

The mixed crowd of working people, trades people and country gentlemen appeared to have been filled with a deep consciousness of the significance of the event. No such scene had ever before been witnessed.

A sense of awe prevailed for an instant, and then the crowd threw off all restraint and streamed across the field in one wild rush. The volume of cheering grew and grew until it became deafening. Men and women shouted incoherently.

M. Paulhan, for it was soon known that it was he by the pair of vertical planes visible in the tail of his machine – flew straight as an arrow at a height of about 1,000 ft towards the goal. Then sweeping in a vast circle eastwards, he passed over the railway and descended lower and lower until some thought he would land on the other side.

He turned however, westwards, and surmounted the raised railway line and the telegraph wires, watched anxiously by thousands of eyes, he completed the half-round and headed towards the south, descending all the time, until at last he touched the earth at 5.30 a.m., welcomed by the cheering of thousands. He had been half frozen with the cold, but he was warm enough in a few seconds.

The one overmastering desire of every man and every woman in the crowd was to grasp his hands. He smiled but could not utter a word. Then, as police forced their way through to his rescue, he realised the generosity of the people who gave their countryman's rival such unstilted honour.

Rising in his seat, he raised one hand, laughed joyously, let his eyes dwell fondly on the sea of faces, and allowed himself to be hauled down. Guarded by two policemen, and surrounded by a ring of protectors, he hurried towards the station accompanied by a dense mass of cheering people, who almost fell over each other in the rush.

It was hard work for the police but they got their charge safely through the wicket and up to the steps of the platform where, a few minutes earlier, the special train had arrived. M. Paulhan greeted his wife as she stepped out onto the platform.

His mechanics left the train and went to the aeroplane, and Paulhan got onto the train, which, seven minutes after his arrival, left for Manchester.

The crowd all this time had continued to cheer and call for 'Paulhan' until the train was out of sight.

A visit to the Lord Mayor

On his arrival in Manchester, M. Paulhan went to the Queen's Hotel, where he took some rest. It was then raining heavily and preparations were being made to put the aeroplane under shelter.

One of Paulhan's first acts after he had had a few hours rest was to pay his respects to the Lord Mayor of Manchester, Councillor Behrens. It was remarked that although Paulhan had come to the city by the latest means of locomotion, he went to the Town Hall in an old fashioned 'growler'.

In the hall, he was introduced to some of the leading citizens, who were eager to learn the incidents of his flight, but he displayed much reluctance in speaking of his achievement.

He asked that he might be excused from taking luncheon with the mayoral party as he was exhausted and as he had no clothes but the aviator's suit, which he was then wearing.

Paulhan afterwards took luncheon with a few friends at his hotel. Paulhan had several engagements to appear at Continental aviation meetings but does not propose to devote himself in future to flying, or to taking part in contests for prizes. He intends to use the money that he has won in effecting improvements in flying machines.

National newspapers, April 29th, 1910
THE SPECIAL TRAIN

Following M. Paulhan's flight in the special train, for which facilities were provided by the London & North Western Railway Company, proved to be one of the most interesting methods of watching the progress of the great race.

The train carried representatives from nearly all departments of the railway, in addition to M. Paulhan's assistants and spare stores, including a quantity of Shell motor spirit, which was used by both aviators in their flights. Madame Paulhan was also a passenger.

Before four o'clock everything was ready for the start after the aviator. When ascended, the train steamed off at once. Just before starting, a message was received to the effect that Mr Grahame-White, who had got away at the early hour of 2.55 a.m., had passed Nuneaton.

The position was exciting. The slightest flaw in the working of M. Paulhan's engine or any trivial obstacle would probably place the prize in the hands of his rival. It was a cold morning, and the passengers in the train spoke of the discomfort of the aviator cleaving his way through the raw air at 40 mph.

While watchful eyes were kept on the tiny figure of the aeroplane far ahead and seldom allowed to get out of sight, problems of aviation were discussed. Everybody was confident that Paulhan would win, and Mme Paulhan appeared to be thoroughly accustomed to seeing her husband facing the danger of cross-country flying.

The aviator kept at a great altitude, apparently about 800 ft to 1,000 ft, and maintained an even, regular flight.

Grahame-White's machine excited great interest in London

FARMAN INTERVIEW

Mr Henri Farman, who accompanied the special train to Manchester, was much gratified at the evidence offered by the fine flights of M. Paulhan and Grahame-White, and of the excellence of his machine.

He said in an interview that there were no reasons for surprise at these long cross-country flights. The flight to Manchester could have been accomplished a year ago. He thought that with ordinary luck, Mr Grahame-White would have won, since, although he is a comparatively new recruit, he had exhibited great skill and courage and the will to make big flights.

He spoke with enthusiasm of the splendid flight, which Mr Grahame-White had made on Saturday, and said that it required great pluck and skill to stand up against the rain and storm as he had done. Mr Farman sympathised with his unsuccessful pupil.

Mr Farman described Paulhan's flight as a wonderful achievement, especially as his machine did not arrive at Hendon until six o'clock on Wednesday morning. He had made his preparations and had completed his flight within 24 hours. It was a great pity, he added, that Manchester had not yet an aviation ground of its own.

It was a matter to which the Manchester Aero Club might devote its attention, as, until they have a ground, there could be no development of cross-country flying.

National newspapers, April 29th, 1910
PAULHAN'S VICTORY

Paulhan had flown from London to Manchester with a Farman aeroplane and won the prize offered by the Daily Mail. The greater experience of the French aviator in cross-country flying and the skill acquired by long and varied practice, which enabled him to start on a difficult journey without a trial flight of nine and a half hours after his machine had arrived at Hendon, have triumphed over the daring and intrepid enthusiasm which Mr Graham-White has displayed from the outset.

Nor were these the only qualities, which elicited the admiration of those who had cherished the hope to the last that the prize might fall to an English flyer.

Mr Graham-White's chivalrous attitude towards an opponent with whom he recognised that it was an honour to enter the field, and the readiness with which he has acknowledged the abilities of the aviator who has wrested from him the reward which so many thought that he would soon claim, have shown him to be well prepared to perpetuate the best traditions of British sport.

The ill luck, which attended him at the beginning on Wormwood Scrubs and followed him until he was compelled to descend on Roade on Wednesday, still accompanied him yesterday.

Seeing that his only chance of retrieving his lost position in the race was to make a start before his rival, Grahame-White faced the danger of a high wind and darkness left Roade at 2.48 a.m. yesterday morning, only to be compelled to descend again at Polesworth about four o'clock.

Undaunted, he ascended only again to be defeated and to learn that the prize was to go to France. M. Paulhan, who was received with great enthusiasm in Manchester when he landed at 5.30 a.m. yesterday morning, did not remain long in the city.

He returned to London last night, and on his arrival at Euston, he was met by Major Kennedy and Mr Cheeseman, of the Aviation section of the Motor Union, which will give a dinner in his honour.

A cheque for £10,000 will be presented on behalf of the Daily Mail to M. Paulhan at a luncheon at the Savoy Hotel tomorrow. The luncheon will take place at noon, as M. Paulhan is anxious to catch the Folkestone boat express, which leaves Charing Cross at 2.20 p.m., so that he may spend Sunday with his family in Paris.

Arrangements are being made in Paris to welcome him on his arrival tomorrow evening. His train is due to arrive at Gare du Nord at 9.16 p.m.

The proprietors of the Daily Mail are giving Mr Grahame-White a 100-guinea cup, and the Royal Aero Club has decided upon a fund for a testimonial to him.

Louis Paulhan's magnificent achievement was duly certified by a committee from the Royal Aero Club as having duly abided by the rules. He was driven from the club to the special luncheon held in his honour at the Savoy Hotel in the Strand.

Additional distinguished guests at that luncheon included: - H.G. Wells the science fiction author; Mr C.S. Rolls, the co-founder of Rolls-Royce, Colonel Capper, termed the father of military aviation in Britain; Sir Hiram Maxim, the inventor of the Maxim gun and flying machine; John Moore Brabazon, another of Britain's early aviation pioneers; and Major B. Baden-Powell, a kite experimenter and brother of Robert Baden-Powell.

Paulhan's rival, Claude Grahame-White was also present at the celebratory meal, where he received his commemorative 100-guinea cup. He was also told that he had achieved two notable records, one for being the first British pilot to fly at night, and the other for flying 75 miles non-stop. He also accompanied his rival to Charing Cross Station.

The unofficial flight times for both competitors taken from 1910 publicity brochures included: -
Louis Paulhan: -
Start in London at Hendon 5.31 p.m.; Harrow at 5.40 p.m.; Leighton Buzzard 6.20 p.m.; Northampton 6.50 p.m.; Rugby 7.20 p.m.; Lichfield descended at 8.10 p.m. Ascended at 4.09 a.m. on April 28th, Paulhan passed over Crewe at 5.05 a.m. and eventually descended at Bracegirdle's Farm, Burnage, Manchester, at 5.30 a.m.

Claude Grahame-White: -
Started from Wormwood Scrubs, London, at 6.29 p.m.; Watford at 6.50 p.m.; Leighton Buzzard 7.41 p.m.; descended at Roade at 7.55 p.m. He ascended from Roade at 2.50 a.m. on April 28th, and then passed over Rugby at 3.30 a.m. before descending at Polesworth at 4.13 a.m.; he ascended again at 4.58 p.m.; descending at Hademore Crossing at 5.02 p.m. He continued his journey and made his final descent at Trent Valley Station, Lichfield, at 5.25 p.m.

And finally....: Letter to the editor of the London Times. April 1914. (A short extract)*

Sir,
Your leading article on 'Trespassing in Aeroplanes' forms an admirable reply to the letter which you published the day before from a correspondent. Such narrow minded, selfish expressions as he uses are unworthy of an Englishman.

The pioneers of progress ought to receive every encouragement, and when they are told by their countrymen that they are a nuisance and ought to be extirpated as vermin, is it any wonder that Frenchmen and foreigners get ahead of us in introducing these epoch-making inventions?

We all know how Count Zeppelin was treated after his unfortunate landing. Why should not we in England, instead of expressing unkind epithets on those who are endeavouring to lead the way, raise a fund to Mr Grahame-White, after his splendid achievement, and after having suffered such hard luck in having the great prize wrested away from him when it seemed within his grasp.

Signed: *Major B. Baden-Powell.*

CHAPTER 14

The Beginning Of The End...

This was a very difficult section to research and publicise for obvious personal and family reasons, and provides a rather dramatic chapter in my great grandfather's life and career.

As a senior police officer, highly respected and much decorated, he was very experienced, and yet became a potentially easy target for attack from vindictive and/or disgruntled officers.

James, I might add, was not the only target during this period for malicious gossip, innuendo and abuse. Many other senior officers also suffered a similar fate from persons unhappy with their lot.

Bribery, fraud and corruption were rampant at this time, and on occasions even within the Manchester force. It was James's job to investigate a great number of allegations against officers and subsequently, it became a most unpopular task.

He acted under direct instruction from the Chief Constable, Peacock, who was a tough cookie determined to rule with an iron rod. From 1913 onwards however, James began to suffer from bouts of ill health.

Family members remained convinced it all began shortly after receiving a thorough soaking during the Manchester to London Air Race in 1910. It is obviously impossible for me to speculate about his troubles, but he certainly caught pneumonia at least once, and ended up with a weak heart!

He also continued to keep up his demanding schedule and hardly took any time off. He was often on call seven days a week, twenty-four hours a day, and like many senior officers, he often lived above the shop and was nearly always on duty. Stress too must have played a key role.

James was one of only a handful of experienced superintendents and since becoming the youngest member to achieve that rank in 1911, seemed determined to prove his worth.

He was called to investigate claims of bribery and dishonesty against two constables, and yet months after completing his report with the aid of two sergeants, both he and they found themselves being sued by one unhappy individual.

The constable made several accusations against James and the two sergeants, and claimed damages for unlawful imprisonment and trespass. All charges were of course denied and defended. The officer in question was investigated and a report passed to the Chief Constable for consideration several months before.

The constables' life was not particularly rosy with poor pay and conditions and many restrictions upon their personal lives. Many left after just a few months service, whilst others enjoyed every moment. It was also a very tough job, out in all weathers with little or no reward, and facing attack and abuse from the public. A great number were simply unable to cope with the strict discipline and regimented routine.

This incident, however, seemed to be blown out of all proportion and happened at a time when James was not in the best of health. The winter weather had taken its toll and combined with the stress and strain of everyday duties and defending the action, he was forced to take some time out to recover. He reported severe chest pains.

This is an honest account of what really happened to James and his co-defendants, and to the accuser. It is supported by press cuttings, court papers and personal records and reveals the behind the scenes drama and interest this story provoked.

It was a massive story for the media with a so-called local hero facing ruin. The nationals followed the story and it became one of the most important actions in police history at that time. It dragged on for some time because of James's deteriorating condition and his inability to attend court to give evidence.

I believe these last couple of chapters provide a highly dramatic conclusion to the action-packed career of a dedicated and loyal servant; and this case perhaps acted as a sharp warning to both investigator and the accused.

It also helped create a new blue print of rules and regulations that are still in use today. It was an unprecedented and unnecessary challenge by what he thought to be one of his own.

It was also a shock from which James never recovered. Justice finally prevailed but it seemed such a high price to pay for a brave man doing his duty as a professional crime beater!

Manchester newspaper, March 1914

POLICEMAN AT LAW

Singular position in a City Action

Defendant's illness – agreement regarding taking of his evidence

Mention of an action between members of the Manchester police force were made before his honour Judge Mellor K.C., at the Manchester County Court today, when an application was made for permission to take the depositions of a witness now ill in Bournemouth, before the County Court Registrar of Hampshire, instead of the witness attending the trial.

Mr P.M. Heath, who made the application on behalf of the defendants, explained that the action was one in which William Buckley, a police constable of Blackley, sought to recover damages for alleged assault from Police Superintendent James Wood and two other members of the force. When on February 13th, 1914, an application was made for an adjournment for three months owing to the seriousness of Supt Wood, his Honour declined to allow more than one month's

A dignified family portrait
James, Letitia and Minnie

adjournment, and expressed the opinion that the case should be tried as soon as possible.

The Watch Committee, Mr Heath proceeded, associated themselves with the remark, and everything had been done to bring the case as early as possible before the court. The application was with respect to the evidence of Mr James Wood.

The judge: He is better now then?

Mr Heath: By no means, your Honour.

A certificate was put in concerning the defendant's health signed by Dr F.C. Bottomley, senior physician of the Royal Victoria and West Hampshire Hospital, Bournemouth.

The judge, after reading the certificate, said he quite saw that it would be impossible to bring the man into the court within a reasonable amount of time and asked if there would be danger in having him called as a witness.

Mr Heath answered that a Dr Sankey in the court was entirely in accordance with the views expressed in the doctor's certificate.

The judge: Dr Bottomley says he does not think Mr Wood could stand the examination.

Mr Heath: The risk is not mine. I shall not say anything to my friend, which might excite him. My friend (Mr Lustgarten) might (laughter).

The judge said he could not make the order asked for, and run the serious risk of affecting Mr Wood's condition.

The Drawback

Mr Heath said that in view of the doctor's letter he could not now ask for the order unless the evidence could be taken in a certain form, i.e., that his friend and he could exchange proofs, and upon them the registrar at Bournemouth could frame questions to put to the witness.

The judge: The drawback to the whole thing is that if anything happens to Mr Wood, it might kill the case.

Mr Heath said his friend could then bring the action against the other two and leave Mr Wood out of it.

Mr Lustgarten, who appears for the plaintiff in the action, said he appreciated the difficulty in making the order. He said that Dr Bottomley did not go so far as to say that the registrar might not examine the witness at Bournemouth. What he seemed to object to is 'my presence' (laughter).

Mr Lustgarten said the evidence might be taken in a series of written questions, but pointed out that it to some extent would be unsatisfactory, as his Honour would still have to draw conclusions from the manner in which the questions were answered.

The judge said he had no practical experience of this sort of evidence by interrogatories. Subsequently, his Honour asked if the case was a personal matter to Mr Wood.

Mr Heath replied that it was, and stated that it was suggested that Mr Wood assaulted Mr Buckley, imprisoned him without lawful authority, caused his room and his box to be broken and entered, and a book to be taken out. "We say we have an absolute answer to it," said Mr Heath.

Mr Lustgarten: The difficulty would be that if Mr Wood were excluded from the case, the others would say they were acting under a superior officer's instructions. It was possible that some good might be done by drawing up a series of questions, and he agreed to Mr Heath's suggestion, provided security were given for the extra costs.

Mr Heath said there was no necessity to apply for security in the case of an officer of 23 years service.

It was further agreed that the questions agreed upon should not be submitted to the witness except with approval of the doctor. The case was thereupon adjourned, the date being left open.

Manchester Newspaper. March 1914

CONSTABLE'S ACTION

Damages claimed against City Police Superintendent
Defendant still an invalid – another adjournment granted

At the Manchester County Court today, before Judge Mellor, reference was made to an action which was mentioned on February 13 – Buckley v Wood and others – and which had been adjourned for a month.

The action is one brought by William Buckley, a police constable, of Blackley, to recover damages for assault from Police Superintendent Wood and two other members of the force – a sergeant and a constable – and when, on Feb 13, an application was made for an adjournment for three months owing to the serious illness of Superintendent Wood, the judge declined to give more than a month's adjournment and expressed the view that 'it was entirely in the interests of everybody that the case should be tried as soon as possible'.

Mr P.M. Heath, Deputy Town Clerk of Manchester, now made an application for an order that Mr Wood should be examined by the Registrar of the Hampshire County Court at Bournemouth.

The judge: Is Mr Wood better?

Mr Heath: By no means.

The judge: But last time he was not fit to be examined?

Watch Committee's desire

Mr Heath replied that the Watch Committee were very anxious to bring the case before the judge as early as possible. They were in accord with the judge's view in that respect, and if anything had been a little too anxious. Mr Wood was a necessary material witness, and they had Dr Sankey in Court to speak as to his condition.

Dr F.C. Bottomley, the senior physician at Bournemouth, had written suggesting that he did not think Mr Wood could stand cross-examination in his present condition.

The judge: There is evidently a good deal of feeling, and an examination might annoy Mr Wood. I cannot order it, if there is a serious danger to his life.

Mr Heath: It has been suggested by Mr Lustgarten that this man is not ill.

Mr Lustgarten: No, I said he was doing his duty.

The judge: Dr Bottomley seems to think he is not fit to be examined.

Mr Heath said his suggestion would be that Mr Lustgarten and he should exchange proofs, and upon them frame questions mutually, which the registrar at Bournemouth would ask Mr Wood to answer. The registrar could be told that the witness must not be in the least degree excited.

The judge: If anything should happen to Mr Wood, it does not kill the case except as regards himself. The man's grievance could still be ventilated?

Mr Heath: He could bring the action against the other defendants.

Mr Lustgarten said the position might be that the other defendants would claim that they acted under the orders of Superintendent Wood, who was their superior officer. He could not, therefore, exclude Mr Wood from the case.

An absolute answer

Mr Heath said this was perhaps not the proper time to say it, but they had an absolute answer to the complaint which the plaintiff had made, which was that Superintendent Wood assaulted Buckley, imprisoned him without lawful authority, caused his room to be broken and entered, and a book to be taken out.

Mr Lustgarten said he would agree to the suggestion made by Mr Heath if security were given for the extra costs. If, of course, Mr Heath would say that the Watch Committee were defending the case he would not ask for security.

Mr Heath replied that Mr Wood was an officer with 23 years' police service to his credit. They need not ask a man in his position to give security.

Eventually, the case was adjourned on the conditions named, with a further provision that the questions should not be submitted to Mr Wood unless Dr Bottomley approved. No date was fixed for the hearing in Manchester but the Judge said he would fix an early date after Mr Wood's evidence had been obtained.

LEAVE OF ABSENCE

Watch Committee report about James Wood's serious illness. Taken from minutes of meeting. Letter, dated 30th April 1914.

The Chief Superintendent respectfully reports that the Watch Committee at their meeting on the 5th February, 1914, considered a report of Dr Sankey, the Police Surgeon of the B Division, in respect of the illness of Superintendent James Wood and resolved: -

That three months leave of absence be granted to Superintendent Wood, subject to the compliance with the advice of Dr Sankey. The Chief Superintendent reports that the three months will expire on Tuesday next, and insomuch as this is the last meeting of the Committee before the expiration of the leave, the Chief Superintendent respectfully asks for the instructions of the Committee in the matter.

The Chief Superintendent had consulted Mr Heath, the deputy Town Clerk, and as a result, instructed Dr Sankey, the Police Surgeon, to make a further examination of Supt Wood. The report of Dr Sankey is attached hereto.

The Chief Superintendent respectfully suggests that insomuch as the Chairman of the Watch Committee and the Chief Constable will be in attendance at the next meeting of the Watch Committee, a short extension of further sick leave should be granted to Superintendent Wood, and that the consideration of Dr Sankey's report should be deferred until the Chief Constable's return to duty.

Dated: April 30th, 1914. This is to certify that I examined Superintendent Wood at 6 Warley Road, Blackpool, and found that he is still unfit for duty.

Signed: Wm Sankey, MB. (B Divisional Surgeon).

Despite a brief, yet temporary improvement in James's health, within a couple of weeks of this latest medical examination, his police colleagues and relatives received the news they had all been dreading; he had suddenly passed away in the presence of his wife and daughter, at his home at Newton Heath police station.

DEATH NOTICE IN NEWSPAPER

Dated: 29th May, 1914
SUPERINTENDENT WOOD
Death of well-known Manchester Police Officer

The death took place last night of Superintendent James Wood of the Manchester City Police Force.

Mr Wood, who was 46 years of age, had been ailing for a considerable period, and for six months had been away on sick leave. He had been to Bournemouth for the good of his health, and when he returned about a fortnight ago, he appeared to be somewhat better.

He had been suffering from heart trouble, and it was known to those who were intimately associated with him, that his death might take place at any moment. He was in charge of the B Division, and died at the station where he lived in Newton Heath.

Mr Wood commenced his police career as a constable in Manchester, and at one time was in charge of the street trading department. Afterwards, he was promoted to be inspector in charge of the City Police Courts, where he became known to magistrates.

He was of great assistance at the courts to those whose business took them there. He had held the position of superintendent for three years with the exception of one month.

OBITUARY NOTICES IN NEWSPAPER: -

WOOD – On the 28th inst, at 627 Oldham Road, Newton Heath, JAMES, the very dear husband of Letitia WOOD, after long suffering (late superintendent, B Division, Manchester City Police). Kindly accept this (the only) intimation.

WOOD – On the 28th May at 627 Oldham Road, Newton Heath. JAMES, the beloved husband of Letitia WOOD, aged 46 years (late superintendent, B Division, Manchester City Police). Internment at Harpurhey Cemetery, Tuesday 2nd June 1914 at 4 p.m. Deeply regretted.

Death Certificate of James Wood, 1914

Evening Chronicle. May 29th, 1914

POLICE SUPERINTENDENT DEAD

Officer who won his way through the ranks

The death occurred last night of Superintendent Wood, who has for several years had charge of 'B' Division of the Manchester Police. He had been ailing for some time.

Mr Wood was a trusted and reliable officer. He joined the force in 1890 and passed through all the uniform, detective and clerical branches of the service. Prior to assuming charge of the 'B' Division in July 1911, Mr Wood had held the rank of inspector and was in charge of the police staff in attendance at the City Police Court. In that capacity, he showed much shrewdness and tact.

When Superintendent Corden retired, the Watch Committee approved a recommendation that Mr Wood should take his place.

Mr Wood was a recognised expert in regulations affecting street trading, the licensing of theatrical children, and the administration of the Explosives Act, in which his last mentioned department, his work had been specially commended by Government officers.

Manchester newspaper cutting. With photograph – believed to be 30th May 1914

LOSS TO THE POLICE FORCE

Superintendent Wood of 'B' Division of the Manchester Police, whose death was announced in the Evening Chronicle yesterday, joined the force in 1890, and passed through all the uniform, detective and clerical branches of the service.

Prior to assuming charge of the 'B' Division, in July 1911, he held the rank of inspector, and was in charge of the police staff in attendance at the Manchester City Police Court. Mr Wood was a recognised expert in regulations affecting street trading, the licensing of theatrical children and the administration of the Explosives Act.

Evening Chronicle. June 2nd, 1914

FUNERAL OF SUPERINTENDENT WOOD

Impressive ceremony this afternoon

The funeral of Superintendent Wood took place this afternoon at Harpurhey Cemetery, and was witnessed by a large crowd, this being the first instance in the history of the Manchester police force that a superintendent on active service has died.

The funeral procession left the deceased's residence in Newton Heath, headed by the police band playing the Dead March and a large body of police in charge of the acting superintendent of the division, Inspector Cubberley.

Minnie, with her husband Tom
The author's grandparents

Accompanying the cortege were the Chief Constable Mr R. Peacock, Chief Detective Superintendent Vaughan, and Superintendents Walker and Gilmour, both former superintendents of the B Division.

The cortege proceeded by way of Oldham Road, Lumb Lane, and Queen's Road to Harpurhey Cemetery. Six inspectors carried the body to the graveside: Inspectors Dentith, Grant, Harrison and Lea (B Division), Liggett (E Division) and Webster (F Division).

The last rites were carried out by Inspector Webster. A large number of wreaths had been sent, including one from the Chief Constable, the headquarters staff and other officers and men.

City News, 3rd June 1914
LAID TO REST

Police Superintendent James Wood of the Manchester City Police Force, who died at the early age of forty-six years, was laid to rest in Harpurhey Cemetery on Tuesday.

Besides the chief mourners, there were present at the funeral, the City Police Band, a large number of constables, most of them connected with the B Division, the Chief Constable (Mr R. Peacock), Chief Superintendent Vaughan, and Superintendents Walker, Cubberley and Gilmour – an impressive tribute to the late superintendent.

Blackley Guardian, June 1914
THE LATE SUPERINTENDENT WOOD

There were some remarkable manifestations of sympathy at the funeral of the late Superintendent James Wood, which took place at the Harpurhey Cemetery on Tuesday afternoon. By order of the Chief Constable, Mr R. Peacock, who was also present, a public funeral was accorded the deceased gentleman.

The police band, together with 50 members of the force, under acting Superintendent Cubberley, who has been in charge of the B Division since Mr Wood's death, marched in procession from Oldham Road to the cemetery, where a short address was delivered by Inspector Webster.

The band played the 'Dead March' in 'Saul' and Chopin's 'Funeral March' and at the graveside a number of hymns were sung. There was a very large crowd of people present, who stood with bare heads as the coffin was lowered.

The late Mr Wood was 46 years of age and for 22 years was attached to the City Police Force. He was at the Police Court as inspector for many years and for two and a half years was superintendent of the B Division.

MANCHESTER POLICE. B Division
(* *Official police notice and records at Manchester Police Museum*)
Particulars of information respecting the late Mr James Wood and his family

Rank, age and length of service in the force: - Superintendent, age 46 years. Twenty-three years and seven months. Joined the service on 30th October 1890.

Full Christian name of widow, age, and her occupation previous to marriage: - Letitia Wood, age 44 years, small ware weaver.
Number of children, their ages and sex: - One, aged 20 years, female.
Whether at home or working (if the latter, state earnings): - At home.
What does the widow propose doing to maintain herself and family? Not definitely settled. Will probably purchase a baby linen or drapery business.
Address of widow: - 627 Oldham Road, Newton Heath (police station).
Cause of death: - Aortic aneurysm & heart failure.
Date of death: - 28th May 1914.
Signed: William Vaughan (Chief Superintendent).

COPY OF MINUTES DATED: June 18th, 1914
(Supplied by the Police Museum)*
Watch Audit Sub-Committee. Present: - Councillor Thewliss in the chair. Alderman Ashton, Carter, Fildes & Harwood. Councillors Fox, Godbert, Grime, Makeague, Moston and Tattersall.

GRATUITIES. Memo from the Chief Constable

The Chief Constable reported that Superintendent James Wood and Sergeant Edmund Barker died on the 28th May 1914, and the 6th May 1914 respectively, and reminded the Committee that they had the power to grant one month's pay for every completed year of approved service.

Superintendent Wood had completed 23 years approved service, and at the time of his death was in receipt of pay at the rate of £210.0s.0d. per annum. The cause of death was certified as aortic aneurysm and heart failure. He leaves a widow, and one daughter aged twenty years.

Sergeant Barker had completed 32 years approved service, and at the time of his death was in receipt of pay at the rate of £125.2s.0d. per annum. The cause of his death was certified as bronchitis and heart failure. He leaves a widow and two sons, aged 27 years and 17 years respectively.

Resolved: That the Watch Committee be recommended to grant from the Police Pension Fund to the widows and children of the late Superintendent Wood and Sergeant Barker, the under mentioned gratuities: -

Superintendent Wood, £402.10s.0d.

Sergeant Barker, £333.14s.3d.

To be paid at the discretion of the Chief Constable.

A copy of the 'Applications from Officers for Pensions and Rateable Deductions, dated Thursday 18th June 1914, confirmed: - Superintendent James Wood (46) joined the force on 30/10/1890. He had 22 years of service. And his present annual pay per annum amounted to £210 with 2 years and 10 months in his present rank, should receive gratuities of £402.10s.0d.

Robert Peacock, Chief Constable of Manchester
who led the mourners at James Wood's funeral

CHAPTER 15

Policeman's Action

Hearing of long drawn out case
Death of principal defendant

The hearing of Buckley v Wood and others, which has several times been adjourned, came on before Judge Mellor at the Manchester County Court today.

The action is one in which ex-officers and officers of the Manchester City Police force are concerned. The plaintiff was William Buckley, Herbert Street, Blackley, and the chief defendant in the action as originally filed was the late Superintendent Wood, whose illness and death have caused several adjournments.

The defendants now were Sergeant Isaac Bennett, Summerville Avenue, Moston, and Sergeant Thomas A. Cort, Waverley Road, Moston.

Mr Lustgarten was for plaintiff, and Mr Sutton for defendants.

Mr Lustgarten said the action was brought to recover damages for an unlawful imprisonment and for trespass on the plaintiff's premises by the defendants. The plaintiff was a constable in the Manchester force. On October 25, some time after six o'clock in the afternoon, plaintiff was on patrol in Bury New Road, Strangeways.

Whilst walking along with acting Sergeant Greenwood, he was approached by a local lad who said: 'What about that arrangement you have made with us tonight?'

His reply was: 'What arrangement do you mean?'

The lad said: 'Didn't you and PC 156 take our names and addresses last Thursday night and say – we will report you for obstruction, and then say, meet us on Saturday night in Bury New Road and give us a shilling each and we will let you off?'

Plaintiff said: 'I know nothing about it,' and the boy went away.

Mr Lustgarten went on to describe how Buckley was subsequently questioned by the superintendent as to the alleged conversation with the boy, and how, in spite of his denial, he was marched off to Derby Street police station, where he was placed in the reserve cell, searched and interrogated with regard to his police book.

He accompanied the superintendent to his (Buckley's) lodgings, where a search was made and a book was found, but not a police book. The matter was eventually investigated by the Chief Constable and in the sequel, Buckley was informed that no case had been made out against him. The case went before the Watch Committee, who did nothing in the matter.

The judge agreed that the questions for the court to decide were (1). Whether in fact an arrest took place and (2). Whether in fact a trespass took place (3). Assuming that, whether it was an act which the officer had a right to commit.

An abbreviated version of the same story also appeared in the national newspapers.

National and local newspaper reports from May & June 1914
CONSTABLE'S SUIT
A dead man's story told in court
Sergeants' sued – action for alleged wrongful dismissal

At the Manchester County Court, before Judge Mellor this afternoon, the hearing was resumed of the action in which a Manchester City police constable sued two sergeants for damages for alleged unlawful imprisonment and trespass.

The plaintiff, for whom Mr Lustgarten appeared, was William Buckley of Herbert Street, Blackley, and the defendants, Isaac Bennett, Summerville Avenue, Moston, and Thomas A. Cort, Waverley Road, Moston, were represented by Mr Sutton (barrister).

This case had been postponed several times owing to the illness of Superintendent Wood, a third defendant, who has since died.

Plaintiff's story was that in October last year, a suggestion was made against him and another officer that they had agreed to accept a shilling each on condition they 'let off' some boys whose names were said to have been taken by them for obstruction.

Superintendent Wood, it was stated, in investigating the allegations (which were denied by both the plaintiff and the other officer), examined Buckley's book. Nothing being found there, search was made for another book, which, it was suggested, was in the plaintiff's possession. Buckley, it was stated, was marched off to Derby Street police station between Wood and Bennett, and there he was placed in the reserve cell.

No police book was found either at Willert Street police station, or at Buckley's lodgings, where search was made, but another notebook, with some pages missing, was found, and afterwards Superintendent Wood told Buckley that he had been telling lies.

The other officer involved with Buckley in the matter was 'sufficiently badgered' alleged Mr Lustgarten, that he resigned and Buckley was also asked by the superintendent if he had not better resign also, but he refused to do so.

After the Chief Constable had investigated the matter, he decided that no charge had been proved. Buckley eventually did resign in February, because, he said, of the snubbing he had received.

The evidence of Superintendent Wood, the defendant, who had died, was read by the judge this afternoon.

Mr Wood's story

His honour observed that when Superintendent Wood was examined, he was very ill and was not physically fit in any way to be cross-examined. He (the judge) put to Wood questions of his own, and then asked him questions which had been suggested by Mr Lustgarten.

Mr Wood told his Honour that he was the Superintendent of B Division and Buckley was transferred to his division in the spring of 1913. Supt Wood referred to the complaints made by two Jewish lads last October that Buckley and the other constable had agreed to accept a shilling on condition that they 'let off' the lads.

The superintendent stated that the lads saw him and told him that the officers gave them to understand they might be summoned for obstruction unless they brought the money. The Supt went on to say that the youths were told to keep the appointment they alleged they had made with the constables and they were given a shilling (marked).

Later that evening, after Buckley had been seen speaking to the youths in the street, he was spoken to by Wood, who asked what the conversation had been about. Buckley told the superintendent that he had not seen the youths before, and Wood then told him of the complaint the lads had made against him and asked him to go to the police station so that they might hear the boys make the complaint.

On the way to the station, Wood walked with Buckley, and Sergeant Bennett walked behind and Buckley was not in any sense in custody, as it was not the custom in the force to arrest officers without the consent of the Chief.

He was asked, when at the station, to go into the reserve room so that the boys could not see him. When asked for his old police book, Buckley declared that he had given it up, but it was not found at Willert Street police station. Wood afterwards asked Sergeant Bennett to go through Buckley's pockets, but he took it that Buckley thoroughly consented to that step.

He (Wood) took a serious view of the allegation against Buckley, but he was anxious to clear him, if possible. Buckley himself assisted in the search, and if he had offered any objection, the search would not have continued. Buckley was allowed to question the lad who had made the charge against him.

The other officer involved in the matter with Buckley told Wood that he was determined to resign, and later Buckley also offered to resign, but after he had been told to think it over, he said he would stay on.

POLICEMAN AT LAW
Evidence of the late Superintendent Wood read by the judge – defendant's case opened

Before Judge Mellor at the Manchester County Court this afternoon, the case for the defence in the action Buckley v Wood and others came on by adjournment.

The action is one in which ex-officers and officers of the Manchester City Police force are concerned. The plaintiff was William Buckley, Herbert Street, Blackley, and the chief defendant in the action as originally filed was the late Superintendent Wood, whose illness and death have caused several adjournments.

The defendants now were Sergeant Isaac Bennett, Summerville Avenue, Moston, and Sergeant Thomas A. Cort, Waverley Road, Moston. Mr Lustgarten was for plaintiff and Mr Sutton for defendants.

Plaintiff's allegations

Plaintiff's case was concluded last night. He alleged that a suggestion was made that he and another officer had agreed to accept a shilling each from three lads on condition they were 'let off' after their names had been taken by Buckley and Spendlove for obstructing the thoroughfare.

Superintendent Wood, it was stated, in investigating the allegations (which both Buckley and Spendlove denied), examined Buckley's police book. No entry bearing on the matter was found there, and a search was made for another book.

Buckley had stated he had handed in his former book at Derby Street police station, but when it could not be found, an inquiry was made at Willert Street and a search of the plaintiff's lodgings, at which Buckley attended, was conducted.

Meantime, Buckley, it was stated in evidence, had been taken to the station and put in a reserve cell. At Buckley's lodgings, a small book was found. There was only one entry in the book, and several leaves were torn out.

Spendlove, it was pointed out, had resigned, but Buckley, when questioned as to whether he had better resign, refused to do so. The Chief Constable having investigated the matter decided that no charge had been proved, and in February, Buckley resigned because he was dissatisfied with the treatment he was receiving.

Dead defendant's evidence

Mr Lustgarten, when the case resumed today, remarked that one of the witnesses, the principal defendant, Superintendent Wood, had been examined privately by the judge, and he asked if he could have access to that evidence

The judge said he proposed at once to read it. Mr Sutton said the judge would observe it was read at the request of the plaintiff.

Mr Lustgarten protested. The witness had since died. The evidence was in fact taken on behalf of, and at the request of the defendants.

The judge mentioned the circumstances under which the evidence was taken. The witness, he said, was at the time very ill, and could not be closely examined. The evidence of the late Supt Wood was that Buckley had joined his division after being removed from A division.

When Buckley joined his division, witness said he would not let bygones be bygones. He had treated Buckley as he did other officers. On one occasion, Wood had interested himself to secure wages for Buckley when laid up after a bicycle accident. He had later to report him for neglect of duty.

Coming to the incidents out of which the action arose, the evidence of the late superintendent was that on October 24th he had had a complaint made to him by the boys, who told him they were given to understand they might be summoned for obstruction unless they brought money for the officers on Saturday night.

The boys were told to keep the appointment they alleged to have been made, but to make no mention of the money until the officers named it. They were given a marked shilling. He (Wood) and a sergeant had the place under observation, but at the time for the fixed appointment, Buckley had passed.

He returned an hour or so later, and the lads approached. The superintendent sent word that he wished to speak to Buckley, and asked him about the interview.

Buckley said he had not seen the lads before. Witness mentioned the complaint and told Buckley to go to the station to hear the complaint of the boys.

In the Reserve Room

On the way to the station, witness (Wood) walked with Buckley and the sergeant (Bennett) followed. Buckley was not in any sense in custody. He was asked to go into the reserve room at the station so that the boy could not see him.

He was asked for his old book and after they had failed to find it in his pockets, it was decided to search his lodgings. Witness then explained that he took a serious view of the matter. Witness told Buckley that Spendlove had decided to resign. Buckley said: 'I think I will do the same.' Witness told him to consider carefully before taking the step and Buckley decided to stay on.

The judge then read the late Superintendent Wood's replies to questions put to him at the request of Mr Lustgarten. Witness denied that Buckley was detained at the police station, and asserted he could have walked out had he wished. The judge added that the superintendent repeated that Buckley was never in fact under arrest.

The old book and the missing page

At this stage, Mr Sutton said another search had been made for Buckley's old book, and it had been found. It was true there was no entry in the book bearing on the incident, but counsel found there was a page missing.

In fairness to plaintiff however, added Mr Sutton, it should be stated that the entries on the page before and after that which was torn out, ran on perfectly regularly.

The judge remarked that even if the conversation with the lads had taken place the entry would probably not be in the book. The officer would hardly have done that. Mr Sutton said an entry could have been made on a loose slip of paper.

Conclusion of trial... 18th June 1914. The County Court
POLICE CASE - Hearing of the action

At the Manchester County Court yesterday, before Judge Mellor, K.C., the trial was concluded of an action brought by William Buckley, lately a constable in the B Division of the City Police Force, against the superintendent of the division (Mr James Wood), and two sergeants named Bennett and Cort, for false imprisonment and trespass.

Since the proceedings were begun, Mr Wood had died, and the action was continued against the other two defendants. Mr Lustgarten appeared for the plaintiff, and the defendants were represented by Mr Sutton.

The case for the plaintiff was concluded on Tuesday. It was, in effect, that in October last, three youths made allegations against the plaintiff and another officer named Spendlove, that they had agreed, on receipt of a shilling from each of the youths, not to report them for street obstruction.

The boys, it was alleged, had brought the matter to the notice of Mr Wood, who asked the plaintiff in the street for his notebook, and as the names and addresses of the boys – which they alleged the plaintiff wrote down – were not found there, Mr Wood directed the plaintiff to go with him to Derby Street police station.

Here the plaintiff alleged he was placed in the prisoners' reserve cell and searched, and as no other book was found, Mr Wood directed Sergeants' Bennett and Cort to go to his lodgings in Blackley to look for it.

The plaintiff accompanied them, and there, another book was found – a private notebook – of which the Sergeants took possession. Spendlove resigned from the force, but the plaintiff declined to do so. He appeared before the Chief Constable (Mr Peacock) and was exonerated.

Four months later, he resigned. He alleged that he had been treated as a prisoner and that the police sergeants had no right to search his rooms without a proper warrant.

Before the evidence of the defendants was given, the judge read the deposition he had himself taken of the late Superintendent Wood. In it, Mr Wood said the plaintiff was in no sense in custody, and he took it that he consented to be searched, and in fact assisted by opening his tunic.

If the plaintiff had objected, Mr Wood said he would have reported the matter to the Chief Constable. He was anxious to clear Buckley if possible. Spendlove gave as a reason for resigning that he was dissatisfied with the police service.

Mr Sutton said that the missing book had been found at Willert Street police station. Examining it, he observed that a page was missing.

The defendants, Sergeants Bennett and Cort, in their evidence said that the plaintiff made no complaint or objection to what was done. The room called a reserve prisoner's cell was not a cell but a retiring room for the sergeants' in the division. There was a gas jet in it, which made for it unsuitable as a cell.

Mr Lustgarten cross-examined the defendants at great length in order to show that they had exceeded their duty. They said that in all they did they acted under the instructions of their superior officer.

Mr Sutton submitted that was a case of leave and licence, to be inferred from a consideration of the relations of the parties to each other. The action taken by the late Supt Wood and the two defendants acting under his instructions were, he urged, right and proper.

The charge made against the plaintiff was one of a serious nature, and in his own interest, his superior officers were the right persons to investigate it. The plaintiff had sustained not the slightest damage, and when he discharged himself, he was repaid the amount he had subscribed to the superannuation fund.

Mr Sutton characterised the action as malicious and one that never ought to have been brought. The judge, after hearing Mr Lustgarten, said the parties in the case were all policemen, and it really affected the discipline of the force.

It was essential that there should be strict discipline, because the police had great powers over ordinary people, and it was imperative that they should be well looked after.

Reviewing the facts, the judge said his impression of Mr Wood was that he was an honest man who would do his duty. He held that there was no case so far as the incidents at the police station were concerned.

As to the searching of the lodgings, he was not quite sure that it was the proper thing to do, but he was perfectly certain that the plaintiff sustained no damage as a consequence. He gave the judgement for the plaintiff for 20s, without costs.

Mr Lustgarten asked for leave to appeal on the matter generally, but the judge declined to accede to the application.

Newton Heath Police Station

City newspaper report, June 1914

EX-POLICEMAN'S CLAIM
Award of 20s damages without costs

The action, which has several times been mentioned at the Manchester County Court, in which an ex-constable of the City Police Force claimed damages for unlawful imprisonment and trespass against the late Superintendent James Wood and two sergeants of the B Division of the force, was concluded yesterday afternoon.

The parties to the action since the death of the superintendent were William Buckley, Herbert Street, Blackley, plaintiff, and Sergeants

Isaac Bennett, Summerville Avenue, Moston, and Thomas A. Cort, Waverley Road, Moston, defendants.

Mr Lustgarten was for Buckley, and the defendants were represented by Mr Sutton. The case for the plaintiff was that in the investigation of an allegation made against him, that he had arranged to accept a bribe, he had been wrongfully imprisoned and that trespass had been committed at his lodgings. He was exonerated from blame in the matter by the Chief Constable.

Judge Mellor held that there had been no wrongful imprisonment, and as to the trespass, he awarded 20s damages, without costs.

June 18th, 1914. National newspaper review of case
CONSTABLE'S CLAIM
Judgement for 20s in suit against Sergeants
Judge's comment: - unable to see any reason for the action

The action in which William Buckley, an ex-constable of the Manchester City Police Force sued two sergeants in the B Division – Isaac Bennett and Thomas A. Cort – for damages for alleged unlawful imprisonment and trespass, concluded at the Manchester County Court yesterday in judgement for the plaintiff for 20s without costs.

The plaintiff's case was that a suggestion was made in October of last year that he and another constable had agreed to accept a shilling each from three lads on condition that they were 'let off' after their names had been taken for obstruction.

The allegation was denied by both officers, but Buckley complained that he was placed in the reserve cell at Derby Street police station and searched, and that in connection with the matter, his lodgings were also searched.

Judge Mellor yesterday read the evidence of the late Superintendent Wood, which was taken when that officer was lying seriously ill. The superintendent told his Honour that he had heard of the complaint against Buckley, and the other officer, from the lads themselves, and the boys were told to keep the appointment they alleged they had made with the officers.

They were each given a marked shilling, but told not to mention of the money unless the officers named it.

Later Wood said he asked Buckley about the interview, and the latter denied that he had seen the lads before. He was then told of their suggestion against him and asked to go to Derby Street police station.

When search was made for the old police book, Wood asked Sergeant Bennett to go through Buckley's pockets, but he took it that it was done with Buckley's consent.

Judge and Late Superintendent

The defendants gave evidence bearing out the late superintendent's version of what occurred, and Sergeant Cort stated that Buckley did not object either when he himself was searched, or when his lodgings were searched.

Sergeant Bennett stated that the room in which Buckley was placed at Derby Street police station was not used for prisoners.

Giving judgement, his Honour said fortunately that kind of case was an uncommon one. It really affected the discipline of the force. Policemen had important powers over ordinary people, and it was necessary they should be well looked after themselves, and that discipline should be strict in the force.

Mr Lustgarten was refused leave to appeal on the main issue of the case, the judge remarking: 'The only doubt I had was whether to give judgement straight away for the defendants.'

'The plaintiff,' he added, 'had been rehabilitated by the Chief Constable, and was in the force for four months after the matter was over.' He could not see any reason at all why he should have brought the action.

SUCCESSFUL CONCLUSION – BUT TRAGIC END TO A POTENTIALLY GLITTERING CAREER

The successful conclusion to this tragic and dramatic case unfortunately came just too late to be of any benefit to James and his family

I am certain his health would have improved, at least slightly, at news of the verdict, and in particular the comments of Judge Mellor, who almost stated the obvious when he said: 'I can see no reason at all why he should have brought this action. The only doubt I had was whether to give judgement straight away for the defendants.'

Some small crumbs of comfort perhaps, but James was buried some sixteen days BEFORE the case was concluded. It had all seemed so totally unnecessary. And yet, the case caught the imagination of the press and public alike, who took James's personal tragedy to their hearts. It also became a cause, or case celebré within the force.

I know from personal records how bitterly disappointed James was that his health problems prevented any court attendance, and that he was only allowed to provide evidence in a statement from a convalescence home in Bournemouth.

At least by this method, he felt he had finally exercised his duty. Both the judge and the verdict exonerated James and his colleagues, but the action almost certainly helped accelerate his demise.

And who knows what would have happened to his health, had the case been concluded a month or two before this date? Certainly the stress, anxiety, and problems of preparing a defence in such a precarious state must have taken its toll.

And to poor Letitia, his widow and the mother of his teenage daughter, the Watch Committee eventually awarded the equivalent of two years' pay, a disappointing £420.10 shillings.

This was supposedly generous compensation for more than twenty-four years of loyal service, and at the same time, she was also given notice to quit their flat at 627 Oldham Road, where they had been living above the shop, so to speak, at Newton Heath police station.

Bemused, bewildered, short of funds and future direction, Letitia told the Committee she would probably try to purchase a baby linen or drapery business in order to survive and help to support her daughter. And like James, she probably wondered what it had all been about!

James had been unfairly attacked by 'one of his own'. I think this was the particular point that hurt him and Letitia the most, and ironically it came from a man that James had tried to help before, after he had experienced some personal problems within the force.

And what about this discredited constable, William Buckley? Not too surprisingly, he took the easy way out and hastily resigned from the force during the latter stages of the trial. He was certainly never heard of again and was thought to have left the area.

It was claimed he made his decision as soon as he realised James had agreed to speak to the judge from his sick bed!

The sad part of this whole sordid affair, is that we will never know the real reasons why Buckley made these false claims, or quit the force at that particular time. Maybe he realised the game was up, and he was about to be 'found out', then disciplined.

Neither will we ever know what would have happened to James and his family, had he lived a much longer life and continued to honour his employers in a similar fashion.

It was a tragic end to a potentially glittering career but at least I am able to record by investigation that he made a positive and invaluable contribution to the development of the force – and to the heritage of Manchester. He was indeed an unsung hero, who, hopefully, will never be forgotten!

Superintendent James Wood
Manchester City Police

OTHER BOOKS
by the same author

TOWN WITHOUT PITY - The fight to free Stephen Downing
Published by Random House, Century.
ISBN 0-7126-1530X

DOWN WEMBLEY WAY
About the controversial former England soccer captain Peter Swan, who was banned and jailed following a bribery scandal but returned to play for Bury and Matlock Town, leading the latter club to victory at Wembley over Scarborough in the FA Trophy success of 1975.

JOE COCKER – VANCE ARNOLD & THE AVENGERS
A unique biography of how the rock legend began his problematic career in a small, smokey club in Sheffield and endured a roller-coaster existence before he finally secured fame and fortune. Published by Voiceprint, www.voiceprint.co.uk, reference VP 214 CD.
ISBN 6-04388-30472-1

CLUB 60 & THE ESQUIRE – Sheffield Sounds of the 60s
This is a unique account of the birth of rock, pop and blues, and includes many exclusive photographs and reports about Joe Cocker, Eric Clapton, Ginger Baker, Rod Stewart, Georgie Fame and a host of others. It was printed and published by ALD Design and Print, in Sheffield.
ISBN 1-901587-26-6

Coming in the spring of 2004:

MALLARD
The dramatic account of Sir Nigel Gresley's battle to take the world steam record from Nazi Germany. Published by Aurum Press.
ISBN 1-85410-939-1.

Printed in the United Kingdom
by Lightning Source UK Ltd.
102189UKS00001B/7-15